Economics of Social Justice
A Handbook for Students

Editors

Miriam Kennet, Iolanda Cum & Sabeeta Nathan

Green Economics Institute Publishing House
September 2015

The Green Economics Institute (GEI)
Registered Office: 6 Strachey Close, Tidmarsh, Reading RG8 8EP
greeneconomicsinstitute@gmail.com

Economics of Social Justice
A Handbook for Students

Published by The Green Economics Institute September 2015
Registered Office: 6 Strachey Close, Tidmarsh, Reading RG8 8EP
Email: greeneconomicsinstitute@gmail.com

Edited by Miriam Kennet, Iolanda Cum & Sabeeta Nathan
Typeset by Miriam Kennet, Iolanda Cum & Sabeeta Nathan
Printed on FSC approved stock by Marston Book Services Ltd.

Economics of Social Justice
A Handbook for Students

Photo by Bogusia Igielska of The Green Economics Institute training course held at Oxford University

The Green Economics Institute has been working to create and establish a discipline or school of Economics called "Green Economics" and seeks to reform mainstream economics itself into a well-defined goals-based discipline which provides practical answers to existing and future problems by incorporating all relevant aspects, knowledge and complex interactions into a truly holistic understanding of the relevant issues. It uses complexity, holism, pluralism and interdisciplinary working in order to widen the scope of economics, adding the science from the green aspects, and the social ideas from economics discourses. This new scope for the first time avoids partial explanations or solutions and also biased and partial perspectives of power elites. The Institute has begun to influence the methodology of mainstream economics, according to Professor Tony Lawson of Cambridge University's Economics Department (2007). It uses trans-disciplinary and interdisciplinary methods so that it can factor in the complexity of nature into economics. It seeks to provide all people everywhere, non human species, the planet and earth systems with a decent level of well-being based on practical and theoretical approaches targeting both methodology and knowledge and based a comprehensive reform of the current economic mainstream. It can, for example, comfortably incorporate glacial issues, climate change and volcanic, seismic and earth sciences into its explanations and thus in this, and many other ways, it is far more complete and reflects reality much more closely than its predecessors on which it builds. The current narrow conventional economic approach using purposely designed methods, is challenged to bring areas and concepts into its scope which have been until now neglected. Existing outdated or inappropriate propositions and solutions are examined and revised to provide a realistic and more comprehensive understanding of the subject.

The Green Economics Institute argues for economic development based on economic access and decision making for all, including respect for cultural diversity and normative freedom. It does this by bringing together all the interested parties, who want to help in developing this progressive discipline, by inviting them to its events, and conferences and by means of such activities as writing books and publications and using its research, its campaigns and its lobbying and its speeches and lecturing all over the world.

The Green Economics Institute created the first green academic journal *International Journal of Green Economics* with publishers Inderscience.

The Green Economics Institute has its own delegation to the Kyoto Protocol, and is a recommended UK government reviewer on the Intergovernmental Panel on Climate Change (IPCC). Members of the Green Economics Institute have lectured or worked in governments and Universities around the world, for example receiving invitations from Surrey University, the Schumacher College, The University of Bolzano, the Tyrollean Cabinet, via Skype in Thessaloniki, FYRO Macedonia, Turkey, the National Government School in the UK with top Cabinet Officials, at University in Cambridge and Oxford, Transition Towns, Oslo, Norway, Liverpool University, Lancaster University, Abuja, Nigeria and Gondar, Ethiopia, Shillong, and Gujerat, in India and attended conferences in many places including Cancun, Mexico and Riga, Latvia and appeared on TV and radio in Italy and Tallin in Estonia and the UK and Bangladesh amongst many others and received invitations the President of Russia and from the governments and several universities in China and from several governments and Princes in several Gulf States as well as several parts of the United Nations and the International Labour Organisation!

The spread of Green Economics is accelerating and hence The Green Economics Institute is pleased to bring these ideas to a broader group of readers, students, policy makers, academics and campaigners in this ground breaking volume and to begin to offer its Green Economics Solutions to help rebalance the economy.

The Directors
Miriam Kennet, UK,
Volker Heinemann UK, Germany,
Michelle S. Gale de Oliveira UK, USA, Brazil

Photo by Miriam Kennet on the side of a school in France. The pen is mightier than the sword. In fighting for social justice and a reformed economy, the pen wins every time !

Contents

Publications of the Green Economics Institute

The Green Economics Institute Publishing House has now published over 300 titles from leading authors and new and innovative thinkers with really new ideas and Change Making solutions for today's pressing issues! Our books are Open Source and many also have around 30 different writers and voices in each book, so that a variety of novel perspectives can be introduced from all around the world.

Titles available from The Green Economics Institute ©:

Economics Books

Handbook of Green Economics: A Practitioner's Guide (2012) Edited By Miriam Kennet, Eleni Courea, Alan Bouquet and Ieva Pepinyte ISBN 9781907543036

Green Economics Methodology: An Introduction (2012) Edited By Tone Berg (Norway), Aase Seeberg (Norway) and Miriam Kennet ISBN 978190754357

The Green Economics Reader c (2012) Edited By Miriam Kennet ISBN 9781907543265

Rebalancing the Economy (2014) Edited by Christopher Brook, Cambridge University and Miriam Kennet.ISBN9781907543845

A History of Economics and Economists from a Green Perspective Edited by Miriam Kennet (2016) Forthcoming

Finance Books

The Greening of Global Finance: Reforming Global Finance c (2013) Edited By Professor Graciela Chichilnisky (USA and Argentina), Michelle S. Gale de Oliveira (USA and Brazil), Miriam Kennet, Professor Maria Madi (Brazil) and Professor Chow Fah Yee (Malaysia) ISBN 9781907543401

The Reform of Global Banking by Professor Maria Madi and Kamile Buskavaite (2015) ISBN 9781907543203

Geographies of Green Economics

Greening the Global Economy (2013) Edited by Sofia Amaral (Portugal) and Miriam

Kennet ISBN 9781907543944

Green Economics: The Greening of Asia and China (2012) Edited by Miriam Kennet (UK) and Norfayanti Kamaruddin (Malaysia) ISBN 9781907543234

Green Economics: Voices of Africa (2012) Edited By Miriam Kennet, Amana Winchester, Mahelet Mekonnen and Chidi Magnus Onuoha ISBN 9781907543098

The Greening of Eastern Europe (2013) Edited By Miriam Kennet and Dr Sandra Gusta (Latvia) ISBN 9781907543418

Green Economics: The Greening of Indonesia (2013) Edited By Dr Dessy Irwati and Dr Stephan Onggo (Indonesia) ISBN 9781907543821

The Greening of Latin America (2013) Edited By Michelle S. Gale de Oliveira (USA and Brazil), Maria Fernanda Caporale Madi (Brazil), Carlos Francisco Restituyo Vassallo (Dominican Republic) and Miriam Kennet ISBN 9781907543876

Africa: Transition to a Green Economy (2013) Edited By Dr Chidi Magnus (Nigeria) ISBN 9781907543364

Green Economics & India (2014) Edited by Professor Natalie West, Professor Indira Dutta, Odeta Grabauskaitė, Kanupriya Bhagat and Miriam Kennet ISBN 9781907543500

The Greening of the Mediterranean Economy (2013) Edited by Miriam Kennet, Dr Michael Briguglio, Dr Enrico Tezza, Michelle S Gale de Oliveira and Doaa Salman ISBN 9781907543906

The European Economy: Crisis and Recovery (2014) Edited by Miriam Kennet ISBN 9781907543463

The Eastern European Economy, Policy and Practise for Recovery,(July 2014) Professor Dr Dzintra Astaja (Latvia) and Odeta Grabauskaitė (Lithuania) ISBN 9781907543890

The Greening of Malaysia (2016) Professor Chow Fah Ye (Malaysia) and Dr Pek (Malaysia) Forthcoming

The Greening of Norway and the Future of its economy Edited by Miriam Kennet (2016) Forthcoming

The Greening of Italy: Crisis and Recovery (2014) Edited by Alberto Truccolo ISBN9781097543920

Social Policy Books

The Greening of Health and Well being (2013) Edited By Michelle S. Gale de Oliveira, Miriam Kennet and Dr Katherine Kennet ISBN 9781907543760

The Vintage Generation, the Rocking Chair Revolution (2015) Edited by Miriam Kennet and Birgit Meinhard – Schiebel (Austria) ISBN 9781907543517

Citizen's Income and Green Economics (2012) By Clive Lord, edited by Judith Felton and Miriam Kennet ISBN 9781907543074

Green Economics Womens Unequal Pay and Poverty. Michelle S Gale de Oliveira, Judith Felton and Amana Winchester ISBN 9781907543081

Young People: Green Jobs, Employment and Education (2012) Edited By Miriam Kennet and Juliane Goeke (Germany) ISBN 9781907543258

The Truth about the Garment Trade and its supply chain (2016) Forthcoming

Ending the War against women (2016) Edited by Miriam Kennet, Michelle S Gale de Oliveira, Professor Graciela Chichilnisky, Professor Maria Madi. Forthcoming

Energy and Climate Policy

Green Economics and Climate Change (2012) Edited By Miriam Kennet and Winston Ka-Ming Mak (Hong Kong and UK)

Green Economics: The Greening of Energy Policies (2012) Edited By Ryota Koike (Japan) and Miriam Kennet ISBN 9781907543326

Renewable Energy (2015) Edited by Iolande Cum and Miriam Kennet ISBN 9781907543784 Forthcoming

Rolling Back the Tide of Climate Change Policies and instruments in the USA and China.(2015) Peter Yang ISBN 9781907543777

Fracking (2016) ISBN 9781907543791 Forthcoming

Renewables are getting cheaper Peter Yang (Autumn 2015)

Biomass and Algae Energy (Autumn 2015) Italian Language Version Iolanda Cum.

Food, Farming and Agriculture

Green Economics & Food, Farming and Agriculture (2013) Edited by Michelle S. Gale de Oliveira, Rose Blackett-Ord and Miriam Kennet ISBN 9781907543449

Greening the food on your plate (2013) Edited by Michelle S. Gale de Oliveira, Rose Blackett-Ord and Miriam Kennet ISBN 9781907543654

Organics (2016) Miriam Kennet and Joylon from Nirvanah Spa. Forthcoming

Biodiversity, conservation and animal protection Books

Biodiversity: The Variety of Life Under Threat (2015) Anna Wainer, Odeta Grabauskaitė and Miriam Kennet ISBN 9781907543227

Animal Protection and Animal Communication (2015) Forthcoming

Ending the 6th Ever Mass Extinction of Species (2016) Forthcoming

Lifestyle Books

The Green Transport Revolution (2013) Edited By Richard Holcroft and Miriam Kennet ISBN 9781907543968

Green Poetry, Art and Photography (2013) Edited by Dr Matt Rinaldi, Rose Blackett- Ord, Friedericke Oeser Prasse and Miriam Kennet ISBN 9781907543784

Abstract Art and the future of Art (2016) Friedericke Oesser Prasse. Forthcoming.

The Green Built Environment: A Handbook (2012) Edited By Miriam Kennet and Judith Felton ISBN 9781907543067

Designing Fairtrade (2015) Jessica Bosseaux. Edited by Christopher Brook and Odeta Grabauskaite

Recycling: Cool, Stylish and Sustainable (2016) Forthcoming

Philosophy Books

Integrating Ethics, Social Responsibility and Governance, (2013) Tore Audin Hedin, (Norway), Michelle Gale de Oliveira, Miriam Kennet ISBN 9781907543395

The Philosophical Basis of the Green Movement (2013) Professor Michael Benfield,Miriam Kennet and Michelle Gale de Oliveira (Brazil) ISBN 9781907543548

Green Economics and the Path to Enlightenment (2015) Miriam Kennet (Italy)

Philosophy of Social Justice (2015) Miriam Kennet and Samuel Gilmore. ISBN 9781907543739

Books about Resources and Basic Needs

Thirst: Water, Flooding and Sea level rise (2016) Dr Indira Dutta and Miriam Kennet Forthcoming

Technology and Technical Books

The Greening of Technology, Innovation and Green IT (2015) Forthcoming Miriam Kennet, Iolanda Cum and Anjikwe Mshelbwala

List of Contributors
The Editors

Sabeeta Nathan read Economics at the University of Leicester. She was born to Sri-Lankan parents and is fluent in Tamil, which is her mother tongue, in addition to French and English. She has visited Sri Lanka many times and is keen on finding ways to grow its economy. Sabeeta is the co-editor of this current volume. She spent a year abroad studying at Universite Toulouse 1 Capitole, France, where she continued to read this subject. During this time, she was fortunate enough to meet the Nobel Prize 2014 Economics Winner, Jean Tirole. She specialises in writing, specifically campaigning for the Reform of Economics. Sabeeta is a passionate speaker and delivered a speech at the 10th Annual Green Economics Conference in March 2015

Miriam Kennet, is a specialist in Green Economics, she is the Co-Founder and is CEO of the Green Economics Institute. She also founded and edits the first Green Economics academic journal in the world, the International Journal of Green Economics, and she has been credited with creating the academic discipline of Green Economics. Green Economics has been recently described by the Bank of England as one of the most vibrant and healthy areas of economics at the moment. Having researched at Oxford University, Oxford Brookes and South Bank University, she is a member of the Environmental Change Institute, Oxford University. She has taught, lectured and spoken at Universities and events all over Europe, from Alicante to Oxford and Bolzano, and to government officials from Montenegro and Kosovo to The UK Cabinet Office, Transport Department, National Government School and Treasury and spoken in Parliaments from Scotland to Austria and The French Senat and Estonia.

She is also a regular and frequently speaks at public events of all kinds, and after dinner speaker. She has a delegation to the UNFCC COP Kyoto Climate Change Conferences and headed up a delegation to RIO + 20 Earth Summit: Greening the Economy in RIO Brazil. She regularly speaks on TV around Europe, most recently in Belgium, and Estonia and this year the BBC has made a special programme about her life and work. She runs regular conferences at Oxford University about Green Economics Publishing regularly and having over 100 articles, Chapters and other publications. She has been featured in the Harvard Economics Review and Wall Street Journal as a leader. Recently she was named one of 100 most powerful unseen global women by the Charity One World action for her global work and won the Honour Award from the Luxembourg Ministry for her work.

Authors

Max Basta has been an Economist at the University of Bristol since 2012, with a particular focus on sustainable growth in developed economies and is now begining to study with The Green Economics Institute.

Sophie Billington is an economist and econometrician at Bristol University. Her main areas of interest are developmental economics and econometrics. Sophie is interested in applied econometrics, econometric theory and the wide ranging and changing approaches to modelling economic problems. She has been instrumental in methodology debates in Green Economics.

Davide Bottos is researches economics at the Universita degli Studi di Udine in Italy. After high school he enrolled in the faculty of economics in Udine, where he obtained his first degree in January 2008 with a presentation of a thesis on the classical theory of price discrimination. In 2009 he studied for six months at the "Skarbek Graduate School of Business Economics" in Warsaw (Poland) as an Erasmus student. He became interested in the Green Economy by reading news that concerned the environment, mobility, energy and climate change. His opinion is that we must act so that governments implement all the policies that drive economic activity to a lower waste of resources and greater sustainability.

Rudolf Bühler founder of ECOLAND Int. and Farmers Association for Schwabisch Hall. Rudolf Buhler, does organic farming at Sonnenhof, Wolpertshausen, Germany, in 14th generation. He founded ECOLAND Int. and Farmers Association for Schwabisch Hall and acts as Chairman of both organizations. In 2013 HRH Prinz Charles visited his projects for integrated rural development in Wolpertshausen and shared views and experiences upon. His contribution to the conference "Charta of Farmers Rights – a needful step to save the social and cultural rights for all indigenous people and small scale farmers around the World" will open eyes and hearts about this important issue: 'Charta of Farmers Rights.'

Dr Susan M. Canney Research Associate, Spatial Ecology and Epidemiology Group, Biodiversity Institute Oxford. Dr. Susan Canney has worked on a variety of nature conservation projects in Africa, Asia and Europe, including living for several years in Niger and Tanzania. Dr. Canney has also worked as a research officer at the Green College Centre for Environmental Policy & Understanding (UK).

Chit Chong Sustainability Manager at Peabody. He has been initiating and implementing projects which reduce impact on the environment. These range from examplar projects like the first construction project in Europe to be certified of its use of sustainable timber and one of the first low energy refurbishments of a Victorian house to acheive over 80% reduction in emissions to large scale carbon reduction project including CHP to 1,500 dwellings and cavity wall insulation to 2,000 dwellings. He is currently working on internal solid wall insulation of dwellings. His aim is to save as much carbon as possible and to provide the practical ways for the UK to turn into a low carbon economy.

Eleni Courea lives in Cyprus but is of Greek, English, Scottish and Indian background. She brings a young scholar's perspective to questions of the importance of geography to green economics. She has participated in several conferences around the world, including World Individual Public Speaker and Debating Championships in Brisbane, Australia (2011) and The Hague International Model United Nations in the Netherlands (2011). She also organised the Youth Voice Conference in Cyprus (2011).

Henry Cox Electronic Engineer has worked as Electronic Engineer from 1950 to 1982, going digital in 1958. Often he has applied in systems of control of infrastructure; in various places - Woomera, Assam, Das, to Strathfarrer. Unpaid work from 1938: mostly in gardens, often growing food for the household; but some repairs of houses and equipment. Green Economics from the Gatherings of 1983 onwards. Present Economics restricting itself to what 'firms' organise; and restricting its concept of "work" to 'work done for money.'

Professor Gary Craig is a Professor of Social Justice at University Of Durham Gary was the world's first Professor in Social Justice when he was appointed at the University of Hull in 2000. He was also founding Fellow at the Wilberforce Institute for the study of Slavery and Emancipation (patron, Archbishop Desmond Tutu) and led the team working on issues of modern slavery. He worked in community development until returning to academic life in 1990 and was President of the International Association for Community Development (with UN consultative status) for 9 years till 2008.

Sandra Gusta Architecture and Building at Latvia University of Agriculture, Doctor of Management Sciences in Economics. One of founders and member of the Board of the LEA (Latvian Association of Economics). Member of the Latvian Association of Civil Engineers, Education and Science section. "Macroeconomics and sustainable development, environmental management, sustainable buildings and building management, sustainable building materials, sustainable building waste management."

Richard Holcroft, economist and mathematician at the University of Durham He is interested in aspects of transport and its environmental and socio-economic impacts. He ran a conference at the House of Commons on transport and climate change. Richard was also a delegate of the Cop 19 in Warsaw and is author of our book The Green Transport Revolution.

Norfaryanti Kamaruddin is Research Officer at the Institute of Tropical Forestry and Forest Products, Universiti Putra Malaysia. She earned her Bachelor of Science and Master of Science from Universiti Putra Malaysia. Currently, she is undertaking her PhD in the field of corporate governance through a collaborative project between CIRAD (France) and UPM.

Professor Dr Maria Alejandra Madi holds a PhD in Economics. She works at the intersection between macroeconomics, finance and socio-economic development. Retired Professor at the State University of Campinas, Brazil, she is currently Director of the Ordem dos Economistas do Brasil and Counselor at the Conselho Regional de Economia–SP. Besides her participation as co-author in chapter books edited by the Global Labor University, she is a regular author with the Green Economics Institute.

Mahelet Alemayehu Mekonnen is an Ethiopian economist interested in economics and political science at Richmond The American University in London. She heads up our Africa team and is editor of our special issue of our academic journal on Africa and our forthcoming book about Africa. She is economics advisor for the management team. She is a firm believer in education and believes in tackling one of the most important problems we are facing in the global world, particularly the issue of climate change and inequality towards women. Her work relates to examining large projects and questions of sustainability – and development.

Dr. Mohammad Naghi M.D, MBA Leadership & Sustainability, is a Lecturer of Pediatrics, October 6 University, Egypt and has an active interest in promoting Green Economics and Healthcare.

Don O'Neal BSc(Hons) in Mathematics and MA in Environmentalism and Society. Don O'Neal has a BSc(Hons) in Mathematics and an MA in Environmentalism and Society. He has been the Oxfordshire Greens Treasurer from September 2000 to date and is a political columnist for The News and The Vincentian national newspapers in St. Vincent and the Grenadines. He is a cofounder of St. Vincent and the Grenadines Greens and a Trustee of the Green Economics Institute.

Michelle S. Gale de Oliveira is a director of the Green Economics Institute, UK.She is a member of the Law School of the University of London School of Oriental and African Studies (SOAS), holding an MA in Human Rights Law with a focus on Islamic Law, Peace-Building, and Developing Countries, specifically South Sudan. Founder of the Gender Progress Consortium, she holds degrees in Political Science and International Relations from Richmond, the American International University in London (RAIUL). She is a deputy editor of the International Journal of Green Economics. Her writing has been featured in Europe's World, one of the foremost European policy magazines. She lectures and speaks on Human Rights, Environmental and Social Justice, Gender Equity, International Development and Green Economics internationally. She also ran a conference on women's unequal pay and poverty in

Reading, UK, lectured at the Oxford University Club on the human rights of land reform, is a regular speaker at international conferences and has appeared in the media in Africa, Europe, and Latin America. In 2010/2011, she was a delegate to the UNFCCC's COP15/16 in Copenhagen and Cancun, and in 2012 led a delegation to the United Nations' RIO+20, Sustainable Development Conference where she ran our three side events on green economics.

Professor Wendy Olsen. Socio- Economics. Wendy Olsen is an economist whose interests span economics, sociology, social statistics, development studies, and the cross-cutting issue of gender. She is interested in realism, comparative case-study approaches, discourse analysis and the use of qualitative coding software for mixed methods. She has international research experience and has carried out primary research in Telugu language as well as English, giving a good insight into the issues of international and multilingual research.

Miriam Prasse was a young student with The Green Economics Institute's Intern's College and was a speaker at our annual conference at Oxford University, starting the trend for young people at school to have a voice in the formulation of Green Economics at the highest level. She is based in Munich in Germany.

Adam Salah has recently joined the institute and he has a strong interest in economics and current affairs. He has studied Business and Administration at the University of Reading at their world renowned Henley Business School. His background is very international and includes numerous family members living in French speaking regions of the world, this has given him a keen grasp of spoken and written French. He is also a keen traveller having visited North America and Australia enjoying the sights and sounds of nature including the Rockies and The Great Barrier Reef. He hopes to gain an international perspective on the upcoming challenges the world economy is facing through working with the Green Economics Institute.

Stephen I. Ternyik MA, is private entrepreneurial economics scholar/educator, with a focus on quantum monetary science, since 1985 (consultancy, innovation, invest-ment). He pursued studies in social science in Berlin, Tokyo, New York and Jerusalem. His recent books are *Economics as Heuristics and New Economics* (2011); *New Ethical Economics Science* (2012);*Monetary Wave Theory* (2013);*Global Wave Energetics* (2014). The recent articles are 'The Monetary Quan-tum/Quantizing Money' (2012, Monetary Economics eJournal); 'Sustainable Monetary Agency' (DPG, Verhandlungen, Berlin, 2015).. He likes biblical poetry and cantorial art.

Enrico Tezza is a senior training specialist and has a background in social research and evaluation studies. After a career in the Italian Ministry of Labour and local public institutions, he joined the International Labour Organisation in Turin in 1992. He is labour market advisor for the Green Economics Institute. Subjects covered vary from training policy to employment and active labour market measures. His current focus interest is on social dialogue for green jobs. His main publication was Evaluating

Social Programmes: the relevance of relationships and his latest publications include Dialogue for Responsible Restructuring and Green Labour Market for Transitions.

Trude Blomseth Thy works in Telecommunications and in her spare time is a green campaigner and policy maker, active both in Norway and is a Representative of the Norwegian Greens the European and International level. She is a Trustee of the Green Economics Institute. She was educated at the University of Oslo and lives in Norway ***Bianca Madison-Vuleta*** is a specialist in holistic, ecological and sustainable living. She has been actively involved in the work of numerous national and international human rights and environmental NGOs as a committed and inspired campaigner, fundraiser and public speaker. A passionate humanitarian and environmentalist and Co-founder of The Sustainable Planet Foundation, Bianca works tirelessly to be the change in the world. She also is a regular writer in our books and an active member of our Trustee board.

Professor Vargas-Hernández is a member of the National System of Researchers of Mexico and a research professor at University Center for Economic and Managerial Sciences, University of Guadalajara. He has a Ph. D. in Public Administration and a Ph.D. in Organizational Economics. He has undertaken studies in Organisational Behaviour and has a Master of Business Administration, published four books and more than 200 papers in international journals and reviews (some translated to English, French, German, Portuguese, Farsi, Chinese, etc.) and more than 300 essays in national journals and reviews. He has obtained several international Awards and recognition.

Part 1: The Economics of Social Justice
1.1 The Reform of Economics

By Sabeeta Nathan

What is Economics? Economics is the study of the way governments and individuals behave in order to produce and consume goods and services. It is based around human interaction within the market and can be linked to the basic theory of scarcity, whereby individuals have to allocate limited resources efficiently in order to satisfy their unlimited wants. Choice is a key determinant. This chapter will focus on the Economics Curriculum being taught to students across many international Universities, right across the globe, from Britain to Brazil.

Since the 2008 Financial Crash, students have been complaining that their Professors are not teaching them about one of the greatest financial recessions of all time and they are now demanding that the Economics course, content and curriculum, are all changed. This has encouraged many protests, such as the Post-Crash Economics Society where individuals are expressing their concerns. Not only do students want the reform of their syllabus, but they are backed by the Bank of England as well as by many economists, including some of the top professors at the University of Cambridge, including Ha-Joon Chang who wrote *Rethinking Development Economics* (2003).

Several questions are hotly debated nowadays. Why did top Economists fail to predict the Financial Crash? Was the crisis predictable or could there be the excuse for the entire profession missing it coming, due to the fact that it was a "black swan event"? This theory was put forward by Nassim Nicholas Taleb in his book *The Black Swan* (2007) describing a type of unexpected event, where predictions would have been difficult to make. However students do accept this justification for the massive failure of the economics discipline and profession to foresee what was round the corner, and to explain it when it arrived.

I hope this book will raise awareness about why a Reform of Economics is essential. I will first offer an explanation of the crisis and follow with the opinions of economists and finally provide an overview of what students think today.

Kennet and Heinemann (2006) argue that economics should treat people (not labour power), the planet, nature, non-human species, and the biosphere as beneficiaries, not just resources or economic factors of production. The aim of economics ought to be to ensure that they are all as well-off following an economic transaction as they were before it. They expand on this idea in their paper, *Green Economics: setting the scene. Aims, context, and philosophical underpinning of the distinctive new solutions offered by Green Economics, (*Kennet and Heinemann *2006)*. In this present book the focus will also be building on those ideas and linking them to the Economics of Social Justice, which I will argue is built on foundations of equality, fairness and justice. Therefore I believe, that policies and theories which do not promote Social Justice need to be reformed in order to promote a healthier environment for the present and future.

A Green Economics viewpoint, for Reform of Economics regards social justice as the essential element, which is why we are currently publishing two books on social justice in order to further a Reform of Economics itself. I regard Neo-classical Economics as too narrow in that it does not accept the validity of other perspectives or theories. I aim, in this book, to explore possible solutions which will help to combat the problems that the economy faces today.

Furthermore, I believe it is necessary to promote this new take on economics, namely green economics because it expands the previous discourses of Social Justice to now include a landscape in which nature, individuals, biodiversity, our planet and society are cared for and looked after. This theory of engaging in positive, practical activity for the economy can be traced back in part to the work of Arthur C.Pigou, who developed the term "externalities" in *The Welfare of Economics*, (1932), which refers to an economic activity that is imposed upon third parties, thus those not actually part to or involved in an action. Impacts and consequences can be the case, even when the person does not take into account the action they have engaged in. They can either be positive or negative. Positive externalities include those such as healthcare or education, which generate beneficiaries upon society. On the other hand, negative externalities impose harmful effects on others, for example pollution or nuclear waste. Pigou argued that there should be government intervention, when there are negative externalities in order to limit such impacts and that taxes could be proposed. In the case of healthcare, Pigou stated that subsidies should be involved, in order to raise awareness. I agree with this theory as it could help to promote social justice and positive environmental effects, especially long term impacts.

The 2008 Global Financial Crisis, caused by the failing of financial markets and the collapse of the American Banking sector, still affects people in many economies, particularly in Europe. The world economic collapse was possibly the most distressing since the 1930's Great Depression. The closure and bankruptcy of Lehman Brothers, the fourth largest investment bank in the USA, caused widespread turmoil, for example, drastically reducing share prices to below $4 on world financial markets. The subprime mortgage meltdown in America, where house prices fell drastically, caused borrowers to default on their loans. Before this turmoil, borrowers with a low credit rating faced high interest rate payments on their mortgages, due to the risk of default. However, as a consequence of house prices falling, borrowers were unable to repay their loans, leading to evictions and individuals filing for bankruptcy. Structural government deficits, economies sliding into recession and overly high debt levels were three major consequences of the crash. European banks which had invested heavily within the American mortgage market faced repercussions, leading to the Euro debt crisis. Greece is one of the countries that has faced bailouts and has received its third financial bailout from the IMF and European Central Bank in order to support its economy and prevent its exit from the Euro zone.

Alan Greenspan, who was the Chairman of the Federal Reserve of the United States from 1987 to 2006, agreed that he had made a mistake in relation to predicting the financial crash. Greenspan was thrown with accusations from Economists, where they argued that he had kept interest rates so low which encouraged the hike in house prices. In his book, *The Age of Turbulence*, he wrote, "*I guess I should warn you, if I turn out to be particularly clear, you've probably misunderstood what I said.*" (2007). He argued that the demand for securities was at a peak in the United States, and that the Wall Street businesses' were to blame for selling mortgage-backed securities. This led to an increase in pressure on financial lenders, who eventually began to print more money into the economy. Social Justice aims to distribute wealth amongst society, create equality and distribute resources efficiently in order to allow an economy to function well. Greenspans' actions have caused misery amongst individuals as well as damaging nature; setting back the cause of social justice. "Why did no one see it coming?" (Financial Times, 2008) a simple yet hard hitting question was voiced by Queen Elizabeth and many other people including today's economics students. Arguments have been made as to why Economists failed to predict the crash. Andrew G Haldane, the Chief Economist and Executive Director at the Bank of England has expressed concern about the Economics Profession and the Graduates it is turning out may not be fit for purpose. He argued in the Financial Times (2009) "*The economy in crisis behaved more like slime descending a warehouse wall than Newton's pendulum.*" Furthermore, the former Governor of the Bank of England, Mervyn King did not even notice the oncoming recession and was adamant that financial institutions and political parties were to blame for their own lack of foresight. He complacently boasted in the Independent Online, (2009) "*It's quite possible that at some point we may get an odd quarter or two of negative growth. But recession is not the central projection at all.*" A statement which in hindsight from the person sitting at the helm of the sinking ship is breathtaking in its arrogance and in its errors!

However some economists were paying attention to what was going on around them in the real world. Nouriel Roubini, an American Economist has published many articles and books on macroeconomic policies. His book *"Crisis Economics: a crash course in the future of Finance,"* pinpointed the fact that the US housing bubble was in danger of bursting and when this bubble eventually collapsed, there would be pandemic impacts worldwide. He laid the pathway for readers to be prepared for the next crisis which could happen in the future. Roubini argues that the crisis was actually a "white swan event" in his *Crisis Economics: a crash course in the future of Finance,* (2010) and that economic predictions are actually quite easy to make if economists analyse the data, rather than rely on Taleb's "black swan" theory. Roubini credibly foresaw the crisis of 2008. However some people think it was merely a lucky guess. Roubini claimed that he made several predictions based upon the state of the economy, which led him to predict the collapse and worldwide recession. Conflicting theories and diverse opinions from top economists have made it difficult to believe if Roubini was right or not.

The continuing aftermath of the financial crisis in 2008 has led many University students to protest against what they were being taught in the field of Economics. This has led to a high level of discontent, as students now realise that one of the biggest phenomena in society and in economics has not been addressed at all and in fact is avoided in many of the courses they are taught. The silence is deafening and students are now beginning to take action. They have noticed that amazingly since the crash, there has been little change to the taught core syllabus. Papers have begun to appear about this with a range of theories about how this could possibly be so. Students worldwide are keen to learn about real world economic problems such as inequality and heterodox economics. There has been an increase in the number of students taking The Dismal Science of Economics since the crash specifically because they want to understand it. Many are noticing that their Professors are unwilling to change the syllabus. Dissent among economics students is growing, even in a subject where traditionally students were very compliant and even main stream and conservative. They are incredulous that the discipline is teaching them a narrow logic of mathematics and avoiding relating anything to the real world. They can feel that there is something very wrong and they can smell a wind of change blowing. There have been walkouts even at Harvard and sit ins. A protest manifesto was signed in 30 different countries and 65 economic student associations were backing this syllabus reform. Economics students have argued that they still have little knowledge about the global economy and current affairs during their time at University, in lectures and seminars. They are embarrassed when their friends ask them to explain about the economy and in spite of their studies they have no more knowledge about it than when they started.

The ISIPE (International Student Initiative for Pluralism in Economics) are worldwide, including in Colombia and Australia. They are a student committee of 82 groups campaigning for the reform of their curriculum and an increase in taught pluralism.

They sent an open letter Manifesto which was signed by numerous member organisations. There was a protest at Manchester University, where undergraduate students formed the Post- Crash Economics Society at the start of 2013. These students have complained about the fact that their Economics course consists of mathematical models and neoclassical theories. They also believe that their syllabus is too orthodox and are keen to learn other economic models, such as Keynes, Marxist, Feminist and Austrian theories. Since the formation of this campaign, many have been arguing that their course should change, and that it is important for there to be the Reform of Economics. They hope that other UK institutions will spread their movement. They want to make a change to the way Economics is taught at University and have held lectures, where they teach theories such as Marxism to other students. Students of the Committee argue that Universities are preparing them solely for jobs in the City, rather than teaching them why it is possible that one of the greatest economics phenomena in history, the Financial Crash, has not been addressed. A student of the committee, Joe Earle, said that Economics was "in danger of losing its broader relevance".

(The Guardian, 2013) Despite this group's protestation, there has been little visible change to the syllabus or curriculum.

The Faculty at Manchester University even disagreed with the campaign and concluded that those who were interested in finding out about the financial crash should join the Business School instead of doing economics. Ha- Joon Chang voiced his concerns over the Economics curriculum, explaining that it was too linked to maths and that economics students were not aware about the global economy and the different situations occurring around the world.

Furthermore, in France, the *Peps-Economie* is a committee arguing for pluralism in Economics and a movement which wants to move away from using purely technical approaches in the curriculum. They are unhappy with the way economics is taught to them and they hope that other Universities will follow in their footsteps and raise awareness about this problem. Several Economics examinations during the University course consist of Multiple Choice questions and the solving of mathematical formulas. Students are of the belief that they are not able to evaluate and analyse Economic problems, and expand on their answers in an essay based exam. They want to develop their knowledge and argue their case based on models, as well as including current affairs awareness. *Rethinking Economics,* is a committee of students and thinkers worldwide, who have collaborated in order to expand the scope of Economics. They aim to teach others in a more thoughtful manner and are keen to diversify this subject. The organisers want to increase social awareness in the present as well as for the future and hope to enhance decision-making amongst students. Several conferences are held during the year where professors, students and many others, such as Nobel Prize winner, Daniel Kahneman, are able to voice their argument and engage in debates and discussions.

I believe that studying Economics has provided students worldwide with many benefits, such as allowing them to develop their business acumen and widen their knowledge about global issues. The range of mathematics on this courses is essential for those who want to pursue careers, in finance for example. What students are protesting about, is mainly the fact that the financial crash was not dealt with enough at University and that their curriculum does not reflect it. As previously stated, students internationally want to learn about Heterodox Economics and to move away from their subject being too "mainstream."

Not only is the Reform of Economics urgently wanted by UK economics students, but also by students in other countries, such as France and Germany. There are many ways to improve the syllabus and allow students to learn about the crisis, one which would be welcomed by many. Students are keen to learn about the background of their economy and how it has changed over decades. Through learning about this, students would be capable of manipulating economic models and understanding why major events have occurred in the past. I hope that the readers of this chapter and book will have a greater insight into our student's viewpoint about why the University syllabus should be changed. This is even more pressing after the Financial

Crash and will help us avoid or prepare better to solve future financial and economic challenges and events. Upton Beall Sinclair Jr, (1994) noted that "It is difficult to get a man to understand something when his salary depends on his not understanding it."

References

Chang, Ha–Joon, Rethinking Development Economics, 2003, Anthem Press: London

Taleb, Nicholas Nassim, The Black Swan, 2007, Random House: London

Arthur Cecil,Pigou, The Economics of Welfare, 1932, Macmillan & Co: London

Kennet M., and Heinemann V, (2006) Green Economics Setting the Scene:in International Journal of Green Economics Volume 1 Issue ., pg 74) Inderscience: Publishers Geneva Greenspan,

Alan, The Age of Turbulence, 2007, pg 19,The Penguin Press: United States Financial Times (2008) The economic forecasters' failing vision. Available at: http://www.ft.com/cms/s/0/50007754-ca35-11dd-93e5-000077b07658.html#axzz3iaplfCXj (Accessed: 01 August 2015)

Financial Times (2014) Students' hopes dashed over 'crash' course in economics teaching. Available at: http://www.ft.com/cms/s/0/07bc8b9e-bf1d-11e3-8683-00144feabdc0.html#axzz3iaplfCXj (Accessed: 01 August 2015)

The Independent (2009) Quotes of 2008: 'We are in a state of shocked belief' Available at: http://www.independent.co.uk/news/business/analysis-andfeatures/quotes-of-2008-we-are-in-a-state-of-shocked-disbelief-1220057.html (Accessed 02 August 2015)

Roubini, Nouriel and Mihm, Stephen,(2010) Crisis Economics: a crash course in the future of Finance,The Penguin Press: United State

The Guardian (2013) Economics students aim to tear up free-market syllabus) Available at: http://www.theguardian.com/business/2013/oct/24/students-post-crasheconomics (Accessed 02 August 2015)

Beall Sinclair Jr, Upton, I, Candidate for Governor: And How I Got Licked, 1994 Reprint, University of California Press: California

1.2 The Balance of Economics and Social Justice

By Richard Holcroft

Economics is the study of how people, governments and firms make choices on how to use our resources. It considers our means of production. We strive to improve the efficiency of the economy so that we can get more out of our nation and planet's limited resources. Social justice is justice in terms of the distribution of wealth, opportunities and rights in society. As the moral zeitgeist has moved forward, we have increasingly advocated social justice. The goals of improving the economy and striving for social justice often intertwine, leaving us with important questions. To what extent will we seek to expand the economy at the expense of equality? What is the optimal top rate of income taxation that will perfectly balance equality and incentives to innovate? What is the perfect balance?

Sometimes the causes of economics and social justice complement one another. For example, improving the efficiency of the economy can improve living standards for the poorest in society by freeing up resources for them. There is a larger pie to share among us when the economy is stronger; or that is the idea. Similarly, a move towards equality can improve our economy. The introduction of the National Minimum Wage in the UK in 1997 has been seen as a dramatic force in increasing the pay of low-income earners while lowering wasteful profits of shareholders, without damaging employment prospects (Holcroft, 2014). In other words, the minimum wage has been seen as a win-win policy, and its success has even led the Conservative Party in the UK, once an opponent of the minimum wage, to introduce a relatively stronger 'living' wage.

Of course, sometimes the two causes result in trade-offs. It isn't implausible to say that income inequality comes hand-in-hand, to a certain extent, with higher absolute levels of income. The extent to which this is true is debatable, since we often see very poor countries with unfavourable gini coefficients. Most people living in the 21st Century have ideals that they wish to achieve collectively, such as equal opportunities for those of different sexes, races, sexualities.

An economy that functions effectively and efficiently provides the resources to pursue these ideals. In the pursuit of these two goals, it appears to me that economics can take up a disproportionately large part of the focus. Often this obsession with economics, which could be called pseudo-economics, can be damaging both to social justice and, ironically, to our own economy. One recent example is Barack Obama's Clean Power Plan. I welcome this plan with open arms, but one thing that stuck out in the video message he released was that in the three justifications he gave for his plan, the economy was announced first (BBC, 2015). The elephant in the room is of course climate change and the prevention of mass devastation, which one might think deserves first place in such a list.Another example is the possibility of an expansion of Heathrow airport. Yes, it may improve the economy for now and bring in more money to the UK, as we often hear Ministers telling us. But at what cost?

Furthermore, I have sometimes looked at the so-called 'Anglo-Saxon' economies and been baffled by the rhetoric on 'growth': that is, producing more output per person each year.2 This is a faceless figure. It could be a very good thing or a terrible thing if the UK were to grow by 2% next year. We could achieve 2% growth by making everyone work twice as many hours. Or we could achieve that growth via an explosion in gun production, petrol sales, or carrier-bag production, but I wouldn't be thankful for such a thing. On the other hand, we could have investment in home insulation, cycling infrastructure, etc., and achieve the same level of growth. That would be the kind of growth I would personally prefer, and it would also improve the efficiency of our economy.

If we moved from the minimalist focus to the whole picture of economics, social justice and more, I think we could achieve a whole lot more.

References

Holcroft, R., 2014. The effects of the National Minimum Wage on employment and working hours in Britain. BSc. University of Durham.

BBC, 2015. Climate change: Obama unveils Clean Power Plan. [video online] Available at: <http://www.bbc.co.uk/news/world-us-canada-33753067> [Accessed 9 August 2015].

Kennet, M. & Heinemann, V., 2013. The Green Economy: Rethinking Growth. In: Holcroft, R. Kennet, M. & Stewart, J., ed. 2013. The Green Transport Revolution. Reading: The Green Economics Institute, Ch 6.

1 The gini coefficient measures the level of inequality in an economy.

2 I would strongly recommend reading The Green Economy: Rethinking Growth

1.3 Karl Polyani on Ethics: Conceptualising Social Justice

By Professor Maria Alejandra Madi (Brazil)

Introduction

In the 21st century, the systemic and institutional analysis proposed by Karl Polanyi is a decisive reference to apprehend the current cultural and social challenges to (re)embedding the economy in society. This historical setting favored shaped ethical and economic patterns that do not favor social justice. As a result of financial and trade globalization, the current driven-forces of institutional change and money commodification have fostered disruptive forces on livelihoods and disorganized solidarity and reciprocity interrelations (Madi and Goncalves, 2007). Indeed, the recent social and economic trends have expressed deep conflicts between the perspectives of sustainable economic growth and the society claims around decent work and income redistribution. Indeed, current economic modernization has fostered social inequality in the frame of the financial-led growth regime that privileges the centrality of the free markets.

Current global business has been overwhelmed by the financialisation of wealth. Beyond financial and "rationalization" strategies, social conflicts and tensions have been strengthened as labor relations need to be adjusted to capital mobility and short-run returns. The expansion of global finance has contributed to the redefinition of labor relations because investors and managers subordinate the business dynamics to a financial model that favors downsizing and cost reduction at the expense of employment. As labor costs are frequently considered large expense items, corporations must tightly managed and documented those costs in order to minimize risk of non-compliance, particularly public companies. In this scenario, changing working conditions result from continuous restructuring to generate cash outflow, redefinition of tasks, increased outsourcing and casualization to cut costs, sell-offs and closures regardless of productivity and profitability, deteriorating working conditions, more control on workers, diminished employment security (IUF, 2007).

Considering the relevance of Polanyi's work to apprehend today's challenging social and political issues, our aim is to provide a more deep and nuanced understanding of his thought on social justice. Section one examines Polanyi's interpretation of modern economic and social history so as to clarify the ethical presuppositions present in his work. Section two addresses how his understanding of the relation between ethics and economics touches on social justice. Section three analyses the concept of social justice as part of Polanyi's contribution to social philosophy. Finally, the conclusions highlight that Polanyi's understanding of modern capitalism really favors a concept of social justice that is overwhelmed by the principles of reciprocity and solidarity.

1 Polanyi's interpretation of modern economic and social history: ethical presuppositions

Current sociability conditions have been transformed by the changes observed in market economy institutions. The outcomes of the neoliberal agenda have stimulated social and cultural fragmentation in the context of the disruption of livelihood conditions. In this scenario, the analysis of social inequality fosters the reflection about the ethical issues that overwhelm the current manifestations of disembeddedness and the commodification of livelihoods. In other words, the current institutional set up created under the auspices of the neoliberal agenda has not been able to protect society, that is to say, it has not been not able to protect livelihoods from the ravages of the "satanic mill." The deep and persistent effects of the neoliberal political agenda can be apprehended considering Polanyi´s concern about the way in which the economy relates to social organization and culture and the impacts of social and political institutions in relation to human livelihood. In fact, after the 1970s, the evolution of the world-wide capitalism system has increasingly expressed the tensions between the expansion of the market economy and its deleterious effects on society. When we examine the current interrelations between economics and inequality, Karl Polanyi´s critic of the liberal myth and of the disruptive forces of the market society is inspiring to analyze the impacts of neoliberal policies on livelihood conditions. As he writes in The Great Transformation, "A market economy is an economic system controlled, regulated, and directed by markets alone; order in the production and distribution of goods is entrusted to this self-regulating mechanism. An economy of this kind derives from the expectation that human beings behave in such a way as to achieve maximum money gains....

Self-regulation implies that all production is for sale on the market and that all incomes derive from such sales. Accordingly, there are markets for all elements of industry, not only for goods (always including services) but also for labor, land and money, their prices being called respectively commodity prices, wages, rent, and interest"(Polanyi 1944: 68-69).

The self-regulated market demands the institutional separation of society into an economic and political sphere, that is to say, in the market society the social relations are embedded in the economy rather than the economy embedded in social relations. The proper self-regulation of the market entails that "Nothing must be allowed to inhibit the formation of markets, nor must incomes be permitted to be formed otherwise than through sales" (Polanyi 1944: 69). Thus, as the commodity fiction is the vital organizing process, labour, land and money turn out to be seen as commodities and are produced for sale. As the result of being the process of exchange the aim of society, the commodification of money may possible to enlarge the subordination of sociability conditions to the market economy and the social relations become an "accessory of the economic system" (Polanyi 1944:75).

Nevertheless, the historical evolution of capitalism has always been followed by the sprouting of safeguards to protect society against the interference of the market practices. Accordingly Polanyi, social and economic changes, in the nineteenth century, were the result of a double movement: the extension of the market was accompanied by a counter-movement to protect society - by a set of measures and policies aimed to restrict the effects of the institutions of the market economy relative to labour, land, and money (Polanyi 1944: 76). As a matter of fact, the deliberate intervention both to "institutionalize" the market economy and to protect society from its harmful effects expresses

".... The action of two organizing principles in society, each of them set special institutional aims, having the support of definite social forces and using its own distinctive methods. The one was the principle of economic liberalism, aiming at the establishment of a self-regulating market ...; the other was the principle of social protection aiming at the conservation of man and nature as well as productive organization..."(Polanyi 1944:132).

The commodity fiction implies that the market economy demands the institutional separation of society into an economic and political sphere. Labour, land and money are elements of industry, but cannot be produced themselves for sale, thus cannot be seen as commodities. Labour is another name for a human activity which is part of life itself; land is another name for nature; money is just purchasing power. As the commodity fiction proves to be the vital organizing process, within the self regulated markets the market society the social relations are embedded in the economy rather than the economy embedded in social relations. Some of the consequences of the social disembeddednes of the economy are clearly presented in The Great Transformation:

"Nature would be reduced to its elements, neighborhoods and landscapes defiled, rivers polluted, military safety jeopardized, the power to produce food and raw materials destroyed. Finally, the market administration of purchasing power would periodically liquidate business enterprise, for shortages and surfeits of money would prove as disastrous to business as floods and droughts in primitive society" (Polanyi, 1944:76).

In other words, in the nineteenth century, the liberal agenda was an important expression of economic and cultural changes because it may possible to enlarge the subordination of sociability conditions to the market economy and the social relations increasingly become an accessory of the economic system. As labour, land and money turned out to be seen as fictitious commodities bought and sold in the market, Polanyi says: "human society had become an accessory of the economic system" (Polanyi 1944: 75).

With the advance of industrialization, the liberal economic theory spread out the statement that the search of individual enrichment is the "natural" characteristic of men. For Polanyi, the social and economic dynamics is not the result of a "natural order." Indeed, he looked for evidences in history and anthropology to show that the priority of the economic sphere as well as the expansion and dominance of the "economic motive" in the markets, are essentially modern phenomena. The spread of individual behavior founded in the economic motive and the disorganization of traditional forms of reciprocity and redistribution threatens the interrelations developed inside the families and neighborhoods that aimed to "… safeguard both production and family sustenance…" (Polanyi 1944: 48). In truth, the new pattern of behavior provokes disruption of traditional livelihoods and intensifies the subordination of the whole society to the commodity fiction.

From the study of early societies, Polanyi highlights the social nature of men as an oustanding feature in societies of all times and places (Polanyi, 1977). Besides, he underlines as an outstanding discovery that the universal motivation of human beings is to protect and enhance social standing. Thus, Polanyi underlines the need to reflect on the relations between material goods and the behavior of human beings towards the aim to achieve social standing within different societies. All societies studied by him other than market societies- protect themselves by promoting values- such as generosity - that foster social standing. At this respect, Polanyi's historical analysis of economic change emphasize the relevance of ethical principles that supports a conception of human being that is social and whose fundamental motivation is to protect and enhance social standing.

Taking into account the current ethical challenges within financialization, the systemic and institutional analysis proposed by Polanyi (1944) in The Great Transformation is inspiring to apprehend the social and cultural tensions inherent to the implementation of neoliberal policies since the commodification of money tends to subordinate the social sphere and the financial markets assume a new role in the possibilities of social reproduction (Madi and Goncalves, 2007). The understanding of the role of the values that shape human behavior is absolutely relevant to apprehend the current ethical challenges in the market society.

As Kari Polanyi Levitt (2013) explains, since the early 1980s, many Western economies observed the declining contribution of manufacturing and the increasing contribution of finance, distribution and business services to gross domestic product. In this scenario, the transnational corporations have increased the monopolistic control over global markets. As a result, millions of farmers have been dispossessed of their land and millions of workers have been dispossessed of good jobs. Besides, financialization of capital has been overwhelmed by short-term market based considerations of shareholder value and the expansion of mass markets. Accordingly Polanyi Levitt, in this Anglo-American variety of capitalism, finance has become decoupled from production and stimulated speculation in the capital markets. Thus, the financialization of capital has had most deep social consequences in the West. In fact, the material and non-material elements of a society should be considered in any attempt to apprehend the challenges to overcome the process of social inequality. Currently, the linkages between finance and culture enclose not only financial strategies, but also values that found the expectations of individuals in society. Thus, it is worth remembering that Polanyi considers that institutions embodied human meaning and purposes (Polanyi, 1944).

Considering this background, we can note that the recent transformations in global capitalism have shown that the current capitalist institutional set up is an embodiment of the "economic motive" as an expression of the global cultural practices spread in the context of financialization. The effects of the big financial business on the enlargement of the market exchange relations could be apprehended in the context of the unrestricted markets where one decisive driven-force of the global dynamics is related to the spread of the "culture of money". In this scenario, the political dominance of high finance comes about by shaping new elites and cultural practices: the free market capitalist culture and its market institutions and values are dismantling the traditional ones, such as the value of generosity. This process turned out to contribute to the loss of social ties since the reciprocity interrelations are being substituted by individual claims that threaten the preservation of collective interests. The outcomes of the expansion of the global disembedded capitalism revealed the trend to the homogenization of national markets at the system level. Among the outcomes, the social tensions emanating from the national market zone -deflationary pressures on expenses, employment and earnings- have been extended to the political sphere and shaped different patterns of social change. As a result, social inequality has turned out to be a global outstanding feature.

2 The notion of economy

In the introductory note to Trade and Market, Polanyi invites us to re-examine the notion of economy since many people is accustomed to think that the only way of organizing men's livelihoods is the market economy. In his own words:
'What is to be done, though, when it appears that some economies have operated on altogether different principles, showing a widespread use of money, and far-flung trading activities, yet no evidence of markets or gain made on buying or selling? It is then that we must re-examine our notions of the economy.' (Polanyi et al, 1957: xvii).

Polanyi proposes a new theoretical construction in order to explain the place ad role of human beings in the social and economic system. And he argues that man values material goods only in so far as they serve the end to promote social standing. In fact, the social question becomes an anthropological question. Reinforcing the role of history and of anthropology to build a new notion of the economy, Polanyi notes:
"But a purposeful use of the past may help us to meet our present over concern with economic matters and to achieve a level of human integration, that comprises the economy, without being absorbed in it" (Polanyi et al., 1957: xviii). Indeed, while taking into account different ways of organizing men's livelihoods, Polanyi provides a guide to examine the non-market economies and claims that empirical observations reveal economic life in archaic and primitive economies to be entirely different from that assumed by formal economic analysis (Polanyi et al, 1975: 243-44).

At this respect, it is necessary to distinguish between the formal and substantive meanings of the term 'economic', as Polanyi also underlines in 'The Economy as Instituted Process'. Reflecting on the epistemological issues that arise in economics as a scientific knowledge, he argues that economics as was being developed at his time depends on formal principles. As a result, a set of assumptions - that becomes premises – were used as the basis for a sequence of logical deductions.

Nevertheless, in Polanyi's view, the method of economic anthropology, as it depended upon principles of economic behavior that were induced from empirical observation, could be known as substantive. From the empirical evidence of economic life in ancient times and primitive economies, Polanyi explains the concepts of reciprocity and redistribution. The reciprocity principle implies that in some societies there is an unspoken agreement and on behalf of it people produce goods and services for which they could do best and shared them with those people that live around who also behave alike. All of them contribute according to their abilities to the common welfare, and all share according to their needs. Their motivation to produce and share is not the economic motive, but the fear of loss of social prestige. In this setting, money also operated within the context of reciprocity. The redistribution principle is found in those societies where a chief or leader, after a harvest or a hunting expedition, redistributes the storage to members of his group. The distribution of communal wealth reinforces the social structure where the allocation of the storage indicates status and importance.

Although Polanyi recognized that market places existed in ancient times and they were present in primitive economies, he highlights that they were not important and existed within a context of reciprocity. Ancient and primitive economies had market places but were not market economies. Daily markets were merely convenient localized exchange places operating within the broad system of reciprocity and those market places for long distance trade, such as ports, such as the ports of trade were specifically isolated by the authorities from the prevailing reciprocity area and served to separate it from external influences. In this way, local craft and provision markets were not linked to long distance markets. These markets sell only items which could not be provided within the local system of reciprocity (Polanyi et al., 1957).

In the nineteenth century, however, a monetary based market economy sprang suddenly into existence and it pushed to the side the old systems based on reciprocity and redistribution. This market economy is an economic system controlled by prices that determine what, how and how much is produced and how is distributed. Money, as purchasing power, enables its possessors to acquire goods and services which are priced in money terms (Polanyi et al., 1957).

As Polanyi explains, in the market economy there are not social considerations in the decisions about production and distribution. The Great Transformation presents an interesting example of this feature of the market economy. Before developing a critique to the explanation of the role of poverty in the economic system, Polanyi synthetized the main (and false) theories aimed to explain "Where do the poor come from?". About these false theories on the increase in pauperism in England in early nineteenth century, Polanyi says:

"On one point there appears to have been general agreement, namely, on the great variety of causes that accounted for the fact of the increase. Amongst them were scarcity of grain; too high agricultural wages, causing high food prices; too low agricultural wages; too high urban wages; irregularity of urban employment; disappearance of the yeomanry; ineptitude of the urban worker for rural occupations; reluctance of the farmers to pay higher wages; the landlords' fear that rents would have to be reduced if higher wages were paid; failure of the workhouse to compete with machinery; want of domestic economy; incommodious habitations; bigoted diets; drug habits."

And he continues arguing that:

"Some writers blamed a new type of large sheep; others, horses which should be replaced by oxen; still others urged the keeping of fewer dogs. Some writers believed that the poor should eat less, or no, bread, while others thought that even feeding on the "best bread should not be charged against them". Tea impaired the health of many poor, it was thought, while "home-brewed beer" would restore it; those who felt most strongly on this score insisted that tea was no better than the cheapest dram" (Polanyi, 1944: 94-95).

However, Polanyi's analysis explains that the deleterious social effects created by the Speenhamland laws led to the emergence of the labor market and the birth of the market economy in the nineteenth century civilization (Polanyi, 1944:87). After land and money had already emerged as commodities, the commodification of labor – that is to say the commodification of human lives- turned out to result from social conflicts and land appropriations via enclosures. In this historical setting, as Polanyi shows, the Speenhamland laws created an obstacle to formation of the labor market. The Great Transformation underlines the process of social change created by trade and industrialization led to the emergence of poverty on a large scale. Polanyi describes the desolation, dehumanization and degradation of human lives as necessary steps for the emergence of a labor market. In his own words:

"Before the process had advanced very far, the laboring people had been crowded together in new places of desolation, the so-called industrial towns of England; the country folk had been dehumanized into slum dwellers; the family was on the road to perdition; and large parts of the country were rapidly disappearing under the slack and scrap heaps vomited forth from the "satanic mills." Writers of all views and parties, conservatives and liberals, capitalists and socialists invariably referred to social conditions under the Industrial Revolution as a veritable abyss of human degradation" (Polanyi, 1944: 41).

Polanyi's concern about the conditions of mankind in the context of industrialization relies on a critique of those economists and public men that, in the nineteenth century, believe that poverty was necessary to the functioning of society. For example, as Polanyi recalls that Townsend, Malthus, Ricardo, Bentham and Burke consider that the provision by the government of extensive relief (such as the Poor Laws) would interfere with the production process (Polanyi, 1944: 132). Reflecting on Ricardo's view, Polanyi condemned not only the hunger of workers as the only way to increase production but also the outcomes of the abolishment of the poor relief. In fact, Polanyi notes that the "iron" laws governing a competitive society are not human laws.

In his own words:
"The true significance of the tormenting problem of poverty now stood revealed: economic society was subjected to laws which were not human laws." (Polanyi, 1944: 131).

Beyond the economic laws, Polanyi highlights the presence of the ideology that supported economic liberalism:
"Economic liberalism was the organizing principle of a society engaged in creating a market system. Born as a mere penchant for nonbureaucratic methods, it evolved into a veritable faith in man's secular salvation through a self-regulating market. Such fanaticism was the result of the sudden aggravation of the task it found itself committed to: the magnitude of the sufferings that were to be inflicted on innocent persons as well as the vast scope of the interlocking changes involved in the establishment of the new order.

The liberal creed assumed its evangelical fervor only in response to the needs of a fully deployed market economy" (Polanyi, 1944: 141). Indeed, the economic changes that resulted from the Industrial Revolution cannot be apprehended if ignoring the political, social and ethical issues underlined by Polanyi. Considering the insights of her father, Kari Polanyi- Levitt's critique of contemporary economics is also related to the objection to the methodological individualism of the neoclassical approach. Indeed, in her view, the representation of the so called rational economic man does not apprehend the multiple set of issues related to human nature and human needs. She emphasizes the importance of history and of a multidisciplinary approach to social and economic change since economic development is overwhelmed by the role of culture, by creativity and diversity.

In fact, the fundamental problem in economics, for Polanyi is the attendance of human needs.[2] Thus, the Polanyian notion of economy certainly offers to us a new way of looking at the "human beings" and at the "economy" around us. This notion of economy is supported by ethical principles that touch on social justice.

3 Human actions and social justice
The Polanyian ideal of social justice can be summarized in the following words: "The economy has to serve society, not the other way around". In his view, human beings act to promote social standing that turn out to be the universal aim that supports social justice. However, the current "market economy" has turned human society into a "market society". The self-regulation of the market creates the

conditions that make the market the only organizing power in the economic sphere, that is to say, the central mechanism for the production and distribution of goods.

In the current context of financialization, private strategies - that search increasing productivity and cost reductions have shaped new labor relations since labor flexibility must be compatible to capital mobility (Goncalves and Madi, 2014). Among the outcomes of the redefinition of global investment flows, the reduction of industrial jobs and the displacement of productive plants favored new management principles that favor short-term profits. As a consequence, the conditions of existence of workers have been redefined. The evolution of labor and capital incomes has expressed the transformations in investment and employment trends that enlarged social inequality.

In the last decades, the participation of labor incomes in gross domestic product fell and the composition of capital incomes revealed the unequal redistributive outcomes of the current financial-led accumulation pattern. Besides, the recent economic changes have also contributed to further commodification of social relations - drawing all workers into the market as consumers - in a market economy where the financial sector dominates economic life (Madi and Goncalves, 2007). Indeed, the business environment has not only expanded the possibilities of economic reproduction, but has also proved to create challenges to the social reproduction. Weil (2014) highlights that today, the employer-worker relationship has been submitted to delivering value to investors.

As Weil's groundbreaking analysis shows, the result has been an everwidening income inequality. Indeed, the current market economy dramatically impacts on the social spheres since the spread of market-based values turns to "disjoint man's relationships and threaten his natural habitat with annihilation." (Polanyi, 1944: 44). Remembering Polanyi's words,

"..the control of the economic system by the market is of overwhelming consequence to the whole organization of society: it means no less than the running of society as an adjunct to the market. Instead of economy being embedded in social relations, social relations are embedded in the economic system. ... society must be shaped in such a manner as to allow that system to function according to its own laws. This is the meaning of the familiar assertion that a market economy can function only in a market society." (Polanyi, 1944: 60).

In our times, the aim of the market economy – the economic motive- is not compatible with the goals of peace and freedom. According to Polanyi, if people want peace and freedom in the future "they must become chosen aims of the societies towards which we are moving" (Polanyi, 1944: 263). Considering this background, the actions of human beings towards social standing, peace and freedom highlight the relevance of aims that foster social justice. In truth, the aim of social justice needs to promote a human-based and community-oriented cultural and economic process that is opened to values that protect society.

Thus, the contribution of Polanyi opens up new perspectives to think about an ethical living in contemporary capitalism different from the utilitarian view of life privileged by the logic of the market society. If economic and social change is to be authentically human, it needs to make room for values that favor social standing, such as generosity. In other words, it needs to make room to values that enhance not only an integral human development but also social justice.Economic change needs to be directed towards the pursuit of the common good for which the whole society – as a political community - must take responsibility. At this respect, Polanyi emphasizes the role of politics to express economic interests but also social aims (Polanyi, 1944). In short, human actions need to encourage the social embeddedness of the economy. As a result, the importance of "economic forms based on reciprocity and redistribution" could indicate how both markets and politics need individuals who are open to values that foster social standing. Basically, what is needed is an effective shift in mentality that can lead to the adoption of new life-styles as a mechanism of "selfprotection" in an otherwise market dominated society.

The decisive issue, therefore, is the overall moral tenor of society. In this context, Polanyi's work is inspiring to dwell on two criteria that govern moral action: social justice and the common good. All individuals are called to rethinking values, also by the institutional path which affects the life of the polis, that is, of social coexistence and excellence.[3] So, Polanyi invites us to think about power and justice today since he reflects on the meaning of human life in history and points out to the existence of values arising from social life.

Considering this background, the Polanyian conception of social justice emphasizes social philosophical foundations where anthropology, economics and ethics are intertwined. Its relevance refers to the current debate about the needs for universal principles in order to rethink ethical choices that could make possible the permanence and cohesion of social ties. This conception of social justice underlines that the economy is an instrument designed to serve the man. The instrument per se does not bear a meaning, but it finds its meaning in the use that is made of it. However, the current neo-liberal economic dynamics, founded on the laws of the self-regulated markets that favor efficiency and productivity, has been strengthening the reductionism of the concept of human being that is also present in the definition of individual in liberal thinking. In this context, the meaning of the human existence is crossed by the promise of productivity gains. The demand for productivity, instead of serving the human purpose, closes on itself to become its own finality. Indeed, such logic of productivity and efficiency is transformed into unemployment, precarious work, social exclusion and impoverishment. In addition, resource exhaustion and the threats against the environment also show deleterious aspects of present-day forms of economic power.

Accordingly Polanyi, a society is a living organism which ethos is the result of a complex combination of customs, norms, attitudes, aspirations that shape institutions.

As a result, his conception of social justice underlines that the economy needs to be supported by ethical values in order to function correctly in order to protect society. It is not any ethics whatsoever, but an ethics which is people-centered. This centrality of the human being at the heart of the ethical values must be the guiding principle of social justice.

4 Conclusions

Polanyi's work is inspiring to think about the ethical issues imposed in the context of globalization on behalf of the primacy of the economic (financial) power. In reality, the ethos of efficiency and productivity have shaped social relations and legitimized social inequality. The idea that the value of a human being depends on the criteria dictated by the principles of efficiency and productivity implies a refusal not only to a holistic conception of man but also to the centrality of human beings in the economic process.

Polanyi's understanding of modern capitalism really favors a concept of social justice that is overwhelmed by the principles of reciprocity and solidarity and the value of generosity.[4] Steps to social change should involve the creation of institutions necessary to translate the shift in mentality into effective actions since he points out to the individual responsibility in the construction of social justice.

The conception of social justice becomes a key-concept in the context of the social philosophy of Karl Polanyi. He emphasizes the social nature of men and warns not only about the morality of human actions but also about the mutability of human institutions. Social justice can be understood in the political dimension of human coexistence where human actions can promote the excellence of human life by preserving social standing and human dignity.

These thoughts underline a humanism in which the human-centered ethics of social justice expressed the universality of human dignity. In this sense, we can say that Polanyi's conception of social justice highlights two central issues: the meaning of the human existence and the ethical orientation of human actions. Considering this background, it is outstanding the need for rethinking the philosophical connections between the economy and the dignity of human beings. More fundamentally, as Polanyi Levitt (2013) suggests, we have to rethink the human needs and the real value of goods and services in current societies where financial power relations shape the evolution of livelihoods.

Ultimately the Polanyian concept of social justice presupposes a universal vision of the human being but also the recognition of a universal aim of men towards social change. The concept of social justice refers to the social problem with "the other" that manifests itself in history.

Finally, following Polanyi's insights in The Great Transformation, we can conclude that poverty, power and inequality are interconnected; and each, in turn, is intricately related to social justice. If the practice of social justice involves the social reembeddedness of the economy, the common good can be built by people that aim the protection of society. Thus, ethical values, such as generosity, cannot be excluded from an ethical living. Without these values, social life will continue at the mercy of private interests and the logic of economic power, with crumbling effects on society. In short, social justice should be the great counter-movement in the context of the great financialization.

References

Hayek, F.A (1937): Individualism and Economic Order, Chicago: University of Chicago Press.

IUF. International Union of Food, Agricultural, Hotel, Restaurant, Catering, Tobacco and Allied Workers´ Association (2007) A Workers´Guide to private Equity Buyouts. Geneve.

Madi, Maria. A. C. And Goncalves, J. R. B. (2007) 'Corporate Social Responsibility: redit and Banking Inclusion in Brazil In: Bugra, A. and Agartan, K.

eds.) Market Economy as a Political Project: Reading Karl Polanyi for the 21st entury, Palgrave.

MEIER, B. (2008). "Book Review: The Great Transformation: By Karl Polayni. Boston: eacon Press, 2001 [1944]" Social Thought and Research, Vol. 29.

http://plato.stanford.edu/entries/markets/

Polanyi, K. (1944) The Great Transformation: The Political and Economic rigins of Our Time, New York: Rinehart.

Polanyi, K. (1977) The Livelihood of Man, New York: Academic Press

Polanyi, K., Arensberg,. H. And Pearson, H. W. (eds.) (1957) Trade and Market in the arly Empires: Economies in History and Theory, Glencoe, Illinois: The Free Press.

Polanyi-Levitt, K. (ed.) (1990) The Life and Work of Karl Polanyi, Montreal: Black Rose Books. (2013) From the Great Transformation to the great Financialization, London: Zed Books

Weil, D. (2014) The Fissured Workplace: Why Work Became So Bad for So Many and hat Can Be Done to Improve It, Boston: Harvard University Press

[1] alejandra_madi@yahoo.com.br
[2] On a different perspective, Hayek proposes that the main fundamental problem of economics is that of coordinating the plans of many independent individuals. The main advantage of a competitive market order, in Hayek's view, is that rational agents respond to price signals, which convey the relevant information available in the markets, for the purpose of economic calculus. In his view, competition, through the price market system, leads to such a coordination. Individuals, acting in their own self interest, respond to price signals. Prices, in turn, reflect the information available in society. Price signals allow the transmission of previously unknown information in the most synthetic and relevant way for the purpose of economic calculus. Now, prices - impersonal signals that provide for an extensive social division of labour - are expressed in terms of money. See Hayek (1937).

1.4 A Farmer's Charter

By Rudolf Buehler (Germany)

The Charta of Farmers Rights Project

Development Process of International Law and Governance for the Protection of the Indigene Rights of Global Farmers' Community.

Gemeinnützige
Stiftung
Haus der Bauern

Definition:
Farmers are individuals of farming families which live on their own land or shared or leased land in the countryside and are cultivating their farmland themselves with sustainable practices.

A: Basic Right of Farmers for free access to nature and natural resources as
 - to crop genetic resources as farmers commons
 - to animal genetic resources as farmers commons.

B: Basic Right of Farmers of farmland in farmers hand; protection against land grabbing.

C: Basic Right of Farmers for the fair share on the value of food and natural products. Additional an economic compensation for their contribution to nature and landscape protection as these are external values to be compensated by the industrial society.

D: The farmers' community's social right on cultural self determination and rural life.

E: The farmers' social right of equal pension claim in comparism to members of the industrial society.

F: The protection of the indigene knowledge of the farmers' societies as their own intellectual property not to be grabbed by multinationals.

G: Further issues are under discussion.

The project aims in a process for the development of an „International Convention on the Basic Rights of Farmers" worldwide.

A number of farming individuals and farming cooperatives/societies/bodies are working on a draft concept for the farming rights convention which will ne introduced after its emerging process and final declaration by an international farmers convent.

In the final stage the „Farmers' Rights Charta" should become an essential part of the UN treaties, f.e. WIPO.

The foundation „The Farmers' House" based in Schwäbisch Hall is promoting this project and coordinates the global activities.

Rudolf Bühler
Founder & Chairman of „Farmers' House Foundation"

1.5 Social Justice: an introductory essay

By Gary Craig

Social justice is a concept that has been debated – in different guises - for thousands of years although it is only since the 1970s, and particularly in the past fifteen years, that it has re-emerged into political discourse, notably amongst governments which have characterised themselves as social democratic or 'Third Way'. As Miller argues (2001), however, in the context of the development of liberal democratic societies, 'the quest for social justice is a natural consequence of the spread of enlightenment' (p.4).

However, the concept remains a contested one, adopted from a variety of political positions, and linking to wider arguments about the roles of the state, the market and the individual. Although contemporary social democratic governments appear to 'own' the approach of social justice, it has also been espoused from the political right in the UK and in Australia, where, for example, the government argues that social justice is achieved best through an approach which privileges individualism - when individuals are able to compete in the market place, unconstrained by the action of the state. Current arguments about social justice also expose the tensions with other overarching political goals of economic competitiveness and environmental sustainability (JRF 2004).

The concept of social justice received prominence within the United Kingdom with the work of the Commission for Social Justice established by the-then Leader of the Labour Party (CSJ 1994). In a context of deepening inequality and poverty, the Commission suggested that the elements of social justice would include:
• the equal worth of all citizens
• the equal right to be able to meet their basic needs
• the need to spread opportunities and life chances as widely as possible
• the requirement that we reduce and where possible eliminate unjustified inequalities.

This begged important political questions and the policy programme of New Labour governments – and similarly disposed governments elsewhere - continue to beg some of them; for example, the question of what basic needs are. Social democratic governments provide systems of social assistance but have not effectively defined the adequacy of that assistance to meet basic needs as defined by a range of participatory research studies. The UK government's programmes to address social exclusion and reduce poverty are titled *Opportunity for All* but most such governments do not go beyond goals related to equality of opportunity to promote equality of outcome, which many would argue was a more robust indicator of a socially just society. ' What is not yet acknowledged is that genuine equality of opportunity and recognition of the equal worth of all our citizens is incompatible with the savagely unequal society we now live in. Equality of opportunity in the context of economic and social structures that remain profoundly unequal is likely to remain a mirage' (Lister cited in NICF 2001). Critics of social democratic governments argue that the state has to intervene more strongly to promote social justice both in terms of the process by which it is achieved and of redistributive policies; the market – covering all the institutions of society which operate to deliver goods and services – distributes those goods and services, as well as opportunities (or life chances) unfairly and the state has a key role in correcting those deficiencies. Governments focusing only on the poor and disadvantaged are also failing one key test of social justice, which is that it is concerned with the fair distribution of the good and bad things across the whole of society and not just amongst the poor.

Within the UK, the adoption of the goal of social justice – with a stated commitment to an agenda of equalities - has been used to mark off the policy agenda of the Scottish Executive (Scottish Executive 2003) from that of the UK Parliament. However, the Scottish Executive goes only some way towards a position of fairness to all: its 2003 spending manifesto argued that 'Scotland must be a society of strong inclusive communities where everyone can live with dignity ... every policy we introduce ... will be measured against success in closing the gap between the most disadvantaged and the average.'

A modern protagonist for the concept of social justice was John Rawls (Rawls 1971). Drawing on Aristotle, Hume, Hegel, Kant and other moral philosophers, he argued that (Social) Justice meant 'fairness ... the principle subject of justice is the basic structure of society ... the way in which the major social institutions distribute fundamental rights and duties and determine the division of advantages from social co-operation...'
(p.6) (that is, he was not concerned with the benefits to be derived for individuals from private association). A 'well-ordered society' was one in which 'everyone is presumed to act justly ...' (p.8), where vested interests are put to one side. Rawls' rejection of the idea of social justice as compatible with a society oriented towards individual gain is echoed in Donnison (1998) who argues that 'standards and values cannot be developed privately' (p.186) i.e. within one institution or in relation to one practice. What, Donnison suggested, 'we apply to others we must apply to ourselves.' These approaches are grounded in the traditions of a redistributive modern welfare state.

Rawls then derived two basic principles:
1. 'each person is to have an equal right to the most extensive scheme of equal basic liberties compatible with a similar scheme of liberties for others ...
2. social and economic inequalities are to be arranged so that they are both (a) reasonably expected to be to everyone's advantage, and (b) attached to positions and offices open to all'. (p.53) Social justice thus has a strong interrelationship with the concept of * inequality.
These were specific formulations of a more general position, that 'all social values - liberty and opportunity, income and wealth, and the social bases of self-respect - are to

be distributed equally unless an unequal distribution of any or all of these values is to everyone's advantage'. (p.59) The obverse concept, injustice, thus becomes in Rawls' view, 'simply inequalities that are not to the benefit of all.' (*Ibid.*) This approach highlights distinctions between equality of opportunity, or access, equality of outcome, and equality of status. Most contemporary politicians arguing for equality tend to argue for equality of opportunity; however, those on the right emphasise simply equality of rules and processes, the state's role being merely to ensure free market exchanges for all (equally), and those broadly on the left for equality of outcome – or at least sufficient equality of outcome to prevent injustice. Rawls observed that if there were to be inequalities, they could only be justified on the basis that everyone had equality of opportunity to compete for the most desirable positions, regardless of their class or status. Rawls' famous test of social justice was through what he called the 'veil of ignorance', through which 'no-one knows his place in society, class position or social status ... they know that their society is subject to the circumstances of justice and whatever this implies..' (*Ibid.* pp.118-119). People thus act without any sense of personal advantage.

Miller argues that social justice – which he regards as interchangeable with the concept of distributive justice - provides the political and philosophical basis for deciding 'how the good and bad things in life should be distributed among the members of a human society' (Miller 1999:1). These things incorporate, in his view, familiar material dimensions of a 'good life' – income, wealth, education, housing, health and so on. Miller identifies three key principles which connect strongly to the concept of social justice: desert, need and equality.

In relation to desert, a just society is one 'whose institutions are arranged so that people get the benefits they deserve' (*Ibid.*:155). This principle must not however become a rigid formulation contingent simply on institutional arrangements within a society, but allow concepts of need to come into play i.e. resources cannot be committed solely on the basis of desert but also of need. The concept of need is 'not merely idiosyncratic or confined to those who hold a particular view of the good life ... it must be capable of being validated on terms that all relevant parties can agree to.' (*Ibid.*: 205). This validation is a political process but one from which many parties have hitherto been excluded because of t heir lack of power, both in a formal and informal sense. Miller agues that the notion of equality relevant to social justice is distributive in its nature: 'it specifies that benefits of a certain kind – rights, for instance – should be distributed equally because justice requires this' (*Ibid.*: 232). To achieve social justice, we must have 'a political community in which citizens are treated in an equal across the board way, in which public policy is geared toward meeting the intrinsic needs of every member, and in which the economy is framed and constrained in such a way that the income and other work-related benefits people receive correspond to their respective deserts.' (*Ibid.*: 250).
The concept of social justice is thus linked closely to other key concepts such as * need to * citizenship and * rights. Marshall's 1950 exposition of Citizenship and social class advanced a taxonomy of rights by which one could identify the characteristics of

citizenship. These incorporated:

• civil rights: property rights, legal guarantees and freedoms

• political rights: right to vote, rights of association, constitutional participation; and

• social rights: entitlements to basic standards of education, health and social care, housing and income maintenance.

Many contemporary commentators on citizenship, such as Lister (1997) and Dean and Melrose (1999) do not regard these rights as of equal weight. Dean and Melrose for example argue that 'Civil rights underwrite the operation of the market economy and are entirely consistent with class inequality' whereas 'political rights and social rights tend to challenge such inequality' (p. 180). Thus citizenship and class to a large extent can embody opposing principles. From this perspective, there remains a major political question about the degree to which social justice is compatible at all with the operation of a market economy. Doyal and Gough (1991) argue that social justice 'stands against fanatics of the free market economy ... but also demands and promotes economic success' or, conversely, that 'social justice is an ideal in its own right but economic success also demands a greater measure of social justice'. (p.130) Plant (2000), however, argues that social justice requires governments to work with the grain of the market. For many commentators, the market is the fundamental cause of much injustice, both social and economic, and the goal of social justice as fairness requires governments to confront the inequities of market systems.

Most contemporary conceptions of social justice generally place social and political rights far ahead of civil rights in the sense in which Marshall used them. Confusingly, civil rights have come in the past forty years, most of all through the political activism of Blacks in the Southern United States of America, more to mean social and political rights - such as freedom to attend mixed schools than the more narrow meaning ascribed them by Marshall. Earlier analyses of social justice are also limited in their understanding of the way in which the dimensions of gender and culture need to be built into a framework of values; to Marshall's typology we would need to add, following Castles (2000), Lister (2003) and others, the categories of cultural rights and gender rights. For minority ethnic groups, this means the right to be culturally different within a society which provides the same social, civil and political rights to all.

This raises a further important theoretical and political agenda, that of exploring the nature of social justice within multicultural societies and particularly those characterised by institutional and individual * racism. Multicultural societies have increasingly been struggling with the difficulties of incorporating respect and recognition for cultural diversity and difference within a framework of universal rights: to date, within the UK, these arguments have been couched in terms of debates about social integration, assimilation and cohesion rather than about social justice. Social injustice might however be said to emerge not just from the unconstrained workings of institutions, groups and organisations through the mechanisms of the market, leading to significant differences in income, wealth and the opportunities and outcomes that these bring, but also because of cultural and socially-constructed differences based on, for example, gender, ethnicity, sexuality and disability (Fraser 2001).

Social justice is also about the non-material aspects of life: these incorporate critically the dimensions of respect and recognition between different groups and individuals (and not just the poor). For Miller, the distributive notion of social justice is not to be confused with 'the ideal of a society in which people regard and treat one another as equals ... [which] ... is not a distributive ideal in itself but does have distributive implications' (*Op. cit.*: 232,241), for example by influencing our attempts at distributive justice. This latter concept he terms social equality, which 'is a matter of how people regard one another and how they conduct their social relations' (*Op. cit.* 239). This complementary 'recognition' or 'relations of respect' aspect of social justice has been strongly argued in recent years by e.g. Young (1990). For her, social justice as a distributive issue needs to be set within a relational context, in particular 'the elimination of institutionalized domination and oppression'. Individuals, as well as the state and the market, have a key role to play in supporting the goals of social justice and answering the sorts of deceptively simple question posed by Miller in relation to social justice between the genders: 'is it fair that women should perform more domestic labour than men?' (2001: 5).

Miller argues that the major challenge posed by multiculturalism is that it widens the notion of the closed political community within which concepts such as need, rights and desert are contested. However, this is not an argument for 'the elimination of cultural differences but the opening up of national identities so that they become accessible to the members of many (ideally all) cultural groups within existing democratic states.' (2001: 263) The political task is to ensure that all cultural groups are, first, recognised and secondly, engaged in the process of determining the principles of social justice and acting on those principles. Miller argues there is little empirical evidence supporting the view that cultural differences translate into differing conceptions of social justice.

Most major conceptions of social justice also fail to consider the role of those most disadvantaged by social injustice, as actors - rather than simply victims - in the search for social justice. The United Nations (see e.g. UNDP 1993) points to the many ways, including organizational, informational, developmental, constitutional and legal, political and economic ways, in which participation by the disadvantaged themselves may promote social justice. Many governments have now also acknowledged the importance of processes which empower the disadvantaged to act and speak on their own behalves. An additional dimension might thus be on the role of community development as the means by which the excluded and the marginalised can act in the search for social justice. To put it another way, social justice is not simply about achieving forms of human welfare – of whatever kind – but the means by which that welfare is obtained.

It has also been argued (see e.g. JRF 2004) that geography has an important influence on the achievement of social justice. Differential equality of opportunity, poverty, access to rights and so on, may be accentuated for those in rural areas as compared with their urban counterparts, (e.g. the costs of accessing goods and services and their frequently poorer quality), or those living in deteriorating neighbourhoods compared with those in well-resourced communities.

Drawing on these analyses, one wide-ranging definition of social justice might be:

• a framework of political objectives, pursued through social, economic, environmental and political policies, based on an acceptance of difference and diversity, and informed by values concerned with

• achieving fairness, equality of outcomes and treatment;

• recognising the dignity and equal worth and encouraging the self-esteem of all;

• the meeting of basic needs;

• reducing inequalities in wealth, income and life chances; and

• the participation of all, including the most disadvantaged.

It is, however, increasingly necessary to consider how the process of * globalisation - that is, the impact of economic groupings which have no allegiance to particular political entities - affects this approach. In Miller's and earlier writers' analyses, it is possible to define social justice within the context of a closed political community in which all relevant actors could be identified and encouraged to engage with the debates about social justice. Globalisation, according to many commentators, has generated increasing divisions, in terms of income and wealth, both between and within all nation states.

Two limited scenarios might be advanced to protect the claims of social justice: one is that each nation state can continue to argue the merits of social justice, the other that a transnational community and its institutions emerges (which the European Union could represent within the context of Europe) which can constitute the new closed political community. Alternatively, those concerned with issues of social justice between states and regions would not retreat within such a closed community but use it as a base for advancing political, economic, social and environmental arguments for global (social) justice.

References

Castles, S. (2000) Ethnicity and globalisation, London: Sage.

CSJ (Commission for Social Justice) (1994) Social Justice:Strategies for national renewal, London: Verso.

Dean, H. and Melrose, M. (1999) Poverty, riches and social citizenship, Routledge, London.

Donnison, D. (1998) Policies for a just society, Macmillan, Basingstoke.

Doyal, L. and Gough, I. (1991) A theory of human need, Macmillan, Basingstoke.

Fraser, N. (2001) 'Recognition without ethics?', Theory, culture and society, 18(2-3): 21-42.

JRF (2004) Overcoming disadvantage: an agenda for the next 20 years, York: Joseph Rowntree Foundation.

Lister, R. (2003) Citizenship: Feminist Perspectives (2nd edition), Basingstoke: Palgrave.

Marshall, T.H. (1950) 'Citizenship and social class', in T.H. Marshall and T. Bottomore, (1992) Citizenship and social class, London: Pluto Press.

NICF (2001) Annual report, Belfast: Community Foundation for Northern Ireland.

Plant, R. (2000) 'Social justice' in R. Walker (ed.) Ending child poverty, Bristol: Policy Press.

Rawls, J. (1971) A theory of justice, Oxford University Press, Oxford.

Scottish Executive (2003) *Social Justice: a Scotland where everyone matters,* Edinburgh: Scottish Executive.

UNDP (1997) Human Development Report, 1993, Oxford: Oxford University Press.Young, I.M(1990) *Justice and the politics of difference,* Princeton: Princeton University Press.

This chapter was written as an introduction to those not familiar with the term or confused by its multiple usages. For a fuller and more up-to-date discussion see Social Justice and Public Policy, (2009) eds. G Craig et al, Policy Bristol: Press, especially the Introduction.

Part 2: Education for Social Justices

2:1 Greening the Academy for Social Justice

By Michelle S. Gale de Oliveira (Brazil) and Miriam Kennet (UK)

"If the bee disappears off the surface of the globe, then man would only have four years of life left," attributed popularly to Albert Einstein. Colony Collapse Disorder is leading to bee losses at 30%.

In the past few years, schools of economics have been dominated by Keynesian or Freedmanite forms of capitalist theory. In the early 1960s and 1970s, the tide began to turn and competing economics platforms began to arise, insisting on a change of focus. These new disciplines were based on a concern for social and environmental commitments, and a reappraisal of economics foundations for human and planetary welfare. Recently, this has led to reforms within academic economic theory and social practise, such as the Corporate Social Responsibility movement (CSR), Environment Economics, and Sustainable Development. The academy initially greeted these movements with hesitant interest and many have now found their way into mainstream economics teaching. This chapter will give a brief description of these reform disciplines, discuss their aims and flaws, and demonstrate that these movements are simply not radical enough. Just as economics in the time of Adam Smith was initially aimed at countering the Industrial Revolution poverty of English cities, as Keynesian economics was constructed to avoid the horrors of a Great Depression and a Third World War, today's economics must be essentially and fundamentally committed to today's crises.

This time, economics must focus on halting environmental and social injustice, and must restructure the system through participatory democratic values. Therefore, the aim of the Green Economics Institute has been to theorize, produce, and mobilize such a discipline – a "green economics" that is acceptable to environmental studies departments at least, if not in business schools. This chapter will thus focus on a brief history of the movement, and examine present debates and challenges facing the discipline, and the future direction of Green Economics. It will touch on important theorists and paradigms that have contributed to the development of this new, progressive discipline. As the economics of doing – integrative, participatory, and dynamic – Green Economics is a distinct aspect of the implementation, discipline and philosophy behind Greening the Academy.

Environmental Economics has been used as a powerful umbrella term for several strands of economics which seek to enhance, challenge or replace the mainstream. In universities, these generally include Environmental Economics itself, along with Welfare Economics, Ecological Economics, lower growth economics, lower carbon economics, degrowth economics, and development economics. Further, it includes many other iterations of pluralist/holistic or Heterodox Economics. Thus the umbrella covers any perspective that challenges the mainstream. This section will discuss a number of theorists and schools in this arena, with a fundamental role in the genesis of Environmental Economics.

First, this section will focus on a several key contributors to the creation of Environmental Economics as a discipline, specifically Barbara Ward, Kenneth Boulding, and Herman Daly. It will then broaden the picture with the creation of sustainable development as a sub-discipline and the "Limits to Growth" perspective. Through this section, the reader will obtain an educated background in Environmental Economics development.

Another important figure in the development of Environmental Economics was Kenneth Boulding. Author of the famous "Spaceship Earth," Boulding wrote much on sustainability, pushing academia to recognize that economics only exists within nature, and that Earth must be protected. With his discourse on the planet as a lifeboat, Boulding expressed a concern that the colonies of his day would eventually be "pried off" of the edges of Europe's sinking environmental and economic lifeboat (Boulding 1978: 302). This prophet of early Environmental Economics encouraged new platforms to break with mainstream thinking patterns, and left a vast literary legacy to Environmental Economics.

"Anyone who believes exponential growth can go on forever in a finite world is either a madman or an economist." – Kenneth E. Boulding.

Furthermore, Ecological Economist Herman Daly had a tremendous impact on the field of Environmental Economics, breaking from the mainstream in many ways over the course of his career. Daly's contributions included his model of the "Steady State Economy" (1993), which involved his addition of biophysical and moral aspects to J.S. Mill's (1848) "Stationary State" model. Further, Daly radically broke from mainstream tradition with his "Means Ends Spectrum." This model describes economic growth – or the production of more goods and services – to satisfy "intermediate ends" as being finite, explaining that technology cannot always be depended upon to solve resource scarcity. Importantly, Daly stated that the trivial wants of some people do not take precedence over the basic needs of others (Hussen 2004:258). Finally, Daly rejected sustainable development, and as other ecological economists, viewed it as a euphemism. As development requires economic growth, and growth requires resource exploitation, development cannot be sustainable.

He was one of the first theorists to promote the "zero-growth economy," which would have a tremendous impact on the field of Environmental Economics and eventually Green Economics. However one aspect of this is that its used to present zero movement of peoples and to prevent immigration which is actually contrary to a progressive green economics approach.

In 1987, the United Nations World Commission on Environment and Development (UNCED) issued the Brundtland Report, establishing sustainable development as a discipline. The report defined sustainable development as meeting "the needs of the present without compromising the ability of the future to meet its needs." Realising that economic development was environmentally unsustainable, this approach insists that the solution is accelerated growth rather than lower growth and development.

Despite the popularity of sustainable development in Environmental Economics circles, many Green Economists mistrust the integration of corporate interests into the umbrella discipline. At one level and one end of the spectrum, the paradigm embodies corporate aims to capitalize on environmental and social justice, or "green-washing," noted in its proximity to Corporate Social Responsibility and Stakeholder Theory. Alternatively, on the opposite end of the spectrum of its advocates, sustainable development is sincerely embraced by veritably green and progressminded organizations, such as ICLEI and the Sustainable Cities Movement. Without a doubt, sustainable development has had a tremendous effect on the development of Environmental Economics as a discipline. Still, its ambiguous aims and unclear scope have led to a false dawn of environmental and social solutions as it fails to reform the current paradigm and instead reinforces it.

The Brundtland Commission's work on sustainable development also led to the growth perspective's predominance within Environmental Economics. First, the growth perspective assumes the potential of sustainable growth to secure environmental justice through the eradication of poverty. Second, this view states that consumption is natural to human beings, who will always require and desire more products. Thus, through this paradigm, the capitalist economic system becomes fiercely consumerist, creating products that consumers believe they need in order to live "the good life." At the same time, consumers learn generationally that the capitalist system cannot function without high growth, and this learning becomes an accepted truth. Part of this led to the high mass-consumption theories that have resulted in the current downturn and economic collapse as commodities, debt and resources are exhausted. The environmental and social reality of our world demands the protection of both ecological and human resources, but in order to change this behaviour, global society must be offered alternatives – alternatives which Environmental Economics and sustainable development in particular have been unable to deliver.

In contrast, a Green Economy would allow every person to maintain comfortable living standards without exploiting other people or resources. The debate tends towards the view that certain absolute limits must be imposed to save people from themselves. The foundations of this approach can be found in Malthus (1817) and issues raised by Hardin (1968) in The Tragedy of the Commons. The debate also questions the root of technological fixes to ecological problems and, one might argue, Environmental Economics and Corporate Social Responsibility.

This chapter will now turn to focus on current developments in the discipline, as well as contributing ideas and schools. Environmental Economics stands at a turning point in global environmental and economic history. Never before has such a combination of environmental, social, and economic changes led to a crisis of this magnitude. Corporate Social Responsibility and market-based sustainable development theories are gradually being received as palpable reforms to mainstream paradigms. Even the mainstream environmentalism of these paradigms is a welcome change. Still, in today's circumstances, a re-humanized economic theory can and should go further. In this next section, the ideas and contributions of various schools will be demonstrated as having great importance to the reform of Environmental Economics. Indeed, Greening the Academia will require Environmental Economics to rapidly evolve and recognize today's most urgent problems. Our planet is changing drastically, and academia must race to process its new challenges. Today, the Earth is experiencing the 6th ever mass species extinction, while climate change is accelerating at a rate that terrifies scientists. Planetary conditions have worsened beyond the rim of experts most pessimistic conclusions. Experts warn that we may see the disappearance of Arctic ice sheets within months. Indeed, these economic costs outpace any previous human dilemma as their scope is truly global and affects our very survivability, underlining the reality that economics has always been engrained in the natural world. Economists may tend to forget this fundamental fact, but the mainstream is now quite literally being "brought back to earth."

Today, Environmental Economics needs to assume a deeper meaning. The discipline must undergo both soul-searching and radically change from the mainstream economic system which has excused hardship, pain and misery for some, while others enjoy wasteful and unprecedented riches. Such exaggeration and inequity is criminal and unethical. Environmental Economics must take this reality to heart – if one fifth of cars crashed and one fifth of aeroplanes fell out of the sky as a result of faulty design, the response would be to immediately return to the drawing board, reworking the system's design.

Our economics system has long been out of balance with nature. It has long been out of balance with people's needs. Greening the Academy will be the first step in opening society to integrative and effective solutions to our current environmental and economic crises. This section will now summarize the contributions of ecological economics, lower-growth school, eco-feminism, nature, and deep ecology school to provide a summary of current developments, debates, and challenges to Greening the Academy from a Green Economics perspective.

An important subset of the Environmental Economics umbrella, Ecological Economics regards the economy as a subsystem of a larger global finite ecosystem – similar to Kenneth Boulding's description in "Spaceship Earth" (1966). Vitally, Ecological Economics recognises the interdependencies of the economic, social and ecological spheres, with the market being brought in only after equity and sustainability considerations are met, and only as a facilitator of the efficient allocation of resources. Markets are never used as an arbiter of (1) the equitable distribution of income and wealth creation or (2) the ecologically sustainable rate of resource use. Ecological Economics takes a major step toward reform, giving due attention to the complexity, value incommensurability and uncertainty in economy-ecology relations. However, it remains predominantly human-centred, with some ecological economists recognizing bio-centrism. This suggests an economy that takes into account the intrinsic values and needs of other species besides maximising human sustainable wellbeing.

Another area that Green Economics sees as intrinsic is the Lower-Growth school. Recently, areas of the British Government have started exploring staff's capacity to deal with today's crises, plunging into new economic and ecological arenas. Surprisingly, this has opened radically new ground, focusing on economic management through The Green Economics Institute. Radical approaches such lower-growth economics, degrowth economics and Redefining Prosperity are being taught and discussed in government departments as they gain in popularity as an approach.

In early 2008, popularity among the French led to a Paris conference on Degrowth. This event was based on the work of Serge Latouche, whose focus is not dissimilar to the work of Green Economics. Green Economics has been heavily influenced by Feminist theory and the idea of other voices, seeing this as lacking within Environmental Economics which continues in the tradition of the mainstream. While the mainstream concerns itself with competitive production and exchange in markets, the economy is underpinned by millions of people involved in care, reciprocity, direct production and maintenance of human beings every day. Their work is completely ignored in GDP figures, balance sheets, economics discussions and text books. One of the main contributions of Green Economics is the notion that production does indeed occur in the home or "oikia," rather than simply by homo economicus or rational economic man. It also points out the links between oikia - economics and ecology. Their approaches warn against theories that legitimise a single gendered homo-economicus version or "story" of reality, ignoring and excluding "gynaika ekonomika" from the public economic sphere.

Feminist methodologies allow us to understand the way in which the foundations of a discipline are laid and then expose them as particular and contingent. Climate change has forced us to remember our role as temporary visitors on Earth rather than its owners or stewards, and leads to a rethinking of our position in the universe. The role of Greening the Academy will be to teach this to society, to untwist the environment from mainstream economics' stranglehold. Now, rather than using science to control nature, scientific knowledge will provide us with the capacity to live within it and respect it. Humanity cannot underestimate the importance of replacing outdated survival strategies, including techno-fixes and environmental overshoot, and wrongly limiting ourselves to mitigation and adaptation. Innovation will be vital to converting the economic system, creating sustainable lifestyles to exist within the planet's means comfortably but differently.

Over the last few hundred years, mainstream economics has tamed and used nature as an expendable given resource, and has only valued resources once they have become scarce or exhausted. Green Economics comprises both the natural and social sciences, making a distinction between values and costs. Again in the mainstream, nature is abundant and therefore has been treated as a "free good" and resource. It has been disregarded even though – as we begin to recognize – nature underpins the world economy. Today, nature has become visibly fragile and "scarce." Should it seek to adjust to nature's entire carrying capacity, the discipline of economics must clearly be rewritten in order to include and account for the whole adjustment. Green Economics is an interdisciplinary economic field, which integrates, explores, and transforms while encouraging democratic participation in the economic re-evaluation and restructuring process. There has been a marked watershed of momentous happenings both economically and in the natural world. For the first time, mainstream policy-makers recognized that humankind could become the first species to destroy itself and its planetary home. More importantly, these mainstream policymakers also realized that this destruction constitutes a choice – and that by altering behaviour, this tragedy can still be averted. Thus, Green Economics emerged as the economics story. It has dovetailed with the launch of the Green New Deal and the TEEB by the UN and EU, the Stern Report's sequel. Green Economics has featured in the most unexpected of quarters – from the headline story at the European Business Summit in February until its launch by the United Nations in December. The discipline has been launched around the world, with the UK-founded Green Economics Institute opening its doors in South America, Africa, and Asia. Its popularity comes from the widespread realisation that the mechanisms for planetary and human-species desecration are embedded, justified and driven by the economics system. Mainstream economics has become completely divorced from its primary purpose in provisioning for the needs of all humanity, all other species, the biosphere, and the planet itself (Kennet and Heinemann 2006). Today, however, policy makers are noticing that just as the mechanism for destruction is embedded in the current system, the mechanism for altering behaviour can be found in another system: that of Green Economics. Policymakers, academics, and leaders in business alike have arrived at a realization that we are on a collision course between Ecology and the Economy.Necessarily, Greening the Economy is regarded as one of the only ways to tackle economic recession and environmental catastrophe. But in order for theory to become practise, Environmental Economics and Green Economics must gain visibility in economics departments and business schools. Mainstream economics resists a surprising level of new thinking – even in the face of enormous market failures and economic meltdowns.

Yet students, policy makers and the general public have embraced the Green Economics strand of Environmental Economics and are hungry for change, demanding that it be reflected in the Greening of the Academy, both in business schools and economics departments. Green Economics requires an emergent and transformative pedagogy, democratic participation of all people everywhere, an inclusion of previously unheard voices, and "lived practise." Refusing to be reduced to a set of definitive principles or timeless truths, it represents a dynamic, expansive, praxis-based economics. Exactly for this reason, Green Economics has been described as "the economics of doing."Leonardo da Vinci (1452-1519) believed that it was important to understand the connections between the "art of science" and the "science of art." His argument was that his success in one field was due to his understanding of another field, namely anatomy and art. The scientific discovery of interconnectedness was a key to the emergence of the New System Theory in the late 20th century, a theory which led to the discipline of Holism. This discipline addresses and links traditions that are foreign to each other. It has no desire to be centralised, over-organised or hierarchical. In this sense, Green Economics and its development is in fact one of the most holistic and multidisciplinary economics the world has ever seen. There is no human activity, no part of the planet that is not of interest to Green Economics, it is the very economics of interconnectedness.

Crucial to the teaching and implementation of Green Economics is an understanding of methodology. Mainstream economics reduces reality by application of simplistic mathematical concepts that make the world appear more precise than it actually is. Mainstream economics remains focused on an infinite growth assumption, and the belief that supposedly innate and uninfluenced consumer preferences should inform economic decision-making. As far as consumption is concerned, infinite growth contradicts scientific findings of ecologists (particularly climate change experts) and psychologists. In response, Green Economics chooses to reflect the world's interconnectedness by utilizing both verbal reasoning and description in addition to quantitative methods.

As a crucial aspect of Greening the Academy's philosophy, Green Economics supplies an integrative, participatory and dynamic teaching approach in conjunction with the appropriate economic foundations for our time. Holistic and interdisciplinary, Green Economics is both a natural and social science that chooses appropriate tools for each problem from its wide portfolio of methodologies. Fundamentally incorporating progressive ideas into scientific thinking and methodology, this discipline is open and able to explore new ideas that may radically change our perspective. This chapter will come to a close contending that Green Economics alone inherently combines a scientific as well as a social science approach. In the past decades, neo-classical economics has misappropriated a narrow interpretation of Darwinism in order to justify its version of capitalism, thus advancing the power of the strongest and fittest, while preserving inequalities. Green Economics, as the "economics of doing," provides a dynamic and transformative pedagogy, focusing equally on practice as well as theory.

Refusing to accept the status-quo, this discipline has managed to resist the static fate of other paradigms, and cannot be reduced to simple "timeless truths" or stagnant principles.

Thus, Green Economics seeks to reintegrate economics and science, addressing injustices by focusing on a broader reality than possible through mainstream economic methods, and by Greening the Academy through a participative, democratic and truly green approach.

A version of this chapter was published in the book by Richard Kahn & Anthony J. Nocella, II entitled "Greening the Academy: Environmental Studies for the Liberal Arts and Humanities." The Publisher is Syracuse University, USA.

References

Anderson V., (2008)Victor Anderson's opinion piece on the economic growth and the economic crisis. Prosperity without growth at http://www.sd commission.org.uk/publications.php?id=832 accessed August 10th 2009 Sustainable Development Commission UK Government Independent Watchdog Paper 10 11 208

Andrioff J and Waddock S (2002) Unfolding stakeholder engagement in Andrioff J and Wardock S Husted B and Sutherland Rahman S Unfolding stakeholder thinking Theory responsibility and Engagement Greenleaf Publishing Ltd Sheffield

Ban Ki Moon (3rd December 2007)Time for a New green economics A test for the world in Bali and Beyond Washington Post http://www.washingtonpost.com/wp dyn/content/article/2007/12/02/AR2007120201635.html accessed August 10th 2009

Barry J., (1999a) The environment and social theory London Routledge

Boulding K., (1966) The economics of the coming of spaceship earth. In H.E Daly Towards a steady state economy, San Francisco W H Freeman and Company 973.

Brundtland G. H. (1987) Our common future. World Commission on Environment and Development OUP 1-11.

Carson R (1962) Silent Spring. Houghton Mifflin

Carroll A (1993) Business and Society : Ethics and Stakeholder Management OH SouthWestern Cincinatti

Carroll, A.B. (1979.) A three-dimensional conceptual model of corporate social performance; Academy of Management Review 4.

Commoner B., (1971) The closing circle Nature Man and Technology Kopf NY (267 276)

Daly H., (1974) The economics of the steady state in American Economic Review (Papers and Proceedings) May vol 64 no 2 (15-21)

Dobson A ., (2000) Green Political Thought London Routledge

Ehrlich P., (1969) The Population Bomb Ballantine

Feiner S., (2003) Reading Neo Classical economics towards an erotic economy of sharing in D. Barker and E Kuiper (Eds) Towards a Feminist Philosophy of Economics. Routledge.

Freeman, E. R., (1984) Strategic management: A Stakeholder Approach, Pitman, Boston. Stakeholder Theory

Goldsmith E., (2005) Rewriting economics. Online: www.greeneconmics.org.uk or Students [accessed: 17th January 2006].

Gramsci A., (2006) Some Theoretical and Practical Aspects of Economism. Online: www.marxists.org [accessed: 17th January 2006].

Hardin G., (1968) The Tragedy of the commons Science vol 162 (1243-1248)

Henderson H (2006) in International Journal of Green Economics Growing the green economy – globally in International Journal of Green Economics- Vol 1 issue 3 4 (2007: 276) Inderscience.

Hussen A., (2000) Principles of Environmental Economics. London: Routledge.

Kaul N., (2003) The anxious identities we inhabit positivisms and economics understandings in Kuiper and Barker (Eds) Towards a Feminist Philosophy of Economics. London:Routedge.

Kennet M., (2007) Editorial Progress in Green Economics: ontology concepts and philosophy. Civilisation the lost factor of reality in social and environmental justice. International Journal of Green Economics. Vol 1 issue 3 4 (225: 2007).

Kennet M., and Heinemann V., (2006) Green Economics Setting the Scene. International Journal of Green Economics Vol 1 issue 1 /2 p 68- 102 Inderscience Geneva.

Kennet M., and Heinemann V., (2008) The second opinion piece for the Redefining Prosperity, third seminar "Confronting Structure - achieving economic sustainability" Prosperity without growth at http://www.sd commission.org.uk/publications.php?id=772 accessed August 10th 2009 Sustainable Development Commission UK Government Independent Watchdog Paper 10 11 208

Kennet M., (2008) The Economics of Doing No 13 e: 51 Green Economics for European Green Activists Berlin December 2007 Green European Foundation: The Green Economics Institute.

Kennet M., (2009) Green Economics and Pedagogy, Developing Teaching Green Economics. In Proceedings of the 4th Annual Green Economics Conference, Oxford University Part 1 (2009: 118). The Green Economics Institute

Lean G., and Shawcross, H., (15 .4. 2007) Are mobile phones wiping out our bees? Scientists claim radiation from handsets are to blame for mysterious colony collapse' of bees.

Leopold A., (1997) A Sand County Almanac. Oxford University Press

Meadows D., (1972) The Limits to Growth: A report for the Club of Rome's Project on the Predicament of Mankind 2nd Ed New York Universe Books

Mies M., (1998) Patriarchy and Accumulation in Scot Cato and Kennet Green

Economics.Green Audit

Mies M., (2007) Patriarchy and accumulation on a world scale revisited International Journal of Green Economics -Vol 1 issue . (2007:268) Inderscience

Mill J.S., (1848) Principles of Political Economy

Mansfield P. and Munro J., (1987) Chemical Children London Century

Mellor M., (2006) Eco feminist political ecology -in International Journal of Green Economics Vol 1 issue 1 /2 (2006) Inderscience.

Naess A., (1995) Deep ecology for the 21st century Shamballa.

Nelson J., (2009) Teaching Economics as if Time Mattered in The Handbook of Pluralist Economics Education Edited by Reardon J., Routledge.

Savage P., (2009) A Bee in our bonnet. You bet: The plight of the bumble bee, in Roundabout RG8 R and A. August 2009:(13-15.)

Salleh A., (2009) Eco sufficiency and global justice. Pluto.

Sachs G., (2005) The End of poverty: How we can make it happen in our lifetime. London: Penguin

Sessions G., (1995) Deep Ecology for the 21st Century. Shambala Publications.

Singer P., (1994) Defence of animals in Singer Ethical Studies Practical ethics in Bowie Business Ethics. Nelson Thornes 1994

Sukhdev P., (2008) TEEB Interim Report UNEP. Geneva

Springett D., (2006) Managing the narrative of Sustainable Development "discipline" of an inefficient concept : Vol 1 issue 1 /2 (2006: 50) International Journal of Green Economics.Inderscience

Stern N., (2007) Stern Review. The Economics of climate change. HM Treasury

Victor P., (2008) Managing without Growth Slower by Design Edward Elgar

Ward, Barbara and Rene Dubos, Only One Earth: the Care and Maintenance of a Small Planet, 1st Ed., New York, Norton: 1972

Waring M., in Salleh A. (2009) Policy and the measurement of Women in Eco Sufficiency and Global Justice. Pluto.

Welford R. (2007) Examining discussing and suggesting the possible contribution and role of Bhuddist economics for corporate social responsibility in International Journal of Green Economics Inderscience vol 1 issue 3 4 .(2007: 341)

2:2 Green Economics and Pedagogy

By Miriam Kennet

Green economics is fast emerging as the economics story for the first 20 years of the 21st century. The European Business Summit in February 2008 told industry leaders, including leaders of Shell and Lufthansa, that the only hope for the European economy is to go green. In October 2008, green economics made the front cover of Newsweek. In the UK, government officials were told that mainstream economics is so fragile that it should be considered radical – and that the only way forward from now on was to use green economics, the only robust methodology. Ban Ki-moon, leader of the United Nations, declared "we are in an age of global transformation – an age of green economics" (Dickey and McNicoll 2008).

More and more people are cognizant that human kind is at a crossroads: we can either save or destroy ourselves and the planet. Either way, the choice is ours. Unfortunately, economics has long been out of balance with the environment, and the hegemony of orthodox economics remains a formidable stumbling block: the two are on a collision course (Anderson 1999). If disaster is to be avoided, they have to become mutually compatible – the voice of the earth has to be heard. Voice comes through diversity, but at present we only have, thanks again to the hegemony of orthodoxy, "monocultures of the mind" which alienate people by precluding other voices from being heard, in turn depleting the strength of the whole. Green economics, on the other hand, has a strong subjective element and is more concerned with life narratives and outcomes than theoretical prescriptions, monoculture or grand narratives. It respects and empowers diversity and other voices. Green economics combines earth voices, green issues, and a practical, real approach characterized by fairness and respect for the environment; it is economics with access for all.

Green economics is by its nature multi-, inter-, and trans-disciplinary: We build on ideas of ecologism, conservation, socialism, feminism, political economy, civil society and counter hegemony, as well as all aspects and limits of natural science. These areas are indivisible – not one of them can be simply a social or positivist science. They are an indivisible unit, which must now be explored in a holistic manner. (Kennet and Heinemann 2006a: 3) This chapter is the first attempt to discuss the challenges of teaching green economics. Green economics is interactive – it is economics by doing. The means are as important as the ends and the ends are as important as the means, so, for example, achieving an equitable distribution of resources without including women or minorities in the decision-making process contravenes the modus operandi of green economics, which includes diversity of methodology and of practitioners within its core. Green economics does not impose one system on the world; we work and create the spaces to allow diversity to flourish.

This chapter will first discuss the core concepts and principles of green economics. The principles of green economics, including the all-important dictum that the means are inseparable from the ends, provides a recipe for teaching: transdisciplinary, providing access for all. Teaching pluralistically is intrinsic to green economics and completely congruent and intertwined with its main principles.

The core principles of green economics
The core challenge for green economics is that rather than imposing a grand narrative we must ensure economic systems meet minimum requirements for social and environmental justice while also incorporating local needs. Unlike traditional economics, which filters out awkward elements as externalities, green economics recognizes the ultimate interdependence of economic justice and the environment.

Three main objectives of green economics are:
1. To create economic conditions where social and environmental justice thrives, benefiting all people everywhere, along with non-human species, nature and the planet;
2. To re-examine new and broader versions of reality, beyond the vested interests, to listen to different voices. Green economics jettisons ceteris paribus as a limitation of scope and rejects "rational economic man" as a benchmark; instead listening and incorporating the voices of all;
3. To establish new thinking in order to provide the means for all people everywhere to participate in the economy with equal power, equal rights, and equal access to decision making. Green economics provides "out of the box" thinking while combining trans- and inter-disciplinary studies to counteract the myopic thinking of orthodoxy. "The world needs a new economics more than it needs a new anything else" (Anderson 1999: 6). Green economics requires that economic models reflect the complexity of the real world; it does not tolerate simplistic economics, which factors out the facts.

The key to uniting the three objectives is factoring nature back into economic theory. Just when people assumed they had completely tamed nature, climate change has forced rethinking of our position in the universe and our role as stewards of the earth. Rather than use science to control nature, we need to use our knowledge to live within nature and respect it. Green economics argues that nature has its own intrinsic value, which it extends to animals (Singer 1985).

Green economics extends this to all life forms. Arne Naess (1973) argued for the preservation of the biosphere, geological and biological systems, and all life forms for their own sake, not only for human benefit. Green economics is highly critical of anthropocentric ethics and the "shallow anthropocentric technocratic environmental movement," concerned primarily with pollution, resource depletion, and the health and affluence of people in developed countries (Sessions 1995: xii).

Since its inception, orthodoxy has assumed nature as an expendable and plentiful given resource, while only valuing scarce resources. It is, however, palpable that nature and the economy are mutually dependent, with the former becoming more fragile and scarce. Georgescu-Roegen (1966) highlighted the continuous mutual influence between economic processes and the natural world, long ignored by orthodoxy. In addition, White (1967) criticized Western attitudes to nature and attributed them to the influence of Christianity on the development of technology and assumption of human mastery through the taming of the natural world. He argued that Christianity has desacralized nature, encouraged its exploitation, and promoted a world view in which humans are superior to the rest of nature.

In order to address these topics and revisions, new and critical ways of thinking are needed that include questioning the scope and meanings of economics, facts, evidence, and reality in positivist economics, as well as so-called "rational and reasonable choices." Green economics welcomes the insights from sister social sciences (Kennet and Heinemann 2006b) as well as Eastern spiritual traditions of questioning the assumed virtues of competition rather than cooperation, and exploitation rather than engagement.

Aristotle argued that reciprocity may not be adequate to account for corrective and distributive justice; thus we need to introduce an exchange bond and exchange justice which provides and governs reciprocity (Meikle 1995: 10). Thus, in reconceptualizing "value," we need further to consider how each individual decision based on value would be assessed in the light of absolute boundaries to consumption that might be imposed by ecological restrictions to human activity.
Despite and probably because of the popularity of green economics, our message has been usurped and distorted for myriads of reasons. Sometimes, what passes for green is more greenwashing – passed off as green but without merit, existing for contrarian purposes. It is easier to comprehend the confusing array of policy outcomes when they are viewed as a continuum. Central is the ambivalent relationship between green economics and the multi-faceted and multi-layered term "sustainable development."Brundtland (1987) as meeting "the needs of the present without sacrificing the ability of the future to meet its standards." The approach argues for a more enlightened globalization to reach these standards and to resolve environmental degradation. Sustainable development has been eagerly adopted by such groups as the World Business Council of Sustainable Development and it nicely comports with Corporate Social Responsibility and stakeholder theory. Acknowledging that many nation states are weaker than global corporations, sustainable development argues for the corporation to be the agent of change. In contrast, many green economists regard corporations as agents of hegemony; and as undemocratic, unelected, lacking in transparency, and the fundamental cause of the problem. Green economics seriously questions how it can be in a corporation's short-term interest to implement equity and environmental justice through the managerial "environmentalist" approach of sustainable development. Dobson (2000) and Springett and Foster (2005) criticize short-term techno fixes which on the one hand

remain within the confines of traditional economics and, on the other, hijack environmentalism and the language of "sustainability" (Welford and Gouldson 1993). Sustainable development is regarded by green economists as an oxymoron, often in reality counteracting existing community economic patterns. Greens instead seek to reverse the trends of neo-colonialism and corporate destruction of local assets, replacing them with new subsistence, local self-determination and community control (Norberge-Hodge 1991; Mies and Shiva 1993). In addition, gigantism, monopoly, and oligopoly contravene green economics arguments for "small, appropriate and diverse production" developed by Schumacher (1976). Nevertheless, given the inexorable complexity of the environmental crisis, there is a growing realization within the business world that business as usual is no longer a choice An ongoing task among green economists is to analyze the growing, complex, and multi-faceted role of the corporation (Reardon 2007b). Needless to say, the nineteenth-century orthodox firm, assumed to maximize profits and externalize any environmental concerns, must be replaced by a more complex and realistic model.

With regard to policy, green economics focuses on the three Fs: fuel, food, and the financial crisis. Just as Roosevelt's New Deal set the stage for the biggest economic growth the world has seen, green economics argues today for a similar vision. Rather than jump-start consumption to aid an ailing economy, however, green economics seeks conversion to greener technologies to enable greener lifestyles so we can live within our means and that of the planet. Accelerating this transition is at the core of the green economy initiative and is the best bet for global sustainable wealth and employment generation for the world's 1.3 billion poor.

A formidable barrier to this transition is the myopic vision of traditional economics, which has been instrumental in the commodification of nature and perpetuation of poverty. Central to green economics is the incorporation of knowledge from other disciplines, particularly the sciences, which helps to circumscribe the forms and extent of economic activity within realistic environmental parameters. Postmodern ideas are absent from traditional economics and from a green perspective this misses important developments in human thought. In particular, the prevalence of the Western-dominated, white, middle-class, "homo economicus" ignores the experience of most of the world's people. Derrida (1978) rejects single narratives and investigates whether reality is fact, truth, myth, interpretation, or one person's view of events. Derrida analyzes binary oppositions and dualisms such as West and East, feminine and masculine, light and dark, civilized and primitive, them and us, to criticize the power structures in which they are embedded.

Green economics and pedagogy
I tend to think of green economics as a slippery eel—if you catch it and think you have understood its imperatives, something else arises and you need to conceptualize

more deeply or in another dimension in order to capture its meaning. Green economics continues to evolve, provoke, and question. So how to teach this evolving slippery eel?

Perhaps it is best to reflect on what it is trying to achieve, which is interaction, responsibility, and accessibility. This suggests that its classroom and lecture hall are very different places from the usual conventional lecture as solution provider. Green economics looks for a new mode of enablement and empowerment as well as a two-way process.

The ambitious aims of green economics to start a new discipline and to change the paradigm of economics to one which creates social and environmental equity means taking the practice of economics beyond the classroom, i.e. making it economics by doing. This means more instruction on site, which differentiates green economics from its sister social sciences. Green economics is holistic, pluralist, and progressive; thus its pedagogy has to reflect its nature. This is one discipline which cannot be amended to the usual macro/micro stuff with a small portion of the lesson looking at the costs of energy. Green economics is different and its foundational concepts are different and this must be reflected in the entire approach of teachers, trainers, and lecturers. A rewarding aspect of green economics is that because it supports diversity and means/ends approaches, it is not country specific. Thus, teaching green economics has to appeal to all kinds of cultures.

Should we equip a new generation of students to learn only the reformed version of greener economics or should we teach our students enough about the mainstream to enable them to cogently critique it? I feel it is important to map previous developments in economics, especially those concerned with nature and social equity, and to provide students with enough knowledge to enable them to understand and respect differences between schools of thought and their modus operandi. This is especially necessary in order to provide students with the tools to begin investigation of newly evolving issue for themselves. Green economics is equally relevant to the very young and the very old, so the Green Economics Institute has been experimenting with teaching the very young and very old together, as the enforced separation of one group has been a disabling factor, similar to segregating different racial groups or disabled and not disabled groups.

In summation, based on the discussion of the core principles of green economics, the following are central elements in the pedagogy of green economics:
1. Incorporate scientific evidence on the environment and how it adapts and changes. This can easily be incorporated into the circular flow diagram usually given on opening day (Reardon 2007a). Throughout the course, additional scientific data can be incorporated, particularly regarding interest rates, externalities, economies of scale, public goods, and the role of government. This will teach students that no one discipline has a unique solution to global problems, and the necessity for pluralist, integrated thinking. Not to do so is to proselytize, which contravenes not only the principles of green economics, but the objective of this book.

2. Continuously discuss the value-laden concepts of economics, such as freedom, the market, externalities, etc. Is, for example, reliance on the continuous, competitive pressure of the market to force people to behave in a certain way antithetical to the classical economists' demand for more freedom from an obtrusive state? Whether markets enable or disengage and whether markets are congruent with the environmental demands is fundamental to green economics.

3. Understand the historical evolution of economics, particularly the visions of classical economics and how they sharply differ from traditional economics. I place economic theories and concepts in their intellectual and historical background, discussing all available information about the economists – their backgrounds, their looks and hairstyles, etc. This provides a vivid, lively, personal account, previously discouraged as hearsay, but which nevertheless elucidates how and why a theory/concept was developed.

4. Emphasize students as the greatest ambassadors for our ideas. As teachers, we should regard each learning experience as a moment in the learning chain which extends into the past and hopefully well into the future, to be handed down like the verbal stories of the ancient world.

5. Teachers must engage in outreach – speaking/lecturing in non-academic settings – as well as in inreach – inviting others to participate in class. If you are passionate about your subject (especially given a rapidly dwindling window of opportunity), in addition to lecturing to traditional students it is incumbent to lecture and teach to potential students, idea makers, policy-makers, and activists. My most successful courses are those where former students continue their presence in my life, where former student and teacher continuously learn from each other. Teaching green economics breaks past assumptions and conceptions of the world. The next generation is witnessing real climate change, species extinction, and festering poverty and inequality. We can no longer assume all problems will be solved by technology and economic growth; but we need a more realistic assessment of human capabilities and the mutual dependency between humans and the environment. And we can no longer assume that the teacher has all the answers; any solutions will be forged in a continuous and ongoing dialogue.

6 We must listen to other voices, from the South, from special needs, voices of older people, younger people, voices of women, and the economically disenfranchised, and engage with them in both outreach and inreach. We need to provision in a more precarious world. We as teachers have to pave (rather than lead) the way forward.

This chapter was first published as Kennet M., (2009), "The Handbook of Pluralist Economics Education," edited by Jack Reardon, Routledge.

References

Anderson, V. (1999) "Can There Be a Sensible Economics?," in S. Cato and M. Kennet (eds) Green Economics – Beyond Supply and Demand to Meeting People's Needs. Aberystwyth, UK: Green Audit Press.

Brundtland, G.H. (1987) Our Common Future: World Commission on Environment and Development. Online: http://www.un-documents.net/wced-ocf.htm.

Derrida, J. (1978) Writing and Difference. Chicago: University of Chicago Press.

Dickey, C and McNicoll, T. (2008) "The Green Rescue," Newsweek, 3 November, www.newsweek.com.

Dobson, A. (2000) Green Political Thought. Abingdon, UK: Routledge

Dowd, Douglas (2004) Capitalism and Its Economics – A Critical History. London: Pluto Press.

Georgescu-Roegen, N. (1966) "The Entropy Law and the Economic Problem," in H.E. Daly and K. Townsend (eds) Valuing the Earth: Economics, Ecology, Ethics. Cambridge, Mass.: MIT Press.

Kennet, M. and Heinemann, V. (2006a) "Foreword," International Journal of Green Economics1: 1–10. (2006b) "Green Economics: Setting the Scene," International Journal of Green Economics 1: 68–102.

Meikle, Scott (1995) Aristotle's Economic Thought. New York: Oxford University Press.

Mies, M. and Shiva, V. (1993) Ecofeminism. London: Zed Books.

Naess, A. (1973) "The Shallow and the Deep, Long-Range Ecology Movement," Inquiry,16: 95–100.

Norberge-Hodge, H. (1991) Ancient Futures Learning from Ladakh. San Francisco: Sierra Club Books.

Reardon, J. (2007a) "How Green Are Principles Texts? An Investigation Into How MainstreamEconomics Educates Students Pertaining to Energy, the Environment and Green Economics," International Journal of Green Economics 1: 381–393. (2007b) "Comments on Green Economics Setting the Scene," International Journal of Green Economics 1: 532–538.

Sessions, G. (1995) Deep Ecology for the 21st Century. Boston: Shambhala.

Schumacher, E.F., (1976) Small is Beautiful. London: Sphere Press.

Singer, Peter (1985) The Animal Liberation Movement: Its Philosophy, Achievements, and Its Future. Abingdon, UK: Routledge.

Springett, D. and Foster, B. (2005) "Whom Is Sustainable Development for? Deliberative Democracy and the Role of Unions," Sustainable Development 13: 271–281.

Welford, R. and Gouldson, A. (1993) Environmental Management and Business Strategy. London: Pitman.

White, L. (1967) "The Historical Roots of our Ecological Crisis," Science 155: 1203207.

2:3 Mountain-eco-Philosophy

]By Trude Blumse
(The title is taken from Dag O. Hessen`s essay "Die Norwegische apparatlantenschaft" in the 2012 etidtion of "Barske glader" ed.)

In Norway we have, and have had, our own special breed of philosophers. What essentially singles them out is that they are, and were, also mountaineers. Some of them met and climbed together in and around 1920-1930 at Kolsas outside of Oslo. They became the inspiration and starting point of Norwegian nature concervacy movements, and one of them founded the well-known deep-ecology.
By now I suppose you have guessed at least one of the philosophers who I am referencing too; Arne Nass. But another important mountain-eco-philosopher, slightly earlier, and in some respects more radical than Nass was Peter Wessel Zapffe.
Peter Wessel Zapffe came from Tromso to Oslo in 1918 to study law, where he delivered his final exam in rhyme, and was later to deliver a 600-page thesis in philosophy called "On the Tragical" (*my translation*). When he arrived in Oslo he was already furious that some outsiders had made the first ascent of Piggtind, the tallest mountain close to his home. It felt wrong. In Oslo he got to know this climber, and soon became part of the climbing environment around Kolsas. Here they climed, and discussed philosophical viewpoints as they did. Somehow philosophy and mountain climbing became interconnected here, for some.

Just after a few years Zapffe had made the first ascent of most all of the mountains in his home region. While still part of the circle who climbed at Kolsas he met the 12 year younger Arne Nass. They became friends. Climbed a lot of mountains together, but also had some philosophical disagreements. Nass was professor in Philosophy by the time Zapffe delivered his thesis, and it was first refused. Later Zapffe found Nass to superficial, he thought he did not take the human predicament seriously enough. But most of the time they were friends.

Zapffe`s viewpoint was that humans are the most miserable creatures on earth. While all the other beeings here have abilities that are suited to their purpose, humans have abilities that way surpasses their purpose in life. We are over endowed. Consequently, our surpluss of acknowledgement leads us on to a desperate search for meaning in our lives, and of ways to not think about what the meaning of life is at all. This leads to a self-destructive over-activity, which will make life even more miserable.
In contrast to his pessimistic outlook on life, Zapffe does not seem like the depressive type. His many texts are full of life, humour and joy. Himself he found joy and meaning in natures` vast beauty. He loved to be alone, surrounded by a nature with no signs of human activities. This lead him to become one of the first outspoken defenders of untouched nature, writing articles to newspapers about how horrible it would be if

the pristine mountain landscapes were marred with red T-s all around, and in protest against tarmaced roads and big hotels out in nature . He became a fierce criticiser of the modern life, and of the modern obsession with "progress", which inevitably always meant more buildings, more people, more things, and less life.

For Zapffe it was extremely important that we kept a lot of nature natural and untouched y human hands. This he meant not for the sake of nature it self, or for biodiversity or anything like that. No, it was so for the sake of humans. Humans need vast spaces of untouched nature to be able to connect with their deeper, more existential selves, to feel alive and live lives worth living.

 This last point was of utmost importance to Zapffe.Was life worth living? In his eyes the world was a brutal place and humans were not properly adapted to it. Our minds are capable of too many things, of too much deep thinking about our own existence. His conclusion was that it was certainly not worth bringing more people into life. For their own sake, the sake of the unborn people.Bringing more people into life he regarded as a very selfish act, while in his eyes it had to be an ethical question. Zapffe treated all his fellow humans with respect and thorough attention. When talking with children he listened carefully to what they had to say, and answered them seriously, like he would answer an adult. For this reason he much enjoyed being in solitude. Being around other people drained him of energy, because he was so attentive.

Arne Nass is in Norway well known for being an incarnation of *homo ludens* - the playing human. He was extremely playful, and he thought that everyone should play a lot more. Arne Nass is for many *the* green philosopher. As Zapffe, and with Zapffe, he started his climbing career in Kolsas while a student at the University of Oslo, but he was soon both a respected philosopher and mountain climber. Nass introduced the technique bolt-climbing in Norway, and has lead mountaineering expeditions in both the Alps and in Himalaya. His group made the first ascent to Tirich Mir (7750 m.o.sealevel). Like Zapffe, and many Norwegian thinkers before him, Nass promoted the easy life, with few possessions and a lot of time in nature. Nass was known a an eccentric, if something could be done in an unusual way he mostly preferred to do it like that.

Like Zapffe Nass found reason and energy out in the wilderness and high up in the mountains. On his many expeditions to mountains in other regions of the world he was bemused by how the locals found him crazy for willingly, just for his own amusement, going up in the arid mountain landscapes. When out in nature Nass felt that he belonged. That he was part of nature. In fact, he would not have said that he was out in nature. He would have said that he was with nature. Not just physically being placed in nature, but with, mentally and physically. Nass felt a strong sense of belonging in nature, and a feeling of being set free from the purposiveness of everything. Because in nature things do not have a purpose, in the normal, human sense. The flowers n the meadow are not there because someone put them there, thet just are there, and that makes them even more beautiful in Nass`s mind.

The place he loved the most was his self-built cabin Tvergastein up in the mountains in Hallingskarvet. Here he worked, and climbed, and had guests. If you are interested to learn more about how it was there you can read Zapffes essay "Barske glader" (*"Rough pleasures"*, *my translation*) from 1942, where Nass is easily recognized as the excentric professor Vinmpelodden.

Arne Nass is the founder of the philosophical direction deep ecology. In deep ecology, nature has intrinsic value, independent of what use it does or does not have for humans, and it views humans as a natural part of nature. A very important feature of deep ecology, that singles it out from regular ecology, is the value it places on emotions and emotive argumentation. Also Zapffe launched a new way to think about the environment, what he called the biosophic method. Some say this was a pre-runner to Nass`deep-ecology, but it seems rather different. The biosophic method is an "ecology for mankind" (Dag O. Hessen, 2012), that is supposed to guide us through the difficulties of a life with an overdeveloped intellect. Deep ecology is rather a way to understand life, and to relate to nature and all living beings.

Nass and Zapffe are not the only mountain-eco-philosophers in Norway. Rather they somehow embody thoughts and feelings that in smaller or larger extent are present in surprisingly many Norwegian hearts and minds. A lot of us do long for quiet times in nature. We treasure ski-trips in winter and mountain hiking in summer, and we all love to sit in the sun outside our cabins with a cup of freshly brewed hot coffee, looking out on to the mountains or the sea nearby.

Part 3: Debating Economics

3:1 The Eco-Energetic Point of View: Globalisatics of Natural Resouces, Economic Value and Money

By Stephen I.Ternyik

Henry George (1839-1897) was the first economist to coin and use the image of spaceship earth, in his groundbreaking work, Progress and Poverty (1879: p.173, NY;reprint by Cosimo, 2005). The quest for the cyclical return of economic depressions, combined with the deep interest in a possible underlying natural law of human progress and decline, is at the heart of his scientific method. It is no coincidence that Francis A. Walker, the first President of the American Economic Association, was a fierce opponent of Henry George as he was also engaged in the research topics of land, economic value creation and money; it is well known that academia is primarily about abstractions of reality, the learning about real life concerns or practices of reality, is viewed as a secondary activity, and even as a disturbance of the discourse to archive knowledge.

What historical event chain caused the creation and publication of Progress and Poverty (and the other elaborations of this economic problem by HG, e.g. The Science of Political Economy, 1898)? The scientific study of available post- mortem data sets is pointing to the empirical fact that the panic of 1873 was the first truly great international crisis of the political economic order as similar phenomena (panic patterns) occurred in different global locations simultaneously. The 50 years of the US National Banking Era (1863-1913) until the Federal Reserve Act ('the child of all panics') were preceded by scattered free banking practices and a slow conversion tendency towards state-chartered banks, with higher monetary reserves and legal business standards. The US population tripled in this period, from about 30 million to well over 90 million. It is also difficult to estimate the real length of the long depression which is normally defined from 1873-1879, but we have to keep in mind that the panics of 1893 and 1907 followed closely.

In any case, this temporal period left a deep psychological mark on Henry George who experienced and observed great progress and poverty at the same time; consequently, humanistic and scientific questions arose: what is causing all this simultaneous gain and pain? Is there any way to balance such events? Are we doomed to repeat these cycles?

We do not want to simply and technically reduce these painful human and natural events of economic suffering and affluence to central/commercial banking techniques, monetary circulation analysis or into the quantitative supply/demand for money (although we know how decisive the velocity and volume of monetary agency effects the modern production economy); abstractions of reality may be sophisticated tools to command or centralize economic policy making and planning, but they tell us very little about the real commercial intercourse in every-day economic exchange and production. Concerning economic growth, business cycles and depressive spiral effects, we have to focus on the productive sequence of natural inputs and processed outputs, like the enigma of the Solow residual explicates. Something happens in between the technical processing of natural resources and the human exchange of economic outputs; it is a quality that the quantitative accounting of total factor productivity does not cover and it can also not be explained by human ingenuity. Let us call this the hidden variable: 'the alchemy of the economic circuit'. As a result, it is imperative that we demystify the quasi-theological omnipotent role of money and view the human economy as an economic energy circuit or eco-logical energy transduction system.

Consequently, human economic activity is not an abstraction of perpetual motion from households, firms and banks, but a real product of natural resource processing via systemic energy transduction. The systems evolution of the modern monetary production economy in the last 100 years has reduced almost all human necessities into the need for money (which has also deeply affected the human psyche, in terms of value preferences); in this economic system, money and energy (natural resources) have become interchangeable, thus nothing (money) equals some-thing (energy). The mathematical infinity of money is computed equal to the physical finity of resources; even the simplest mind can grasp that an optimal economic resource allocation and distribution cannot be achieved via such an artificial accounting system as it is not balanced by a natural ratio. This economic development is insofar dangerous as almost all social systems collapses in human history have been induced by an energy crisis; on the contrary, the developmental imperative reads that the higher advancement of an economic system demands to attain a higher level of energy efficiency and natural resource allocation, i.e. the direction (pattern) of the natural selection procedure is to limit entropy and to extend bio-social life physically; increasing energy consumption of all kinds increases the material entropy of the economic system, it costs energy to convert energy from one form to another and it comes always with a loss of energy by friction. The Snooks/Panov algorithm calculates and confirms the eco-energetic fact that every important techno-economic wave took only about a 1/3 of former temporary evolution intervals.

As in our times, money grants access to natural resources; we can read the eco-energetic circuit of production cycles as follows: energy/quantifies/time; time/quantifies/production/; money/quantifies/energy. This is the essential working body of the economic quantum space of energy, time, production, and money. The increasing conversion of energy quantifies the temporal acceleration of economic cycles; the economic behaviour of acute and chronic monetary excess increases the exponential need for energy and causes the temporal acceleration of economic production cycles, i.e. shortening the cyclical intervals of depressive and regressive crises. Consequently, the operating scheme of our monetary system needs economic reforms; Henry George envisioned a form of public currency, issued by government agency, to satisfy our desires with least exertion and to perform the indispensable office of interpersonal (temporary) exchange.

Reaching such a stage of economic systems sustainability would require separating money (central banking) from credit (commercial banking) by the following legal reform steps:

A) Removal of natural resources (land) as collateral for bank loans/land value=public revenue;

B) Decrease<labour taxation/increase>taxation of capital gains (interest);

C) Banking regulation=100%money/narrow banking.
The systemic interplay of natural resources, economic value and money lies behind all monopolies (tax, credit, land) and privileges (inherited wealth/unearned income), but monetary emission and circulation drive the economic cycle via ecological energy consumption (non-physicality performs a physical office).Henry George could simply not foresee this type of economic systems evolution which is defined instrumentally by gaining monetary purchasing power as access to the not man-made goods of this earth (extracting physical value for no-thing).
Regarding the cyclical and spiral interplay of this physical foundation of human economic activity, it is vitally important to understand that the methodical tools of the economics profession are, since 5000 years and starting in Sumeria, derived from private wealth management and asset maximization via money, credit and interest. From this knowledge system follows a scientific vacuum and bias, concerning the sustainability and stability of the public body economic; in addition, global processes of the world economy remain a blind spot. As a result, professional microeconomics (in practice: management models) and fragmentary macro-economics (in practice: economic and monetary policies) do lack the integrative level of meta-prudent cybernetics. Consequently, an economic sustainability science is currently gaining momentum, with different and distinct levels of human economic activity. This science in the making is a humanistic response of survivalist rationality (logic) and morality (ethics); it will lead most probably to economic accounting methods/models that allow for optimal resource allocation and distribution (with or without monetary agency; possibly with 'new monetary technology').
Advancing Georgist thought can play an eminent role in this learning process of knowledge systems evolution, referring to the global science of political economy and to world economic waves of progress and poverty.

The psychological realization and scientific research into cyclical progress and poverty was the Georgist and humanistic response to unbearable conditions for millions of people. N.Kondratieff (1892-1936), J.Schumpeter (1881-1950) and H. Rosenberg (1904-1988) have explained these painful events as contractive dynamics of capital formation, on the physical foundations of land and labor; Kondratieff was punished to death in the Bolshevist system as he rendered a very different interpretation of long wave movements in the stages of techno- economic evolution although the studies were derived from observable empirical data. It is interesting to note that Central European Georgists like G.J.Pikler (1864-1952) of Hungary and A.Damaschke (1865-1935) of Germany discovered such long wave assumptions as students of the Biblical account in Moses 3 (chapter 25); what both economic points of view have in common, refers to the ca. 50 year temporal regularity of expansion vs. contraction, related to possible human and scientific remedies of this money-based capital dynamics. The eco-energetic point of view can help us to operationalize the involved factors and to identify key variables for practical remedy formulation. The scientific observations of Henry George fall mainly into the temporal period (1850-1900) of modern economic history that is associated with the 3rd Kondratieff industrial wave of railway and steel. What is the mystery or alchemy of this deflationary wave circuit? The progress of technological innovation is always accompanied by unsustainable debt levels, caused by the privately capitalized land value (rent) of natural resources and unfair taxation techniques; in addition, this dynamic inefficiency is reinforced by monetary and banking practices that support private rent seeking over public economic health and entrepreneurial spirit, i.e. monetary policy does not make a behavioral distinction between private rent seeking and public wealth creation. However, there exists a strong empirical relationship between, for example, real estate value and economic wealth creation. One important point is to elaborate the public revenue system from traditional taxation methods to the capturing of rent-seeking via the land value of natural resources, according to the Georgist formula: $P-R=W+I$, and not according to the classical formula of: $P=R+W+I$.

The resources of nature will be actually freed from rent-seeking and productive activity will be freed from taxation. Consequently, unsustainable debt levels can be removed from firms, households and banks via the removal of total private property over land titles or the free goods of nature; land titles will lose their economic value as traded items. Public revenue is derived from capturing land rent via a simple estimation of annual economic value, valuated by locational quantity. All types of employment will increase, because taxation is no longer based on labor-intensity; commercial banks will have to develop more expertise in the assessment and viability of all types of entrepreneurial projects, because land value can no longer serve as collateral or security for credit (interest) or loans. As a result, our discourse slowly deciphers the 'alchemy of the economic circuit' which is also an energy transduction system; as in the modern money- based production economy, money and energy (natural resources) have become interchangeable, a legal banking reform towards narrow banking or even 100%money is unavoidable to removing the speed out of rent seeking momentum of all kinds.

Beginning around the 1850s, the US transformed from a land-based economy towards a money-based economy until the 1910s when the tricky calculations of banking replaced the physical visibilities of a natural economy; this was the life period of Henry George and the observed economic problems of rent-seeking, monetary gambling and wage reduction have grown into a global eco-energetic conflict for natural resources (land value) since the last century.

There exists no alchemy of the economic circuit; the mystery of cyclical motion (and possible development) is hidden in the physics of the economic wealth and value creation chain. The long-term dynamic efficiency of the eco-energetic circuit in economic cycles (and eventually spirals), in terms of sustainability or stability, is disturbed in regular intervals by non-productive rent-seeking (from natural resources), monetary excess (minimizing reserve ratios) and labor taxation (taxing human resources); the extraction of value for no-thing begins with unearned rent and ends with unearned capital gains from interest, i.e. the public body economic is maintained via taxing wages and the private body economic gains from this type of value creation process a more solid capital pool (for even more gambling), i.e. increased physical mass-momentum.

Entrepreneurship and employment are discouraged under such an unstable system, because it makes no more economic sense to toil and try. The logical consequence of these productive imbalances is an increased energy consumption level which leads to a temporal acceleration (entropy) of the economic crises intervals, observable in technical progress and human poverty worldwide. As a result, the ecoenergetic sustainability of a money-based economy requires to tax rent seeking and capital gains (to serve as public revenue), must remove natural resources (land) as collateral value from bank credit and interest (loans), free labor and production from taxation, and introduce narrow banking (strict reserve requirements).The social science of economics is not a branch of morality or physics, it is a science of human action; the concealed laws (construction principles of reality) of right or false direction of human economic activity can be discovered by empirical, rational and methodical inquiry. A deterioration of ethical, moral and human values is well observable in our times and cyclical economic crisis is always a systemic feedback signal of behavioral mal-adaptation (this topic is about communicating with economic complexity and deserves our separate attention); the establishment of a just legal system, in economic terms, is a vital commonality between all nations on the most basic level of social existence and such a just legislative system, the economic rule of law as rational imperative, is discoverable and applicable by logic and reason.

References
Broch H. (2003). The Spirit in an Unspiritual Age (Zeit and Zeitgeist).NY: Counterpoint.

Foldvary F. (2007). The Depression of 2008. Berkeley (CA): Gutenberg.

Friedman M/Schwartz A. (1971). Monetary History of the US (1867- 1960).Princeton: UP.

Grinin L/Korotayev A. (2012). Kondratieff Waves.Volgograd: Uchitel. Gaffney M. (2009). After the Crash. Chichester (UK): Wiley.

George H. (1879). Progress and Poverty. Reprint: NY: Cosimo (2005).

Hall C/Klitgaard K. (2012). Energy and the Wealth of Nations. NY: Springer. Lough A. (2013). The Last Tax. PhD diss. Brandeis U.

Ternyik S. (2013). Global Wave Energetics. Bloomington: Penguin.

Ulmen G. (1978). The Science of Society. The Hague: Mouton. Vapnik V. (1998). Statistical Learning Theory. NY: Wiley.

Zgurovsky M.(2010). Metric Aspects of Periodic Processes in Economy and Society. Cybernetics and Systems Analysis. Vol.46(2): 167-172.

www.commongroundnyc.org
www.cooperativeindividualism.org
www.politicaleconomy.org/history.htm

3.2 Good Jobs: the double dividend of Green Employment

By Dr Enrico Tezza

Introduction
The discussion about green jobs seems to be primarily focused on the employment impact of climate change policies underestimating two phenomena of the so called socio-ecological transition. First, layoffs caused by industrial restructuring, and second, the real employment impact of the energy sector which is the main sector addressed by climate change policies. It is recognized that green industries account for 1% of the total employment and so far they are too small to create the millions of jobs needed for recovery and development. In the short run, figures are not promising when layoffs are combined with green jobs created in the energy sector. The perspective is better when the long run is considered. The technological variable and scientific applications could generate an adequate multiplier effect transforming business and economic models through net job creation.

The quantitative dimension of green employment is widely debated alongside new job creation for the future. Surprisingly, few studies are focused on the qualitative dimension of green employment. This chapter seeks to address this issue by pointing out the decent work dimension of green employment and its implications for Labour Market Analysis.

The methodological framework lies on the so called emphatic civilization going beyond the market regulation mechanism or the greenhouse gas emission restriction targets. Full employment and well-being become the key aims to be reached by humanity in a world where there should be a balance between humanity and nature. As nature and social justice go hand in hand, green jobs are an opportunity to reconcile the working life decency and sustainable nature.

As a result, adaptation and mitigation policies should be re-examined along with both quality of life and decent work for all. Nature and decent work are two parts of the same development model coin. This chapter stresses the decent work dimension of green employment so as to shed light on an integrated approach to Labour Market analysis: green and decent jobs.

After introducing the elements of the 'rethinking employment' concept within the new socio-ecological scenario, the second section reviews the drawbacks of current labour statistics involving green job classification. The third section deals with labour market analysis and attempts to highlight past issues with emerging questions raised by the green job movement. The debate on green job quality gauging is outlined in the fourth section, while the fifth section reports on the application of decent work indicators to green jobs highlighting the risks when they are indecent. The need for a systematic "good jobs" approach is explained in the conclusion.

Elements of Rethinking Employment
The time horizon between the 1970s and 2004 corresponding to the studies drawn by The Limits to Growth (1972), Beyond the Limit (1992) and the subsequent book, Limits to growth: the 30 Years Update (2002), is considered to illustrate the transition cycle to sustainability (*D.H.Meadows, J. Randers, D. Meadows, 2004*), in which scientific and humanistic disciplines became oriented towards sustainability. The sustainability concept, developed in 1987 by Our Common Future, had a paradigm shift brought by the Oxford School of Green Economics. Rather than the relationships between generations, Green Economics raised issues such as the inequalities between current generations, social justice, ethics and Good Life Theory (*M Kennet, 1999*). A parallel conceptual evolution is sought in the socio-ecological transition realm. These studies (Viennese and Dutch School) share the same view on sustainability transitions and agree on the same family theories of socio-ecological change that oppose the mainstream idea that change is incremental, generally linear, predictable and even controllable *(Jan Rotmans, 2007).* The mentioned "green" movement highlights three key dimensions of transitional change: the time horizon, the spatial scale and the pattern of human development. First, the human activity impact on ecosystems should be analyzed in the long run rather than being restricted to the contingent horizon. A different time scale is needed for the socio-ecological transition: decades and centuries rather than the usual business or electoral cycles. The second component concerns the actors' interaction across different scales or levels. The analysis of the impact of human activity should be applied globally, at the level of nation states and of communities, in fully industrialized and developing countries from various world regions. The third dimension refers to the symmetry between the overexploitation of nature and the underutilization of labour as pointed out by the European Union in 1993 (*EU, COM 1993, 700*). If society is an autopoietic system, then everything that affects the environment will also affect the society itself. Hence, GHG emissions affect the environment and human health as well.
In short, the quality of life options, or the Good Life Aristotelian imperative, should lead to the rethinking of the interaction "society-nature" which is different from the means-end principle: not by transforming natural systems to make them more useful for society's purpose, but by conceiving a co-evolutionary process between labour, technology and ecosystem.
The mentioned paradigm shift in sustainable development mirrors the debate on the separation between humanistic and scientific cultures and focuses on employment and social inclusion not competitiveness as key modeling variables, leading to a rethinking of green jobs along three strands:
1. Green Jobs Classification
2. Green Jobs Analysis
3. Green Jobs Measurement
A succinct explanation about these strands is described below as well as implications of indecent green jobs and related workers risks.

Green Jobs Classification

Any green job classification can be used against the huge debate on Green Jobs. The below salient review highlights the need to classify the new and emerging job profiles and occupations called "Green Jobs".

The historical background
Green Jobs before 2007

The green colour in job profiles is rooted into the so-called Ecological Revolution of the 1960s. A move from anthropocentrism to eco-centrism characterized this period, bringing about a shift in perception, values, and lifestyles and redirecting the ecologically destructive path of modern industrial growth societies. In 1999 the book *Green Collar Jobs*, written by Alan Durning explained the changing economic base of rural towns in the Northwest Pacific to a more sustainable community. Afterwards, the term 'green jobs' began turning up in the speeches and articles in politics and economics (*A. Durning, 2002*). Unionist referred to green jobs as specific jobs such as retrofitting, solar panel installation and weatherization which would create a pathway out of poverty. In 2004, Raquel Pinderhughes used again the term 'green collar jobs', defining them as manual labour jobs whose products and services directly improve environmental quality and identified 22 sectors in which green jobs are located (*Raquel Pinderhughes, 2007*). The link between the environment and occupations as a way to overcome poverty shapes the first meaning of green jobs. Rather than opposing brown jobs, green jobs entail a new development model based on the equilibrium amongst the economy, society and nature. The new green economics discipline has deepened the realms raised by the ecological movement with the 1999 book "Green Economics" (*M Kennet, 1999*). The need for a development model based on less GHG emissions and a better quality of life for all is highlighted and green jobs become the priority in the economic framework and related public policy.

Green Jobs after 2007

The ILO Director General's introduction to the International Labour Conference 2007, along the Bali Road Map, launched the Green Job Initiative to promote a socially just transition to green jobs. Green jobs are defined as those contributing to fighting global warming and building a green economy (*J. Somavia*, 2007).

The 2008 Green Jobs Initiative (*ILO, UNEP, ITUC, 2008*) highlighted that the pace of the green job creation is likely to accelerate in the years ahead. A global transition to a low carbon and sustainable economy can create large numbers of green jobs across many sectors of the economy and indeed can become an engine of development. Green jobs are defined at large as occupations in agricultural, manufacturing, R & D, administrative and service activities aimed at alleviating the myriad threats faced by humanity. This includes jobs that help to protect and restore ecosystems and biodiversity; reduce energy, materials, and water consumption through high-efficiently and avoidance strategies; de-carbonize the economy, and avoid the generation of all forms of waste and pollution. Stating green jobs as a relative and dynamic concept, not linked solely to climate change and not necessarily to new occupations but also to existing jobs, was a good policy option without a concrete effect on statistical classification. This broad definition exacerbated the distinction with decent jobs. In effect, green jobs are not necessarily good jobs or "decent jobs". This important distinction was raised during the ILO Conference on Green Jobs (*ILO, 2008*) where it was shown that green jobs may also be indecent if the Decent Work Agenda criteria are not met (a photovoltaic unpaid worker who is green but not decent and a chemical polluter engineer who is decent but not green).

Every week, new green products, new green services, and new green processes are introduced without generating new green jobs (restyling BAU strategy). This explosion is creating new business opportunities for the rich and new consumer opportunities for the affluent but it is not bringing direct benefits to low income people and communities. On the contrary, poor people experience unhealthy conditions and indecent work, living in polluted environments. (*D. Campbell, 2009*).

The ILO criticism against the Washington Consensus, in contrast with the development strategy promoted by the Bretton Woods institutions, is a key indicator of the paradigm shift in the Development policy. The Green Development advocates for a more holistic approach with long term perspectives respecting historical specificities and a development no longer as a monopoly of economists (*P.M. Krugman, 2006*).

The real change, asked by both the Green Movement and ILO, involves not just opposing exploitation and injustice but implementing social and ecological alternatives which directly target human development and ecological regeneration. In short: from opposition to alternatives, the shades of green towards the low carbon economy show a paradigm shift in the labour market in different ways, according to job creation and job destruction processes.

In fact, new and additional jobs will be created through the adaptation of existing production equipment, manufacturing of pollution control etc., while existing jobs will face the impact of transition to a low carbon economy. In particular, existing jobs will be substituted by shifting from fossil fuels to renewable energy. Furthermore, existing jobs will be eliminated without replacements due to the restructuring processes and existing jobs will become redefined.

Green Jobs encapsulated into the Global Jobs Pact.

The 2009 ILO Resolution on Global Jobs Pact (*ILO, 2009*) which follows the 2008 ILO Declaration on Social Justice for Fair Globalization, encapsulates green jobs within the global policy instrument, addressing social, economic and environmental development.

The new Global Jobs Policy is based on the Decent Work Agenda and represents the tripartite agreement towards socio-ecological and just transition. The ILO World of Work report 2009, focusing on the Green Employment Policies impact, shows an increase of about 15 million new green jobs in 2008.

That said, a new classification of occupations adequate for new jobs typology, deriving from the green economy, is expected. The related revision of the International Standard Classification of Occupations (ISCO, 1982) goes hand in hand with the clarification of employment statistics, whose purpose is to provide indicators of the number of people who, during a specific period, contribute to the production of goods and services in a specific society.

Labour Statistics
Definition of Employment
The Green Jobs movement offers the chance to sort out incongruence in the Employment definition. In this regard, the international definition of employment (Resolution on statistics of the economically active population, employment, unemployment and underemployment adopted by the 13th Conference of Labour Statisticians in 1982) is broad enough to leave a certain margin for national interpretations. As for Employment for instance (*SNA, 1993*) it is defined in terms of a reference period, which can either be short (one day) or long (one year). A short reference period provides an instant image of the employment situation at given time, missing the measurement in economies where the seasonal or casual work is common or where transitions in and out of employment during a year are significant. On the contrary, when a long reference period is applied, employment statistics are derived from information on the number of days or weeks of employment, unemployment or inactivity. People are usually considered as employed when they are economically active most days over the long period. As result, casual and seasonal workers at work only some days during the reference period are excluded from employment statistics, as can happen for seasonal green workers. The seasonal adjustment statistical method in labour statistics tries to overcome the mentioned drawbacks.

Employment Age Limit
A second concern is the age limit. Since a specific value is not set out in the international standards, in many countries the minimum working age is established by legislation. Whatever the lower age limit, younger workers are inevitably omitted from the statistics, hampering efforts to identify child labourers in the green economy.

The Nature of Work: Just for Profit?
A third issue related to the social work has given rise to a great debate. In fact, the System of National Account covers the production of goods or services for sale in the market but services or goods for personal consumption are excluded in the SNA. Hence, women carrying out social services and childcare are also excluded. Most green jobs are located in the social sector which is a sort of "hidden" employment sector. A further concern regards people who not at work during a short reference period. How do you consider whether a person is absent from work and yet still in employment?

Statistics on employment in countries whose laws allow workers to take long leave without losing their jobs tend to show a higher share of people absent from work than statistics in countries whose laws are less favourable in this sense. Furthermore, different statistics can be used for the same employment status. According to those contexts based on regular work, a person can be considered employed even if she or he does not work (sick leave), while according to a context where irregular work is the rule, statistics count a person unemployed even if she or he works (informal jobs).

Employment and Working Time: is One Hour Enough?

The International definition of employment counts people who work for only one hour during that period and therefore encompasses a very heterogeneous group of workers. This group includes the self-employed, workers in paid employment, full time workers or persons who actively look for work while working a few hours in marginal activities. The one-hour limit gives priority to employment activities over unemployment activities, hindering the classification of other social domains. People who work "voluntarily" short hours are known as part time workers, while those who are compelled to work short hours as an alternative to unemployment are classified within underemployment status. Due to the strong link between underemployment and unemployment, in countries where unemployment is low, the number of underemployed tends to be high. This case involves even the USA green collar jobs, where people are often classified as underemployed when they are actually full time employed.

Sources of Employment Statistics

Our last concern refers to different statistics methods and conflicting estimates. The two main sources are household surveys covering the whole population and labour market surveys each with its own methodology and different time frame. As a result, employment and labour market statistics have different features. In conclusion, the updating of the ISCO classification (*ILO, 1988*) so as to include green jobs should be accompanied by the effort to improve the labour statistics towards a more equal representation of the "green employment".

Green Jobs and related labour market analysis

The Purpose of Economic Activity and Employment Meanings.

The rethinking of the purpose of economic activity touches both micro and macroeconomic studies. There are a growing number of microeconomics studies on the relationships between green workers motivation to work in the green firms, which are socially responsible firms observing the related higher productivity and low pollution pattern (*K.Arne Brekke, K, Nyborg, 2007*). Leaving apart microeconomics, this section focuses on macroeconomics as promoted by ILO. Considering that the purpose of economic activity is to increase the well-being of individuals (*J. E. Stiglitz, 2002*), economic sectors (green sectors) that are able to do so, generating social, economic and environmental good cycles, are more desirable than those which do not. Well-being can be achieved through employment and the relevance of employment, following Keynes' teachings, is the main contribution brought by ILO to socio-ecological transition.

Employment is important not only for income but also for the individual meaning of life. For individuals who lose their jobs, it is not just the loss of income that matters, but also the individual's sense of self. Due to a casual connection between employment and unemployment, the meaning of employment lies on the recognition of the workers contribution by employers through pay. Hence, the most serious economic hazard that a worker has to face is that of unemployment. The focus on employment, rather than unemployment, entails a radical change in the economic theory and related policies. Among economists and politicians there is no general agreement on what precisely is meant by full employment, though everyone would agree that zero unemployment is impossible to achieve since changes in the demand of technological change can lead to structural unemployment and frictional factors cause temporary unemployment. It must be pointed out that a person cannot expect to be continuously employed throughout his or her life at a particular job in a particular place. In 1944 Beveridge defined full employment as a condition of having always more vacant jobs than unemployed working out a 3% unemployment rate as a full employment state. What Beveridge regarded as full employment, neoclassical economics would consider to be "over-full" employment with a negative effect on inflation.

Tricks of Neoclassical Economics

The great tricks of neoclassical economists' are to treat labour like any other factor of production. On the contrary, the ILO states that labour is not a commodity. Different from steel, individuals decide how hard they work and with what care (*J. E. Stiglitz, 2002*). The second assumption of mainstream economics is the perfect mobility of labour. This is a crucial issue in the green economy since it is expected that workers move from one sector to a greener alternative through training, which adapts their skills. Imagine how different the labour market might be if labour were perfectly mobile. It might threaten to leave countries that did not provide adequate air quality or which otherwise had a degraded environment. Adam Smith declared that a man is of all sorts of luggage the most difficult to be transported *(J.L Hanson, 1969).* Mobility of labour is of vital importance, essential if full employment is to be successfully maintained. For many reasons people are often reluctant to move to another occupation or to another country. The third assumption says that jobs are not lost due to the international competition, but merely relocate elsewhere and that wages of the low paid workers will rise. This seems not to be the case, even in the green sectors, where wages remain very low. The fourth assumption concerns training. It is supposed that investing in training leads workers to earn more and to be more competitive in the labour market. For those who survive in the competitive jungle, the idea of a knowledge society may ring true, but this may not be the case for those who have been trampled underfoot. The last trick refers to the self-adjusting principle. Markets automatically quickly lead to full employment. Now that market failure is universally recognised, if policy makers want to achieve mobility and act towards full employment, they should be kept away from mentioned economic assumptions. Instead of profit, the welfare of workers becomes an end in itself if living standards are the main objective of economics.

The Green Economy as Transition Paradigm Shift
The green economy is more than just the adaptation of industrial processes towards less pollution patterns or the reduction of energy inefficiencies. It is a transition of

society, a departure from the traditional ways of doing things and traditional modes of thinking. If the green economy is to be broader, then it must pay much attention to workers, their security and social inclusion. They must be persuaded that change and transition can benefit them. Making the socio-ecological transition requires large scale changes in the way that labour markets are structured, changes in the consumption and production models, the technology used, the location of firms and the distribution of modalities. There is not a need for a greener capitalism, but a change in the nature of development, turning to capabilities and human development. Within this transition scenario, the discussion on labour market analysis should be focused on employment rather than unemployment, taking into account that job numbers are only half of the story. The nature of the jobs created by the green economy may differ from the nature of the jobs lost with the repercussion on labour productivity and pay. While there is a rich literature on the employment effect of renewable energy, there are only few studies of the employment effect of climate change policy and green policies. It is worth noting that the energy sector is a relatively "small" direct employer and source of value to the economy (1% of jobs across the 27 Member States of EU and 3% of the value added by non financial businesses) (*J. Stiglitz, 2009*). In the Government's stimulus packages, the number of jobs created by the green economy is often overestimated. For instance, 3 million jobs are expected from the USA stimulus package in the next two years. The other half of the story refers to jobs already lost (2.5 million), the jobs which we are still losing (600 000 per month), and the new entrants into the labour market (2 million each year). According to this data, the conclusion is that by 2010 there would be a very large job deficit in the USA. Hence, green employment analysis should be put within a worldwide framework, where the local context plays the central role in employment and development so that the sustainability path for the local community is considered.

The Time Horizon of Labour Market Analysis
The space dimension is accompanied by a time dimension entailing the need to analyse the green labour market in three stages: the short term, the medium term and the long term. The short term effect of green policies on employment is considered to be the direct employment effect since jobs are lost in directly affected sectors and new one are created in replacement green industries (*N. Stern, Climate, 2008*). An economy wide effect on employment happens in the medium term when the impact of green policies ripples through all sectors of the economy. The creation and destruction of jobs should be studied along the value chain of affected industries. The long term effect takes into account the innovation and the development of ICT and new green technologies. The investment on research and development for green products creates new opportunities and multiplies demand.

Training Policies Analysis
The scenario dimensions of green job development raises the debate on dynamic theories in the labour market. There are a number of different economic theories aimed at explaining some or all of the dynamic aspects of the labour market, such as the reasons why workers enter and leave jobs, why wages change within and between

jobs, etc. The debate focuses on the human capital theory, pointing out green employment changes in the green workers behaviour and their decision to move from brown jobs to green jobs as above mentioned (*K.Arne Brekke, K, Nyborg, 2007)*. The human capital theory stated in its canonical form by Becker in the 1960s remains valid but soft variables replace the monetary ones. As for the dichotomy between general and specific human capital, many green skills acquired during a job, for example in the renewable energy sector, may have some specific elements but also general elements. The concept of generality of green skills also requires elaboration. Whilst some skills and green competency may be useful to a vast number of green businesses and sectors, such as environmental engineering, other skills may be useful only within a particular green industry. The labour market transition from high carbon to low carbon sectors gives rise to a scope for bargaining between firms and workers over returning to specific human capital (*M.Myck, 2005*). If training is necessary for green competency to be accumulated, the question of *who* funds training becomes important and the European Social Fund plays a new role in green employment policies. Other models, labelled as "search-matching models" depart from the perfectly competitive paradigm which was used for early exposition of human capital theory. Here, the key assumption which is dropped in the search model is that of costless information. The worker's decision whether to accept a job or continue searching depends on an optimal stopping strategy which examines the expected value of the accepted job net of search cost. Given the wrong assumption of perfect information, as earlier outlined, these models can be considered obsolete. Instead, studies on the green sectors' potential, (energy and building) to attract and retain transitional workers from low carbon sectors, are very interesting in explaining the workers' behaviour and their mobility choice.

Labour Market Flexibility
A further dimension relating to the transition of jobs from brown to green is the labour market flexibility which refers to the speed of the adjustment to economic changes or changing labour market conditions. In general, flexibility means the degree to which labour input or labour costs adjust to economic changes. Since green jobs involve transitions from firm to firm or movement within the company, either internal flexibility or external flexibility is analysed. Moreover, the numerical flexibility refers to changes in the numbers of workers, whilst functional flexibility covers the change in the competency profile. Green workers need reasonable employment and income security to be motivated in accepting higher mobility and flexibility. Hence, to avoid "deregulation", choices must be made on the basis of various combinations of the different components of the employment and social protection regimes, which need to be analysed to ensure a balance between labour market flexibility and employment security. Flexible forms can be defined as labour contracts with a limited duration, such as fixed term and short term contracts, agency work (temporary work), part time employment, multiple-job holding and work arrangement between two parties for a certain activity. The level of labour mobility and intensity of green job repositioning is measured by the labour turnover as a sum of recruitments and separations from enterprises divided by the level of employment. Job turnover is used to describe structural change as the sum of job creation and job destruction rates, and it helps in

understanding the green employment structural change in a specific territory (*S. Cazes, A.Nesporova, 2008*). Low level indicators are a symptom of the slow pace of the economy. The green sectors should expand new jobs and encourage more workers to change their job voluntarily. In contrast, in the traditional and carbon based sectors, enterprises seek to cut costs by reducing new hires and by resorting to redundancies. Due to the development of the green sector (energy and energy saving in particular), new data sets are now available to work out the green job tenure (the length of time currently green employed individuals have spent with their present employers), which is another variable commonly used in studies focusing on green labour market stability.

In conclusion, the employment priority and socio-ecological transition highlight the need to adapt the labour market analysis in terms of time horizon, labour market flows and training policies, towards a green economy. A new green labour market analysis should be coherent with emerging green policies in a way that employment flows from the traditional sector to the new green sector are facilitated and streamlined. In short, socio-ecological transition requires a transition in the labour market concepts and methods to be applied, so that the Decent Work Agenda is easier implemented.

Green Jobs measurement

The classification and analysis of green jobs has led to their measurement. In the measurement lies the quantity and quality of jobs and the distinction between green, brown and decent jobs. Indicators are the common tools that measure the extent to which a specific labour issue has to be studied. They are the last stage of a demanding research process (method) which starts with knowledge objectives and definitions. It was mentioned earlier, the difficulty in defining employment, even by official statistics, and one can understand the related difficulty in measuring the dimensions of work or labour. Take for instance the concept of "remunerative employment". Here the problem is increased by the need to define and measure the concept of "remunerative". This section discusses the difference between green jobs and decent jobs, so as to highlight the need to orient the green employment policy towards the principle of decent and good jobs as defined by ILO in the 1999 International Labour Conference (*D. Ghai, 2003*). How to measure the current state and future progress of green jobs? The suitability of a range of indicators applied for decent work is useful in understanding how green jobs should be measured.

The indicators' value also defines the closeness between green jobs and decent jobs. The fundamental components of decent work are those related to employment and the relationship issues. As for employment, the three most common indicators traditionally used are those applied in the labour statististics: participation rate, employment rate and unemployment rate. Focusing on the employment rate, this indicator does not provide information on working time. As said earlier, working an 8 hour day in a multinational is quite different from a shorter working time in a micro company covering informal business. The differences in definitions, sources, and the level of measurement leads to the first remark on green jobs measurement: green jobs are not yet comparable, both for traditional jobs adapted into green and new green jobs.

Green Jobs and Decent Employment Dimension: Contract and Social Security

The debate on the remunerative employment concept involves the quality dimension of green jobs as well. Two measures are applied for the adequacy of remuneration: the proportion of workers earning an income less than half of the national median wage and the number of people living in absolute poverty. Many countries have developed their own national poverty lines whilst the World Bank employs a standard of US$1 and $2 per day per person, in order to estimate the number and proportion of the working poor. If green jobs were classified on a remunerative basis, the remuneration scale of those workers included in the 15 million new green jobs reported by ILO would have been known. Employment relationships and social security schemes are key dimensions to evaluate the quality of green jobs, considering not only the environmental or energy sectors but also all occupations associated with quality of life, such as those in the health and care sector. The condition of work indicators can be of some help to measure the quality of work carried out by green workers. These indicators include night work, hours of work, weekly rest and paid leave. Recent discussion, however, is mainly concerned with occupational safety and health such as, the number of accidents and deaths at work and how many of these accidents or deaths are green coloured? The balance between work and personal life is another issue of green employment, both for female and male workers.

Workers protection standards are a key issue for green jobs according to ILO Convention 155/1981. Stress and strain caused by certain types of work also need attention in green employment policy. The ILO Convention on Social Security (102/1952) establishes social protection classes, medical care and benefits related to sickness, unemployment, employment injury, family, maternity, invalidity and survivors. These social protection regimes are designed to cover wage employment but are not adequate for countries where wage employment is a small proportion of the total working population. Now, one can imagine how green workers are protected in the USA or in China. The measurement of social protection (social security) is covered by two indicators: public expenditure on social security as a proportion of GDP and adequacy of the workers coverage. ILO estimates that only 20% of the world's workers and their dependants have adequate social protection. In developing countries, social security measurement is grouped into three categories: basic needs, contingencies, and natural disasters. The first one includes the access to adequate nutrition, primary health care, primary education, clean water, sanitation and shelter. The second one concerns sickness, accident, death of the principal breadwinner, disability, old age. The third one comprises floods, droughts and earthquakes. It is understood that green policies in these countries should be designed to be coherent with green employment policies covering all social security categories as well.

Green Jobs and Relational Dimension: Rights and Dialogue

Rights at work and social dialogue among social partners characterize the relational dimension of decent work.

As for the rights at work dimension, the ILO Conventions 29/1930 and 182/1999 on forced child labour should not be underestimated for green workers, given the application of the Convention 5/1919 on the minimum age. How many children of green collars are included within the 300 million child labour phenomenon? Considering the discrimination issue, discrimination at work refers to the equality of treatment and opportunities for individuals in their own right as a member of a social group being employed or unemployed, according to the Convention 111/1958 (race, colour, sex, religion, political opinion, social origin). Labour force participation rate, employment to female working age population ratio, unemployment rate, differences in earnings and the distribution of skilled labour show disparities even in green employment, where the gender discrimination seems exacerbated.

Green policies should also be concerned with the freedom of association as a fundamental right at work. A number of indicators are suggested to measure the achievement of freedom of association. The number of countries having ratified ILO Conventions or the number of workers belonging to organizations concerned with work related matters are a few examples. The relationship dimension of decent work is mainly focused on social dialogue. Here, the proportion of workers covered by collective bargaining agreements, the union's density and the workers' participation in the functioning of their company, all provide useful indicators relating to green employment as well.

The Risks for Green Jobs

Without underestimating the relevance of green jobs as new employment opportunities pointed out by environmentalists, it is worth insisting on the role of working conditions to achieve the just transition. Together with employment contract or wages (*F. Eyraud, C. Saget, 2005*), working time is the key element to examine the "decent" nature of a green job. According to the ILO perspective (*J. Messenger, 2006*) five dimensions of working time are relevant for green workers. The first concerns health and safety, and suggests that green employment could improve the conditions of work, consequently reducing the negative effect of working time on the health of workers. Secondly, green employment should give priority to family friendly policies exploiting the green philosophy as a lever to promote gender equality and obtain what brown jobs were not able to make up. The balance between work and personal life allows the two birds (working time and productive time) to be killed with the same "decent stone. Yet a decent working time broadens the workers' autonomy and their life control.

Following the ILO approach (*Ghai, cit*), three worldwide contexts can be drawn to classify the alignment of green jobs with decent work. The first, labelled the Classical model, refers to the wealthiest nations (USA and Europe), where GDP per person is high, wage earning is the predominant form of employment, the poverty rate is low (little more than 5%), and collective bargaining is the regulating framework between social partners. The second refers to Central and Eastern Countries (former socialist regimes), where there is a comparable level of GDP, a rebirth on industrial relations and the social security system is under transformation. Lastly, the rest of the world, where the agricultural sectors dominate the economic structure (from 60-80%), the informal economy is large, the wages are very low, poverty is the reality, unions movement is still in its infancy and public expenditure on social protection is much lower than in the other regions.

Green employment should overcome the workers' vulnerability brought by the free market economic approach and the Business as usual principle. As previously said, with reference to conditions of work, different risks are distinguished in the literature (*F. Eyraud, D. Vaughan- Whitehead, 2007*). The main risk is of remaining excluded from the labour market. This risk could be associated to the new form of green jobs which give priority to green skills and competency. Green employment studies provide evidence on this risk, with particular emphasis to women and gender disparities in the green economy. Other risks of green employment are associated with working conditions, as highlighted by the ILO, in terms of low wages, a greater number of working hours, stressful working rhythms, health and safety problems, poor access to training facilities and difficulties in reconciling the balance between work and private life. Green employment and green polices should fight these vulnerability risks, promoting the inclusion of vulnerable works. Again, women are more affected by the low employment rate in the green economy. Furthermore, women workers tend to receive lower wages, even in the green sectors. Young people remain a group at risk. The case of "green engineers" in precarious employment relationships or energy engineers with temporary work contracts are increasing with the same tendency as the green employment rate. Older people are also at risk due to discrimination in green recruitment and the processes in the green restructuring, where carbon based sectors are forced to generate redundancies. New green jobs, in fact, are mirrored by massive layoffs in traditional sectors due to the socio-ecological transition. Minority groups, migrants and low educated workers are other vulnerable groups at risk of exclusion from the green economy. As said, atypical employment, low pay, social protection and no coverage, plunges vulnerable workers into a situation of long term social exclusion, where they remain trapped along what is called vulnerability vectors (*F. Eyraud, 2007*).

Conclusions for Good Jobs

Observing these vulnerability dimensions, the quest for the interaction between these components arises: are they actually completely independent of each other? Isn't analysing and acting on one simply the same as analysing and acting on another? Regrettably, a vulnerability chain seems to determine the economic and social status of current generations, who are in need of green employment social justice and decent work. Can green jobs overcome the persistent inequality and the vulnerability trap caused by the current development model? Are there sufficient conditions towards good jobs? Accepting the failure of the reconciliation between economic, social and environmental development, and experiencing the debatable sustainability of the economic and financial component, green employment could be seen as a new dawn towards good sustainability. Questions mentioned raise the holistic issue, since green jobs should be put within a logical framework, where nature and development, ecosystem and societal transformation, social justice and industrial change, all receive the equal treatment as good life components. To recap the integration between nature and society, an occupations map is drawn where the combination of green and decent jobs is represented using two dimensions, one relating to the ecosystem, the other one referring to decent work. Each axis with two extremis: Ecosystem +, Ecosystem -;

Decent Work +, Decent Work -. The resulting map is useful to illustrate the "good jobs". In the first area (E-; DW-) are located social, ecological and employment circumstances to be avoided. In the second area (E+, DW-) are located those green jobs that need improvement in the decent work conditions. They are green but not decent. Third area (E-, DW+) needs improvement in its ecosystem component and its focus on nature: decent but not green. Fourth area (E+, DW+) gathers socio ecological jobs, which are decent jobs as well: these are good jobs according to Aristotelian Theory of Good Life. This area of good jobs should be the focus of green employment policies so that social justice and nature protection are achieved.

In conclusion, the outlined review of green employment towards socio-ecological and just transition highlights the need for rethinking labour market analysis. This could be achieved by starting from the green jobs classification within the labour statistics and then by incorporating the green jobs movement and concepts raised by green economics. A coherent analytical method should be applied in order to understand green job flows and decent work characteristics. Good jobs epistemology offers the logical framework aligned with ILO employment policy and its Decent Work Agenda. The measurement of the employment relationship between green policies, the social security schemes applied to green jobs, rights at work and social dialogue building good jobs, confirms the strands of a training policy to be designed and enacted in achieving the double dividend of green employment.

References

Kennet M, (1999) Green Backlash Strategies, in Scott Cato M., and Kennet M., (1999 Green Audit

Lunn C E, (2006) *The role of green economics in achieving realistic policies and programmes for sustainability*, International Journal of Green Economics,

Vol.1, No. 1 Nitnitiphrut K, (2008) The Concept of Happiness

Eyraud F, Vaughan-Whitehead D, (2007) The evolving world of work in the enlarged EUThe Gross National Happiness Abridged Survey, (2006)

Easterlin R A, (1974) Does Economic Growth Improve the Human Lot? Essay in Honour of Moses Abramovitz, NY Academic Press

Hodge B J, (1996) Organisational theory, Prentice Hall

Packard A, (2009) Cultivating the future: integrating idealism and rationality

Schumacher E, (1973) Small is Beautiful

3:3 Green Economics: its recent Development and background

By Miriam Kennet and Michelle S. Gale de Oliveira (Brazil)

1. Introduction
a) Increasing interest in Green Economics and the Green Economy
Ban Ki Moon General Secretary of the United Nations, said that "We are living in an age of Global Transformation, an Age of Green Economics."
There has been a dramatic increase in interest in environmental and green economics and the transformation towards Green Jobs and a Green Economy.
Partly in response to concerns about unprecedented and rapidly accelerating anthropogenic climate change there are worries that "the very survival of the human species is at risk." We are also living in the 6th ever mass extinction of other species that the earth has ever experienced, (IUCN) with many mammals, fish and birds under threat. A growing population predicted at 9 billion, means the poor are more directly dependent than ever directly on the ecosystem, and geo political instability is becoming more common.
Inequalities between people, within and between nations, and between present and future generations as well as social and environmental injustices are now significantly affecting the world economy. The bundle of natural capital resources, (forests, productive seas, agricultural land, healthy soil, air and water, food resources, rainforests) we can leave to future generations may actually be smaller than those of today. Climate change and sea level rise mean that current and future generations may inherit a world in which there will be less land available for cultivation or habitation, as well as depletion of forests, bleaching of coral reefs, protective mangrove swamps and other resources of all kinds including viable fish stocks or productive oceans. Massive dead zones are appearing in the sea and increasing desertification and soil erosion and declining forests and whole Ecosystems services are declining and the economy will be under threat.

b) People and institutions are looking for alternative solutions and innovation in economics
The current economic crisis has exposed deficiencies of mainstream economic concepts and the creation of new ones. These include for example by Paul Krugman in the USA and Stigilz and Sen and Green National Accounting from President Sarkozy in France and McGlade at the European Environment Agency and more fundamental changes in Ecological economics (Daly) introduces absolute limits on "more is better than less."
The mainstream regarded ecology related decision-making as having infinite natural boundaries, and simply aggregated human behaviour and "optimal" solutions from it.

If the air or sea is so polluted that they can't sustain life, or the soil removed, or we have passed certain thresh holds or tipping points from which the natural systems can't recover, green economists propose doing different things, rather than substitution of one raw material with another. Standard neo-liberal economics models are insufficient for today's issues and are in urgent need of not only a major overhaul and has become "unfit for purpose," but also need replacing.

c) The broadening of scope and the arrival of "Inclusion" in economics

According to traditional market explanations "*the invisible hand*" (Adam Smith) mechanism ensures that everyone benefits from the investment and activities of homo economicus or "rational economic man" and his spending preferences and choices. In spite of arising from selfish aims, they are presumed to benefit the whole of society. Most people on the planet are not white western educated wealthy men and cannot choose how to earn a living or how or become wealthy.

So the absolute hegemony of markets is being fundamentally questioned in all its aspects: from the need to separate investment from savings banking, to its ability to solve climate change and its ability to solve the problem of poverty for which absolute as well as relative evels continue to rise. Similarly the role of "homo economicus" in the collapse of for example Icelandic banks, has led to laws to increasing the number of women at the helm or are brought into corporate board rooms and to correct long standing imbalances of power, representation and wealth between men and women.

d) Mainstream economics solutions have reached a crossroads

Human economic development has always relied on technological advancement to address challenges in the past. So the switch from fossil fuels to biofuels to allow for the continuation of current transport modes, as business as usual, was a logical step which was fully embraced by large companies and large trading blocks such as the European Union. However, this competition over land uses and pushed up the price of fuel, caused a scarcity of land for dwellings, and food riots all over the world, creating more poverty and land price spikes. This increasing investment and speculation culminated in the bursting of the "bubble economy" and a complete collapse of land prices in several countries leading to a serious economic downturn. It has ended the economic period called the "Great Moderation" and we are now in a period called "The Great Contraction."

e) Vulnerability of the economy to Global environmental change: the example of Italy

In common with many other places today, the OECD has warned that the economy of Italy in common with several other countries is particularly vulnerable to the economics effects of global environmental change. There are changes in the climate, leading to health effects of encroaching tropical vegetation, "Alien Species" invasion, malaria and dengue fever reappearing. The warming world is causing sea level rise andaffecting specific environments such as the city of Venice and its lagoon and many other coastal towns and in other countries whole small island states may disappear. The increase in temperature is causing micro climate environments, leading to more warming in certain Alpine Regions, upsetting watersheds and the available Hydroelectric Power which drive the economy and industry. In particular the warming has led to melting of the glaciers, leading to the re-emergence of "Oetzee the Ice Man" for the first time in 5000 years. These changes are affectng tourism as the mountain tops are no longer snow covered. The rich agricultural traditions such as wine, apples and meat may be damaged in South Tyrol. Slope instability, caused by changes in water courses and other global environmental changes, has meant more train derailments in mountain areas too such as occurred this year in Bolzano.

A transformation in the role of the car has led to large scale shut downs of car factories in the south and bans on using cars on certain days in larger Italian cities. Agriculture has to cope with advancing climate change and in general species moving northwards in the northern hemisphere according to some studies by up to an observed 5 metres per year. Plankton in the sea are moving significantly northwards affected by increasing acidification in the sea. In Italy tourism, a significant part of the economy, is threatened by the encroachment of a warmer tropical world, replacing it as a reliable and comfortable Mediterranean attraction and as a ski and winter walking holiday destination.

The rapidly expanding Green Economy is particularly useful in offering the hope of Green Jobs and the creation of 1000s of new ones to create a more sustainable economy.

f) Mainstreaming Environmental and Green Economics

The climate and biodiversity crisis solutions evolve into a blueprint for leading the world in the Green Economy

Solving the complex mesh of social and environmental justice is included in all aspects of Green Economics thinking, as are the costs and effects of climate change on the world economy. For example, the Stern Review of the Economics of Climate Change (2007) showed that spending up to 1% of GDP (recently corrected to 2%) would actually be a cheaper option than allowing runaway climate change to persist. The TEEB Report in 2010 by Sukhdev has done similar work in highlighting the even higher costs of biodiversity loss as we are now causing the 6th ever mass species extinction. For example, bee colonies are disappearing due to microwave disturbance to their navigation systems from mobile phones, and the cost of hand pollination (already happening in China) of crops would be catastrophic in the west. Einstein said that once the bees disappear humans will only have another 4 years to survive on the planet.

Green Economics is an interdisciplinary science; on the one hand it is concerned with the theory and practical management of Global Environmental Change in all its aspects and on the other with the development Economics providing provisioning, sharing and distribution of the wealth of nature and human and naturally occurring resources.

It is a developing progressive holistic approach which cannot be explained by simplistic, typically linear mathematics and fixed preferences of individuals.

It extends beyond ecological issues to wider considerations of ideology, history of thought, evolution of society, the level of objectivity and the time specificity of solutions in a social science environment to be taken into account. These provide a much stronger basis to criticize and replace current reductionist mainstream economics. It embraces a wider set of values, including but not exclusively ecological values.

2. The arrival of Green Economics
a) Green Economics Strategies for addressing current crises
The Green Economy Initiative of the United Nations (2008) describes the crises as "Fs", Food, Fuel and Finance" and advocates a more growthist solution and the Lisbon 2020 Agenda also suggests Smart, Green, Growth is possible and desirable. A Green Economics perspective instead regards the crisis as a mixture of the current economics downturn, a crisis of poverty, climate change and biodiversity loss and proposes a composite set of solutions. These consist of a mixture of market instruments, such as carbon trading under the Kyoto Protocol, regulation, carbon quotas or even rationing of carbon use,as well as technological innovations and green developments. It advocates, most of all, a change in public attitudes and reduction in unnecessary consumption of the earth's resources and individual carbon footprints and for *life style changes*. A progressive holistic approach extends beyond ecological issues to wider considerations of ideology, history of thought, evolution of society, the level of objectivity and the time specificity of solutions.

The European Greens propose that the economy must adapt to what the natural environment can tolerate, aiming for ecological sustainability, equity and social justice as well as self-reliance of local and regional economies, encouraging a true sense of community, based on democracy, transparency, gender equality and the right of all people to express themselves and participate fully in decision-making.

b) Environmental Economics
Environmental economics aims to factor in the costs of activities and impacts external, to a particular economics transaction. Market failure, its central concept, means that markets fail to allocate resources efficiently and this occurs when the market does not allocate scarce resources to generate the greatest social welfare. The best and most famous example is that of climate change in the Stern review. Biodiversity loss is also as serious, if not even more costly. The previous discipline of Environmental Economics has quite a main stream framework and does not specifically change activities or prevent impacts and only aims to simply find out how much things cost.

Although useful information, it will not change what is done. It so omits the point thatother options are available, or reassessing what is actually required.
Similarly surveys are used to establish "Willingness To Pay," for its existence of a species, or its conservation or to visit a natural amenity for an environmental benefit popularised by David Pearce are often used for example in deciding on the fate of a natural amenity such as whether to conserve a species.
The Stern Review proposes introducing a price for carbon, REDDS -debt for nature swaps and Carbon Storage and Sequestration and Discounting the future.

Common Property Rights are another concern first identified in this context by Coase and Hardin. When it is too costly to exclude people from accessing a contested environmental resource, market allocation is likely to be inefficient. Hardin's (1968) The Tragedy of the Commons popularized the challenges involved in non-exclusion and common property. "commons" refers to the environmental asset itself. Hardin theorizes that in the absence of restrictions, users of an open-access resource will use itmore than if they had to pay for it and had exclusive rights and thus will often cause environmental degradation. Ostrom (1990) won the Nobel Prize this year for work on how people using real common property resources do establish self-governing rules to reduce this risk.

c) Ecological Economics

Ecological economics moves towards the primary role of energy and the laws of thermodynamics and energy flows and democratic decision making as subsets of the natural environment in its discourse.

Ecological economics includes the study of the flows of energy, and materials and material flows and ecosystem services that enter and exit the economic system. For the first time we have a change to the core concepts and a move towards the human economy as a subset of the natural world. Ecological Economics now is being used in global institutions. Use and non use value for measuring costs of Ecosystems services degradation are being used for example by the United Nations.

d) The Renaissance of Economics; the Green Economy rediscovers the roots of economics

Green Economics works in what it terms the four pillars of scope or activity, namely-1. Political and policy making, 2. academia especially science and economics, 3. business and 4. civil society including NGOs and most recently adding in a fifth, the general public and consumers.

Everyone and everything on the planet is acknowledged to have economics or provisioning requirements to achieve desired optimal conditions. Green Economics describes itself as "Reclaiming Economics, for all people everywhere, nature, other species, the planet and its systems. " As a result even the volcanic activity which cost European Economies dearly this year, was able to be incorporated. For example it has been discovered that allowing the glaciers and ice caps to melt will increase seismic activity. The earth has a self regulatory mechanism, Gaia Theory by James Lovelock) which controls the temperature at 14 degrees centigrade. Too much warming and the volcanoes erupt cooling down the planet. Too much cooling and the ice sheets form pressing down the magma and preventing earth quakes!

Green Economics a participatory approach is a development which includes natural science data and works with it, as many of its teams are physicists and natural scientists who also have economics qualifications, so it is able to weld both natural and social science together.

It is at core multi- disciplinary, and inter – disciplinary and pluralist and its decisions are based on the twin imperatives of human and natural science futures. It fully accepts that we all inhabit the earth and there is no economy outside of it. It reflects the current knowledge about the complexity of reality,. It is characterised by a holistic perspective, the involvement of nature, and is very inclusive.

It has evolved from a complete and fundamental philosophical renaissance of the origins of economics from the Greek Word oikia- meaning household or estate management, now evolved to meaning the *earth*. The "oikonomia" -of Xenophon is now the economics and provisioning for the needs of all people everywhere, nature other species, the planet and its systems and also of the "Good life" of Aristotle.

3. The Cultural, Institutional, Academic Umbrella and Positioning of the Green Economy and its Chronology

a) The Transformation of Economics Disciplines and Schools of Thought

Under the Heterodox Economics Umbrella, are found alternative, holistic interdisciplinary,pluralistic set of methodologies and contributions. Pigou (1920) working on external effects and Coase examining the role of property rights. The USA and the UK struggle to decide who is liable for BP 's huge oil spill in American waters. The debate is evolving into a robust economics school or discipline and widening the scope of an alternative economic framework further, into Environmental economics by authors such as Hartwick and Solow, Ciracy Wantrup, Daly, Tietenberg, Markandya, Pearce, Boulding, Jacob, Hillman, Ekins, Chichilnisky) and Ecological Economics (Soderbaum, Daly, Martinez- Alier).

Green Economics is influencing the economic debate and transforming existing policies and decision-making. 'Green' and Writers include Kennet, Heinemann, Hillman, Ekins, Reardon, Porrit, Gale De Oliveira, Dobson, Anderson ,Barry, Gale, Reardon,Rao and Turk and Jociute..

A rapidly growing branch of economics, Green Economics is spreading into policy development in governments for example the Korean Government and also in Global Institutions such as the United Nations and the International Labour Organisations and the OECD. Each of these has a Green Economy Initiative or a Green Jobs Programme. Green Economics is being taught in Universities around the world and is also featured by the Dow Jones and Wall Street. The Green Economics Institute was founded in 2003 and its academic journal, *The International Journal of Green Economics* founded in 2005. Its background is in the "Green movement " hence a strong policy orientation combined with Economics Heterodoxy, as well as Environmental Science and Global Environmental Change and Management.

The discipline builds on enlightenment ideas of reason and rights, post-modern ideas of different and power struggles and elites, and Malthusian limits to growth and the search for sustainability, and on eco-feminism. The Enlightenment brought a major impact on modern understandings of economics and the role of humanity in the natural world. However it tended to look for logic and reason rather than wisdom in nature, as Bacon explains : "The human mind which overcomes superstition is to hold sway over a disenchanted nature. What men want to learn from nature is how to use it in order to wholly dominate it and other men. That is the only aim." The backlash against 10 000 years of the domestication of animals, plants and women and the colonies is in full swing within Green Economics. So it is the acknowledgement that the quest for domination is over.

Green Economics argues that nature has its own intrinsic and existence value and extends this value to all life forms, (Deep Ecology Arnae Naess) and thus seeks transform economics to "provision for all people everywhere, all other species, the biosphere, systems, and planet."

It is sometimes part of a broader ideology, sometimes part of Buddhist economics (Welford, Guenter Wagner 2006) advocating de-centralist, non materialist, and cooperative values and the concept of "enoughness" or sufficiency is important, as well as leaving enough resources for future generations.

One key development was the book "Silent Spring" by Rachel Carson which exposed the effects of DDT and the practices of the chemical industry and the relationship between the economy, industry , the environment and our over all well being.

b) Sustainable Development Economics

Another important key development was the Sustainable Development Economics, developed by Professor Graciela Chichilnisky, and our Common Future which addressed this area of futurity In 1987. the United Nations World Commission on Environment and Development (UNCED) issued the Brundtland Report, defining sustainable development as meeting "the needs of the present without compromising the ability of the future to meet its needs."

Sustainable Development economics gives equal weight to economics, environment and social aspects.

c) Green Economics as Practice

The Green Economy has been called the Economics of Sharing the earth and its economy amongst ourselves but also with other species and systems of the planet in addition but not exclusively also to ensure it remains hospitable for us and our way of life.

It is also the economics of doing and is intensely practical. For example this means that there is much focus on green supply chains and the greening of procurement with the aim of creating social and environmental justice. It also advocates greener transport methods and slower local smaller scale production, even with slow travel and more train travel, slow food and degrowth to keep withing the earth's Carrying Capacity. It advocates *"Reduce, Reuse, Recycle, Repair, Restore, Relax, Recover"*

Green IT

The role of IT, once hailed as the ultimate saviour, is now regarded as a significantcause of climate change and so there is a move to decouple the big monopolies such as Microsoft and move towards more community owned human style, open source IT and to limiting the carbon usage of server farms, saving carbon by virtualisation, using recycled and also recycling materials and managing and limiting the power usage much more.

Environmental and social dumping and checking for green and transparent supply chains Large outsourcing of environmental and social standards to where they can't be seen (called dumping) is coming to an end. Equity, social and environmental justice are acknowledged as providing attractive competitive advantage in a modern economy.

Green Jobs
Increasing numbers of jobs are being created in this vast and innovative transformation- this green economy. The Green Jobs Initiative of the United Nations and the International Labour Organisation and the International Federation of Trades Union describes a green job as *"work in agricultural, manufacturing, research and development (R&D), administrative, and service activities that contribute(s) substantially to preserving or restoring environmental quality. Specifically, but not exclusively, this includes jobs that help to protect ecosystems and biodiversity; reduce energy, materials, and water consumption through high efficiency strategies; decarbonize the economy; and minimize or altogether avoid generation of all forms of waste and pollution."* A Green Economics perspective of a Green Job is anything that is sustainable and contributes to social and environmental justice.

4. Instruments and Tools in Green and Environmental Economics
a) Geo engineering and Green Technologies
The use of technological solutions (also called Eco technology or Geo engineering or Technical Fixes). These include, solar radiation management, iron fertilisation of the sea, stratospheric aerosols, sucking carbon using giant artificial tree scrubbers, albedo management, air capture, urban albedo and algal-based CO_2 capture schemes, Carbon Storage, Sequestration or Capture.
There is increasing concern with the idea that "Unintended Consequences" could occur if for example we seed the clouds as the Chinese Government has done this year to create rain or we use Sulphur Aerosol Particles to mimic the action of volcanoes in cooling the global climate.
The "Precautionary Principle" is a major feature of a green economy which advises against trying untested technology. This would for example be used to prevent the kind of the oil spill or engineering at great depth without a clear strategy for clean up by BP.
The change to green technologies involves the use of Rare Earth Materials, which are nearly all mined in China. Significantly this year, China ceased exporting them in order to supply its own home market and so made the production of green technologies more expensive and more difficult.
"Local Production for Local Needs" will mean that the private car will be slowly replaced by modern and attractive lower carbon public transport, including car clubs, car-sharing, more cycling, and train travel. Governments introduced a green Car Scrapage scheme to encourage purchases of new cars
Greener alternatives such as slow travel are taking off, and train-travel is once again fashionable. Slow travel, slow cities, and the Italian idea of slow food are gaining in popularity.
Lower carbon economies are now actively being created, to combat the current average of 10 tonnes carbon equivalent usage in Europe, 25 tonnes in the USA, 5 in China, and 1 in Africa. Policies include "Contraction and Convergence" firstly to limit each

person's carbon to 2 tonnes of carbon equivalent per year, secondly to equalise global economies.

Additionally, the acceleration of melting permafrost and the release of catastrophic amounts of methane would set in motion rapid climate change and sea level rise. Mainstream fossil fuel dependence has unacceptable costs, including pollution damage to fisheries and geopolitical struggles over supply chains from Russia to the Middle East. Fossil fuels are being replaced by microgeneration, Renewables and SMART grids, (linking areas of high wind to areas of high solar availability) more self sufficiency. Local and micro generation of energy is possible with Feed in Tariffs introduced in Germany and the UK.

b) Changes in attitudes to energy production and use: Lower carbon economies

British Petrol (BP)'s Deepwater Horizon oil drilling leak in the USA is an example of how the role of oil and fossil fuels in the economy is starting to be acknowledged as a limiting factor and is being questioned. Roughly 10 per cent of UK pension funds are linked up with BP and so the cancellation of the dividend from BP has deeply affected the UK economy but the oil spill has affected the economy of the US ruining for example fisheries but also coastal tourism and wildlife. The cost of oil is also a feature of the much criticised Iraq war too which reduced public acceptability of the costs of our current life style and how the idea of freedom, liberty and nonviolence fits with the idea of safe energy supplies from hostile, undemocratic or unstable regimes.

Additionally there have been concerns about the effect of CO2 use on climate and the acceptance that the 20th century economy was characterised by mass-production and economies of scale, ending the century with huge outsourced supply chains in human conditions for workers.

c) Carbon trading and market solutions Climate crisis : Kyoto Protocol and the Copenhagen Conference COP15

The Kyoto Protocol, (a market-based attempt to trade carbon to solve climate change), held its regular Conference of the Parties Conference in Copenhagen COP15 in December 2009. It received unprecedented interest, and over 40 000 people and most of the world's Heads of State flocked there. Small island states would disappear unless climate change is stabilised at an agreed at 1.5 degrees of warming. Other more powerful countries decided to ask for costs of stabilisation of the climate at 2 degrees of warming. The huge response led to an actual failure of the Conference as the organisers UNFCC were completely overwhelmed with the level of interest people showed in limiting climate change.

Lord Stern said that "Climate Change was the biggest market failure the world had ever seen." Although he continues to remain within the market mechanisms promoting ever more growth as a solution, green economics tries to solve the climate problems by looking beyond only market mechanisms. Main stream Economics methods have to some extent relied on Cost Benefit Analysis and Discounting The Future but in a world where future resources may be depleted, and a weaker economy we should be doing the reverse. What is needed is to do different things differently.

d) Environmental Taxes and Regulations

An external effect was defined by Arrow as a "a situation in which a private economy lacks sufficient incentives to create a potential market in some good, and the nonexistence of this market results in the loss of efficiency." Externalities are examples of Market Failures in which the unfettered market does not lead to an efficient outcome, such as the costs of clean up of an oil spill, or the raising of the climate by fossil fuel use, or wastes collected and treated and can include energy products, transport equipment and transport services, as well as measured or estimated emissions to air and water, ozone depleting substances, certain non-point sources of water pollution, waste management and noise, in addition to the management of water, land, soil, forests, biodiversity, wildlife and fish stocks and on unleaded petrol and the fuels efficiency and climate change impacts of vehicles, the CO_2 emissions per km driven.

e) Regulations

The current economic crisis was caused in part by deregulation of the banking system which had separated casino banking or speculation in investment banking from that of the savings of the small investor. Regulation is a cornerstone of a green economy. Some of which include: REACH Directive on Hazardous Chemicals and the WEEE Directive on recycling of components for electronic equipment when purchasing electrical or electronic equipment, batteries and accumulators.

f) The Green New Deal – Keynsian Investment

Very popular with UNEP and with the Greens and with governments, implemented by the UN and by the Korean Government and many others using a Keynsian stimulus package to pump money into the economy and targeting it towards green innovations and sustainable projects. The age of stimulus projects is now over as the big clean up starts and frugality and living within our contemporary means is the order of the day.

5. The Broader Background of the Green Economy – Changes in Focus in Economics Today

a) The Limits to Growth

There is an increasing realization that we may have reached what has been termed the "limits to growth." We are brushing up against the finite limits to the earth's adaptability and its "carrying capacity" in the face of our human and continualonslaught on sustainable the climatic conditions, and use of resource assets have "overshot" beneficial levels. A green economics perspective argues that empowered and educated female citizens decrease population size faster while increasing a country's GDP. Some even suggest that overall "equity is the price of survival."

b) Prosperity without Growth

Currently gaining popularity, Prosperity Without Growth dialogues are spreading around Europe, and a fashionable Degrowth Movement has originated in France, promotes the kind of Steady State Economy envisaged by John Stuart Mill. Rather than being seen as a failed attempt at growth, Growth by Design is gaining in interest, if not in acceptance.

This is partly a result of growth actually stalling in many Western Countries and the realisation that growth above 2 tonnes of carbon equivalent per person is no longer a good long term proposition. The European Environment Agency and many other institutions are working on this and other aspects of Green Accounting and Indicators. In particular important benchmarks are progress towards the Millennium Development Goals, and the Millennium Ecosystems Services Assessment Goals, The GRI for measuring Corporate Social Responsibility, (O' Carrol) the GINI Co- efficient index,The HDI Human Development Index, the Happiness Index from the State of Bhutan and many other sustainability and social indicators as well as measurements of unemployment, trade deficit and sovereign debt. Since WW2 there has been an economics policy of encouraging high mass consumption but this has begun to be questioned. Conspicuous consumption is going out of fashion and we are moving into an age of more austerity and rebalancing. Commodity prices are fluctuating and there is a global economic downturn, large sovereign debt and rising unemployment all over Europe. Many countries and national institutions are exploring a green economy as the one ray of hope in this rather bleak landscape. The European Commission believes that this green technology will drive competitive advantage, and encourages green venture capital and Smart, Inclusive, Green, Growth as part of the Lisbon Agenda.

Conclusion

The Transformation into the Age of Green Economics is a very exciting period of economics innovation, offering choices of strategies from right across the spectrum. Much has happened in terms both of the evolution of Green Economics, Green Jobs and a much more effective economics system. It has spread as an important driver from Korea to the EU and as an important aspect of decision making such as in the successor to the deep sea oil spill. Environmental, ecological and green economics are all playing their part in this process as we move towards the development of an economics for the 21st century- an Age of global transformation- An age of the widely predicted 4th Industrial revolution, decarbonising our economies and working to enhance the future not to discount it!

A previous version of this chapter was first published in Encyclopedia Trecanni (in Italian), in 2010.

3:4 How useful is Econometrics for Green Economics?

By Sophie Billington

In this chapter, I shall address the contentious issues relating to the use of econometrics within the field of green economics and I will argue that, in many cases, econometrics *could* prove to be a useful tool for analysing specific problems in green economics. I shall start by defining the key terms, 'green economics' and 'econometrics' and then go on to suggest some of the reasons why econometrics could be of use as well as some of the reasons why it may be applied inappropriately in the context of green economics. I will conclude by reflecting upon the future for econometrics within the discipline of green economics.

Green economics is an alternative approach to thinking about economics in a world where our actions are beginning to have huge implications for the natural environment. This developing field of economics highlights the inter-dependence of human civilization and natural ecosystems, and considers the impacts that our own decisions have on all aspects of life on earth. Research in green economics typically aims to find solutions to problems such as, climate change, resource depletion, poverty, damage to ecosystems, loss of biodiversity and population pressure (Kennet, 2007).

The research tends to be based around instinctive and practical ideas; it rarely makes use of econometric models, which are often thought to be too narrowly defined for the issues which are dealt with in green economics.

Econometrics can be described as the application of statistical techniques to economic theories. It can be used for modelling purposes i.e. to test hypotheses and infer the relationship between a set of variables. It could also be used for forecasting purposes, in order to predict future trends in the data.

Let us now consider a simple econometric model, $Y_i = \beta_0 + \beta_1 X_i + \varepsilon_i$. That is, for each individual observation, i, and with fixed parameter values, β_0 and β_1, the dependent variable, Y_i, is determined by the value of X_i, plus a random component, ε_i. For the model to be unbiased, the expectation of ε (its mean value) must equal zero. Furthermore, to find the most suitable estimator to use, we must also minimize the variance of ε. Therefore the primary aim is to find the estimator with the minimum variance, subject to the condition that the model is unbiased. This will be our best linear unbiased estimator, and will be used to obtain an estimate of the parameters in the model (in this case β_0 and β_1).

Why might this type of analysis be useful for green economics? Let us, for example, consider the model

$Y_i = \beta_0 + \beta_1 X_{1i} + \beta_2 X_{2i} + \varepsilon_i$ and define Y as the number of people living in absolute poverty, X_1 as government expenditure on education, and X_2 as government expenditure on social security benefits. We are then able to use either time-series data (taken over a period of time), or panel data (from a sample of different countries), to determine the effect that expenditure on education or social security has on the level of absolute poverty within a county. We can establish whether these variables are statistically significant in the model and can evaluate their parameter values to find the effect they have on the level of absolute poverty. This analysis would therefore be extremely useful for informing decisions related to government policy. Should a government invest in education or social security if their primary objective is to reduce absolute poverty and they only have a limited budget? The model I used is, of course, highly simplified, and therefore our estimates are likely to suffer from problems such as omitted variable bias, which is referred to later in this chapter. We could add more variables, which may improve our model, provided that they were statistically significant.

Other examples of using statistical models to make informed decisions on green issues include regressions to find out: how significant is the effect of a carbon trading scheme on carbon emissions reduction; to what extent are rising sea levels affecting the seagull population; what effect do democracies have on the level of absolute poverty within a county. Using similar regressions to these, we may determine crucial relationships between variables which may not be obvious or instinctive if the analysis had not been carried out.

There are, however, various problems with the use of econometric analysis, many of which are indeed acknowledged by mainstream economists. In the next few paragraphs, I will briefly describe some of these issues before expanding my discussion into further concerns which are held by many supporters of the green economics movement.

The most obvious fault with most econometric and mathematical modelling is that the models are often highly simplified. For example, there may sometimes be a case of omitted variable bias, where explanatory variables from the true model are omitted, either because no data for that specific variable was available, or because the relationship between the variables was not recognized. This will therefore bias the estimates of the parameters in the model. As a consequence, the results will be incorrect and therefore, the conclusions drawn will be wrong. This is a classic example of when critics describe econometrics as being precise, but wrong; whereas they often claim that a more intuitive or philosophical approach will be less precise, but closer to the truth. Moreover, supporters of green economics believe that the world is characterized by extremely complex and inter-dependent systems and relationships between human and ecological factors.

Furthermore, the models used in economics can often depend on questionable assumptions which can affect the 'practicality' of the model. We need to ask ourselves whether these assumptions are realistic enough to be acceptable in the model. If the assumptions are not satisfactory, then when too much emphasis is put on the models, we can end up with significant economic consequences. An example of this is the recent financial crisis. The financial models used by the banks were established on the assumption that house prices would continue to rise. When this key assumption broke down in early 2007, a huge 'credit crunch' led to a global economic recession, the effects of which are still prominent 3 years on.

A further critique of econometrics is that it deals with variables which must be measured quantitatively. There is, however, considerable difficulty in measuring many variables this way. For example, what value do you put on the loss of the entire Amazon rainforest? What value would do you put on the entire elephant population becoming extinct? Economists' answer to this is to apply CBA (Cost Benefit Analysis) to these situations, whereby a monetary value is assigned to each and every social, environmental and economic aspect which may occur in a specific situation. The values are typically calculated by considering how much people would be willing to pay, to prevent one of these scenarios from occurring. Inputs are evaluated in terms of their opportunity cost. The effect that the scenario will have on GDP is also commonly used as a way of measuring total cost. Surely though, some of these scenarios are impossible to valuate. Indeed, money, our own invention, is too narrowly defined to be used to evaluate the impact of major a disaster, one which could, for example, wipe out the entire human population. This is an extreme example, but it illustrates why many supporters of green economics have criticised the use of econometrics as failing to deal with these issues in a practical way.

Furthermore, economists have often discussed the fact that some variables which we use in econometrics are inappropriately employed as a proxy for a variable which is more difficult, or even impossible, to measure. The alternative variables which are used can sometimes prove to be a poor substitute.

One final observation is that econometrics is very good at showing us the relationship between specific variables in the past, but it tells us very little about future solutions to problems which we are only beginning to experience now. We have not yet compiled enough data to calculate the extent to which we have already been affected by climate change and predicting the magnitude of future climate change involves a very high degree of uncertainty. It is these types of issues which are at the core of green economics and perhaps a more creative wisdom is necessary in order to find possible solutions and ideas before it is too late.

In conclusion, I do agree that there are certain problems with using econometrics to analyse issues in green economics. Using statistics in the practise of economics is very different from analysing statistical relationships in most other sciences, where conditions can be appropriately controlled and inputs carefully monitored. In economics, it is more difficult to create these perfectly controlled conditions in order to conduct a 'social experiment'. Tony Lawson (2007) questions whether human behaviour is predictable and queries whether the same results would occur if we were to repeat a social experiment in the exact same conditions.

However, I think that econometrics should not be dismissed when considering its usefulness for green economics. It is a fact of life that we must make decisions. Choices must be made and trade-offs will be involved. From deciding whether to invest in solar power or wind-turbines, to deciding what rate the Bank of England should set interest rates at, the only current method of objectively analysing their impacts in order to make an informed decision is to apply econometrics to the problem.

This chapter was first published as a paper in the Proceedings of the 5th Annual Green Economics Conference at Mansfield College, Oxford University, July 2010, published by the Green Economics Institute.

References
Kennet and Lawson, T. (2007) 'An orientation for green economics?', *International Journal of Green Economics*, Vol. 1, Nos. 3/4, pp. 250-267.
Bergheim, S (2006) Measures of well-being: There is more to it than GDP. Current Issues Deutsche Bank Research
Hodgson, G (2008) What is Wrong with Mainstream Economics? And How Could Economics be Improved? www.feed-charity.org
Kennet, M and Heinemann, V (2006) Green Economics: Setting the scene. Aims, context, and philosophical underpinning of the distinctive new solutions offered by Green Economics. International Journal of Green Economics, Vol. 1, Nos. 1–2, p68-102
Lawson, T (2007) An orientation for a green economics? International Journal of Green Economics, Vol. 1, Nos. 3–4, p250-267

Part 4: Debating Social Justice
4:1 What opportunity do poorer people have to participate in the Green Economics Debate?

By Don O'Neal

1. Introduction
In traditional economics, it has all been the wealthy and the powerful that have defined what economics guides global trade. The poor have had no voice in traditional economics and are casualties of an imbalanced economic order. In 1990, 31% of the population of the developing world lived on less than $1 a day - close to 1.4 billion. (Alexander, 2012).

2. Rio Summit 1992
In recent decades, there has been a backlash against traditional economics. Five years after the Brundtland Report, the United Nations held a Conference on Environment and Development, in June 1992 at Rio de Janeiro in Brazil. The Rio Earth Summit was the largest environmental conference ever held, attracting over 30,000 people including more than 100 heads of state. Aside from Rio, there have been numerous sessions of the Conference of the Parties (COP 17) to the United Nations Framework Convention on Climate Change (UNFCCC) and other global initiatives such as the Millennium Development Goals. One has to wonder how much the voice of the poor was represented at these negotiations and how much poor people were able to participate. The Rio summit, though, offered hope and real possibility for change. For once it seemed as though the plight of the environment and world development was being put high on the agenda.

3. Rio+20 in 2012
Twenty years on, one can ask again how much has the voice of the poor been represented at these negotiations and how much poor people were able to participate? How much has changed for the poor of the world? Rio, like Kyoto, and the COP sessions has been a succession of meetings where global leaders and big business have set agendas to satisfy themselves and absolve themselves of doing much at all. Has the past 20 years been a success for poor people? (Box 1. Poverty statistics)
Still 2.7 billion people struggle to survive on fewer than US$ 2 a day.
More than 50 per cent of Africans suffer from water-related diseases such as cholera and infant diarrhoea. More than 800 million people go to bed hungry every

day. 300 million are children. More than 2.6 billion people-over 40 per cent of the world's population-do not have basic sanitation, and more than one billion people still use unsafe sources of drinking water.
Source: http://www.unmillenniumproject.org/resources/fastfacts_e.htm [Viewed 27 July 2011]. Bearing the above poverty statistics in mind, what opportunity do poor people have to participate, or lead, in the Green economic debate?

4. Maslow's hierarchy of needs

The problem for most people living in poverty is that they do not have the luxury to participate in the Green economic debate as they are too busy trying to satisfy their basic needs. American psychologist Abraham Maslow stated that people are motivated to achieve certain needs. When one need is fulfilled a person seeks to fulfil the next one, and so on. The earliest and most widespread version of Maslow's hierarchy of needs includes five motivational needs, often depicted as hierarchical levels within a pyramid. This five stage model can be divided into basic needs (e.g. physiological, safety, love, and esteem) and growth needs (self-actualization) (McLeod, 2007). One must satisfy lower level basic needs before progressing on to meet higher level growth needs. Once these needs have been reasonably satisfied, one may be able to reach the highest level called self-actualization. Every person is capable and has the desire to move up the hierarchy toward a level of self-actualization. Unfortunately, progress is often disrupted by failure to meet lower level needs. (Figure 1. Maslow's hierarchy of needs).

To ponder about Green economics and to participate, or lead, in the Green economics debate, people need to be able to function adequately at the self actualisation level of Maslow's hierarchy of needs. Most of the world's poor are stuck trying to conquer the lower levels of physiological and safety needs.
Until these lower levels have been overcome, it is difficult for poor people to have opportunities to participate in the Green economics debate.

5. Example of 'hierarchy of needs' problems and proposed solutions

A real life example of these problems can be illustrated by life in St. Vincent and the Grenadines (SVG). Discussed with these problems are policy ideas of SVG Greens.

5.1 Access to food, water and electricity

Although, some food is grown locally in SVG, a substantial amount is imported. In 2011, ☐ 52 million worth of food was imported, which is significant when public debt was ☐ 305 million and the SVG Government Budget Estimates 2012 were only ☐ 199 million (SVG Government, 2011). SVG Green's policy is to set up farming co-ops and create incentives for supermarkets to substitute foodstuffs they buy from abroad with locally available foods. Imported food is very expensive and by using more locally grown food, food prices will come down and farmers will start to earn a decent living again.

Many households in SVG are not connected to the mains water supply. About 21,600 households were disconnected from the mains water supply during the period 2006 to 2010 (Letter from Central Water and Sewerage Authority - SVG). This is a substantial amount considering the population of the country is only 104,000. SVG Greens' policy is to reduce the cost of water by 50% and to make sure every household is connected to the mains water supply. Also, we intend to make the first 1000 gallons used each month free of charge.

Electricity in SVG is expensive and many households do not have electricity. SVG Green's policy is to reduce the price of electricity by 50% and to make sure every household gets connected. Also, the first 200 KWh would be free. This will be managed by moving away from oil-produced electricity to making SVG 100% reliable on renewable energy sources.

5.2 Access to safety, employment and resources
Crime is a major problem in SVG. In an article entitled 'Is this Caribbean idyll the worst place in the world to be a woman?', it was noted that over the past decade, more than 4,500 refugee claimants — or 4.3 per cent of the tiny Caribbean archipelago's population of an estimated 104,000 – sought asylum in Canada (Yang, 2011). In 2007, SVG had the third-highest rate of reported rapes in the world per capita, according to a UN report. SVG Greens' policy is to reduce crime by strengthening the economy, partly by starting a tuna fishing and canning industry using its deep-sea fish licence.

Unemployment is very high in SVG because the economy is on the verge of collapse. SVG Greens' policy is to strengthen the economy by moving away from tourism and focusing on education and science and technology. Also, we intend to make education free and build a first university for the country.

The internet is very expensive and only a minority of people has access to the internet.

SVG Greens' policy is to make internet free in the whole country to encourage innovation and entrepreneurship. Also, provide access to micro-credit schemes to help small businesses and start-ups.

6. Abolish Apartheid
Abolish the scheme whereby Taiwan and a super-rich minority in Mustique does pay tax in SVG, whereas everyone else has to pay tax.

7. Conclusion
If the foundation in people's lives is not there - no food, water, shelter, security and education – then they will fail to participate in Green economics and Green economics may not help them. I believe that Green economics will be richer when more of the poor are involved. We have had the Adam Smith 'trickle down' economics: that has not worked for most of the world. I think that 'trickle down' Green economics will not work either. What's needed is a kind of 'trickle up' economics, to provide more realistic solutions for the poor and empower them to be part of, and benefit from, Green economics, rather than being casualties of Green economics. Stalagmite economics – where the poor are the architects of the solutions and architects of the methods to achieve the solutions. Poor people need to be empowered to participate, or lead, in the Green economics debate.

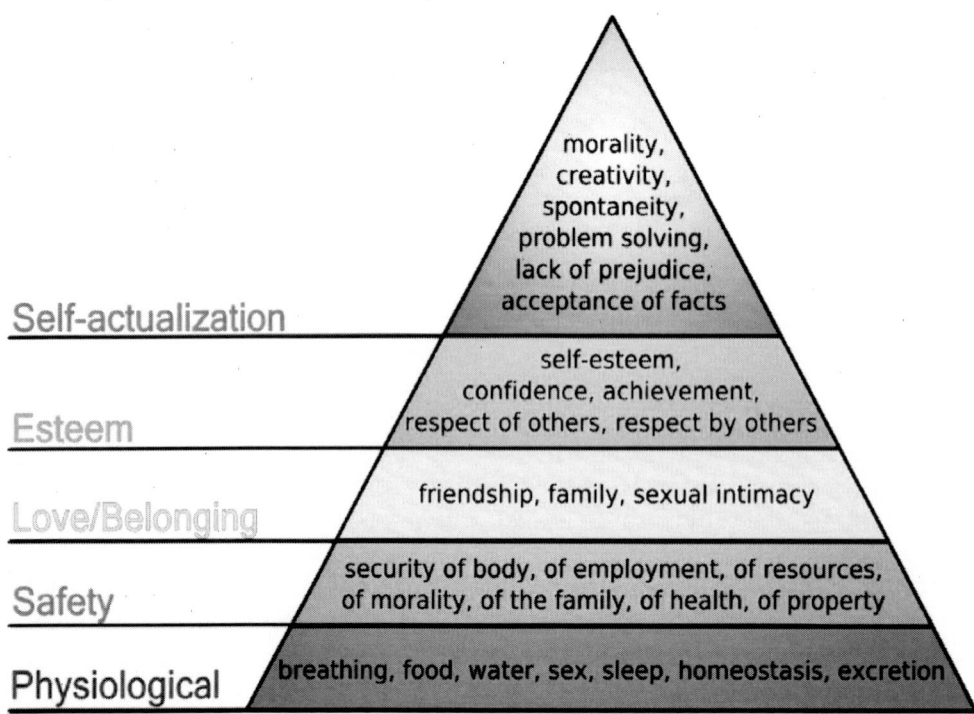

References

Alexander, R. (2012) Dollar benchmark: the rise of the $1-a-day statistic. [Online]. Available from: http://www.bbc.co.uk/news/magazine-17312819

Letter from Central Water and Sewerage Authority, SVG.

McLeod, S. A. (2007). Maslow's Hierarchy of Needs - Simply Psychology. [Online]. Available from: http://www.simplypsychology.org/maslow.html

Millennium Project (2006) Fast Facts: The Faces of Poverty [Online]. Available from: http://www.unmillenniumproject.org/resources/fastfacts_e.htm [Accessed: 20 July 2011]

SVG Government. (2011) SVG Budget Estimates 2012. Kingstown: Government Printer

Sustainable Environment (2012) Earth and man: Action > Rio Earth Summit. [Online]. Available from: http://www.sustainable environment.org.uk/Action/Earth_Summit.php

Yang, J. (2011) Is this Caribbean idyll the worst place in the world to be a woman? [Online]. Available from http://www.thestar.com/news/world/2011/11/12/video_is_this_caribbean_idyll the_worst_place_in_the_world_to_be_a_woman.html

4:2 Tragedy in Zolitude: A lesson for contemporary society

By Sandra Gusta

On November 21, 2013 Maxima shopping center's roof collapsed in Riga, Latvia causing 54 deaths and creating international news. The collapse of the supermarket in the Latvian capital Riga has been described as "murder", by the country's president Andris Berzins. It is the deadliest disaster in Latvia since it regained independence in 1991.

Figure 1. Maxima shopping center roof collapsed in Riga. Photo by Gatis Smagars
(Source: Latvia...,2013)

Figure 2. FLAWED: Inspections of buildings in Riga are exposing numerous problems
(Source: Lawsuit, 2013)

The causes of the collapse need to be studied in detail. This report is the authors' independent attempt to find the cause based on photographic evidence and literature observes. This article is based on a study conducted by the students and teachers of Latvia University of Agriculture.

The chapter provides the reasons for this tragedy basing on the analysis. The author considers that the tragedy was the result of the coincidence of circumstances caused by mistakes in the calculation of building structures.

Introduction

According to the "Regulation (EU) No 305/2011 of the European parliament and of the council" of 9 March 2011 laying down harmonized conditions for the marketing of construction products and repealing the Council Directive 89/106/EEC Member States have introduced provisions, including requirements, relating not only to safety of buildings and other construction works but also to health, durability, energy economy, protection of the environment, economic aspects, and other important aspects in the public interest (Regulation...,2011).

In *ANNEX I* the BASIC REQUIREMENTS FOR CONSTRUCTION WORKS are mentioned: 1.Mechanical resistance and stability 2.Safety in case of fire 3.Hygiene, health and the environment 4.Safety and accessibility in use 5.Protection against noise 6.Energy economy and heat retention 7.Sustainable use of natural resources. The author offers to view some of them :

The 1st requirement - Mechanical resistance and stability.

The construction works must be designed and built in such a way that the loadings that are liable to act on them during their constructions and use will not lead to any of the following:

(a) collapse of the whole or part of the structure;

(b) major deformations to an inadmissible degree;

(c) damage to other parts of the construction works or to fittings or installed equipment as a result of major deformation of the load-bearing construction;

(d) damage by an event to an extent disproportionate to the original cause.

The fourth requirement - Safety and accessibility in use. The construction work must

be designed in such a way that it does not present unacceptable risks of accidents or damage in service or in operation such as slipping, falling, collision, burns, electrocution, injury from explosion and burglaries.

Materials and Methods

Hypothesis: Safety and durability of constructions are the basic conditions for the buildings' longevity and sustainability in the future.

There is an increasing tendency of the sustainable development principle implementation in all Latvian companies including building, construction and architecture companies and this is what can be done, improved and developed by every company.

However, one should keep in mind that while implementing the sustainable development projects, the key is to ensure the safety of the structures, thus also human security.

In order to confirm or refute this statement, the following goal was set:

To analyse the causes and consequences of the tragedy in Zolitude using the information available to the author, so that lessons could be learnt by society to avoid similar tragedies in the future.

The objectives set in order to achieve the goal:

1. To analyse the theoretical basis for sustainable development and assess the necessity for it.

2. To analyse the causes and consequences of the tragedy in Zolitude.

3. To view similar structural collapse cases in Latvia and abroad.

1. Maxima Tragedy in Riga

On November 21, 2013 the roof of Maxima shopping center in Riga, Latvia collapsed, causing 54 deaths and international news. The collapse of a supermarket in the Latvian capital Riga has been described as "murder", by the country's president Andris Berzins.

It is the deadliest disaster in Latvia since it became independent in 1991.

The causes of the collapse need to be studied in detail. This report is an independent attempt of the author and Rural Engineering Faculty students of Latvia University of Agriculture to find the causes based on photographic evidence, numerical and analytical calculations.

2. More defences are founded

Ongoing inspections by the Riga Construction Board of public buildings over the past several weeks have shown cracks of various sizes, specifically at 18 Rimi and 13 Maxima supermarkets in Riga. Overall, the Riga Construction Board has carried out inspections at more than 200 public buildings in Riga, including 100 Rimi, Supernetto 124

Economics of Social Justice; A Handbook for Students

and Maxima supermarkets, establishing "certain problems" in 31 of them.

Several years ago, the Riga City Council eliminated the local government's Construction Supervision Department, the functions of which were largely the same as the previously-eliminated State Construction Inspection, while the function of supervision of the construction process was completely handed over to local governments. The department, then part of the Riga City Council Construction Board, was liquidated in 2009. Riga City Council said this was due to a shortage of funds. It is notable that construction of the Maxima supermarket in Zolitude that collapsed began in 2010. The Construction Supervision Department's functions were not taken over byany other unit of the Riga City Council. It was a "political decision by the Riga City Council" to weaken the Construction Board so it would not impede the various construction projects implemented in Riga.

In late November, a 100 million lats lawsuit was filed in Riga Regional Court against Maxima Latvia, construction company Re&Re, the company Tineo - the owner of the collapsed Maxima supermarket building, real estate developer Homburg Zolitude, and Riga City Council. [3]

Results and discussion
"Maxima" supermarket was not the only ruined building, where the Maxima construction team participated in. In 2011 the roof of one of the two recently completed "Cemex" factory warehouse collapsed causing millions of measurable losses. The "Maxima" supermarket tragedy is largely similar to the disaster at the International Exhibition Centre (Międzynarodowe Targi Katowicka) in the Polish city of Katowice on 28 January 2006.

The investigation was completed in 2008, in late June. Katowice District Court in late July found the guilty ones of the tragedy,12 persons were indicted, among them two hall designers, who were accused of "directly endangering lives of other people" and faced up to 12 years in prison.
In general, the experts concluded that the major catastrophe was due to errors in the design, which changed several times in order to reduce the cost of building. It was also demonstrated that the company was aware of the problems and needed to clear the snow from the roof of the building, but ignored the warnings, not wanting to take on additional expenses. (Kā Polijas..., 2013)
Thinking about safety and durability of constructions – the basic condition of the building longevity and sustainability in the future, the Latvian government should react adequately.
These problems are also in tune with the present political situation in the country and the world. They clearly show that the society has forgotten about the signals which should not be ignored and the problems should be noticed and solved in time. The society which does not understand or does not want to understand the problems has to be addressed and convinced.
By analysing them, it appears that the company is oblivious to the existence of economic laws to the business environment. Thus, for example:
☐ Law of value (lowest price problem in the building area)
☐ Law of expanded reproduction - "It is necessary to develop and expand production, constantly researching the needs of society";
☐ Intensive Development Law - "As the resources of our planet are limited, the ill considered
extensive or incomplete use of them may lead to the collapse of manufacturing and global natural disasters."
☐ Law of interest - "positive cooperation with any human being can be best achieved if the people's interests – moral , material, social, etc. are are taken into consideration;
☐ Law of harmonization of interests - " harmonious cooperation and development will only be achieved if the parties cooperate (buyer – seller, employer - employee , entrepreneur – state, etc.)". Participants will have consistency and common interests.

3. Possible cause and consequence analysis of Maxima supermarket tragedy

According to the author the main causes of Maxima supermarket tragedy were:
• mistakes in the calculation of the building structures:
• mistakes in the construction process
• incorrect response to an emergency:
• problems with the lowest price of construction in public procurement
• other reasons

The main consequences of the Maxima supermarket tragedy are:
• collapse of the supermarket in Zolitude;
• causing human suffering and claiming the lives of people;
• increased attention to the construction process and building exploitation
• revaluation of values and attitudes;
• problems with the lowest price of construction in public procurement.
• other reasons.

Conclusions

The author's main conclusions and recommendations arising from the results of students' and teachers' study regarding the tragedy:

1. Simultaneous public building construction and exploitation is not allowed. How was it possible to allow large-scale construction work to take place on the roof while inside the store there were several dozen people?

2. Completey *inadequate* staff response to the alarms. Alarms sounded, but the shop staff responsible reacted incorrectly. People were not evacuated in time.
3. If substantial changes were made in the structures in the project (the side truss was split into two parts), it was mandatory to do iterative calculations and carry out re-approval of the project.

4. The need to carefully analyse construction materials and conditions, such as checking the strength of the steel bolts class.

5. It should be noted the designing work involves high level of responsibility and great work load,and the professionals are are remunerated inadequately.6. The lack of independent control of building sites. It is necessary to restore building inspection in Latvia.

7. In recent years, too little attention has been paid to the supporting structures for safety and sustainability. For public building design and construction the constructive solutions should be introduced in such constructive solutions of overload: upon the first noticeable appearance of distortion.

8. Nowadays in construction the wrong slogan is dominating, and the prevailing principle is that the best offer is the cheapest one. There shall be no material

savings at the expense of people's safety.

9. Delegation of responsibility.

10. It is very important to improve the legislation in Latvia's building sector (Building Law).

11. In conclusion, the author wishes to express her belief that society as a whole will be able to identify, measure and draw the right conclusions from this tragic human and economic lesson.

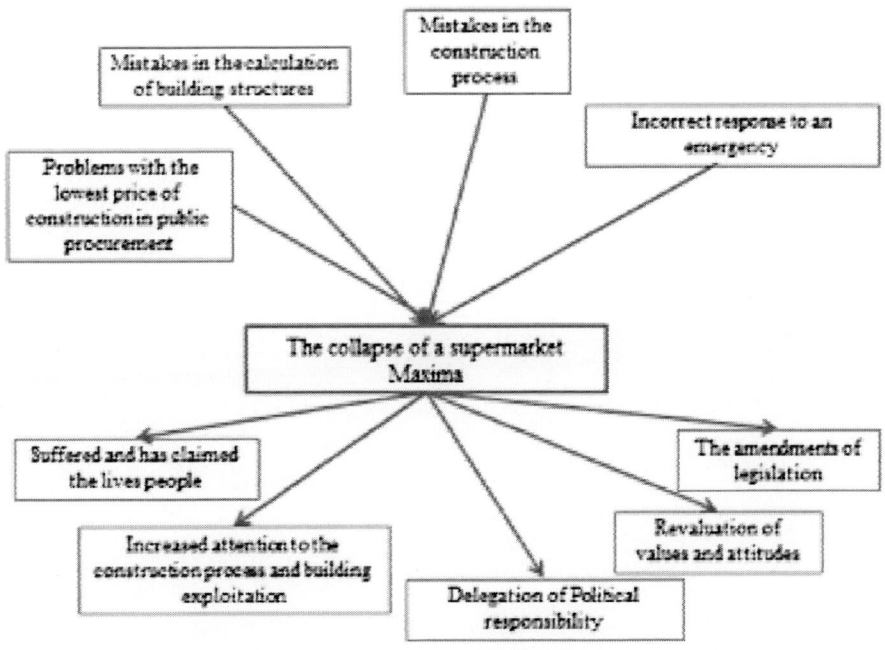

Figure 4. Reflective scheme of causes and consequences of Maxima supermarket tragedy (Source: by the author)

References
Kā Polijas varas iestādes rīkojās pēc Maximas traģēdijai līdzīgās 2006. gada janvāra traģēdijas Katovicē [online] [accessed on 25.11.2013.]. Available: http://blog.kapitals.lv/2013/11/25/ka-polijas-varas-iestades-rikojas-pecmaximas-tragedijai-lidzigas-2006-gada-janvara-tragedijas-katovice/

Lawsuit filed in Maxima aftermath The Baltic Times [online] [accessed on 01.11.2013.].
Available: http://baltictimes.delfi.lv/news/articles/34011/
L.Pakrastins Priekšlikumi būvniecības nozares profesionālās vides
sakartošanai[online] [accessed on 27.11.2013.]. Available:
http://lbpa.lv/2013/11/priekslikumi-buvniecibas-nozares-profesionalas-
videssakartosanai/
Latvia mourns victims of Riga suppermarket collapse [online] [accessed on
01.11.2014.]. Available:
http://news.bbcimg.co.uk/media/images/71281000/jpg/_71281211_71281210.
jpg
Regulation (EU) No 305/2011 of the European parlament and of the council [online]
[accessed on 01.11.2009.]. Available: http://eurlex.
europa.eu/LexUriServ/LexUriServ.do?
uri=OJ:L:2011:088:0005:0043:EN:PDF

4:3 Towards Economics that provides for Social Justice

By Henry Cox

Introduction

The overall objective, in a context of SJ, is to improve the condition of people – with a long way to go. Here, and a first stage, the concern is about changing the Economics – the words and terminology used to describe the economies. This includes describing, or setting, what is meant by "the economy". Which is distinct from changing the various economies ('transition' of them). But much that is written is proposals (policies) to change an economy (not change the Economics), or is examples of practice that could or should be followed. Some proposals do not fit with present Economic theories, doctrines, and terminology; and depend on the Economics being changed to allow description of the economies intended. Green Economics being often heterodox. Also one limitation is that above a certain amount of change people will reject the change, as beyond what they think is feasible, or thinkable.

From 2009 I have had Papers, of up to 10 pages, at Green Economics Institute conferences and published in the proceedings; and a few Chapters published in books of GEI. Much of them is about having economies that are sustainable and pleasant; and using, within them, some terminology and words that are different or unusual relative to what is now usual in Economics. This Paper is an attempt to be short, and keep mainly to thinking about changes to Economics - not policies for economies. I first wrote about sustainability for a Green Economics Gathering in Huntingdon, in 1983. Much I write is from memory. My practice ('work') has been in applications of electronic engineering, and in gardening (growing plants for food andornament) for households – not for money. A longer description is in Cox 2014, 1.

Economics of (for?) Social Justice

The word "Economics" derives from an ancient Greek word - "oikia" - for household.(Kennet) But much has changed since then; such as the rise of trading and manufacturing firms that Smith sought to fit into Economics. A basic topic now is whether the objective of 'the economy' should be to 'grow' firms; or to improve the lot of people; as distinct from the few who grow rich from firms - buying, owning, selling them.

The ancient Greeks probably had little or no money involved within the economies of their estates or households; and their "democracy" was of a slave owning society; in which only the male citizens had votes. Further there is now a need for economies to be changed to be sustainable; a global topic as climate change is a global problem – eg changing the level of the sea. Basically, to have social justice and to have economies, requires people – societies – to continue to exist. Which means the economies are to be sustainable.

Present Economics, in its view of 'the economy', appears to be concerned – only – with what is done by and for firms - "bodies corporate", and with what is done for money. For 'the economy' is now measured in GDP – which is in a metric of money. People are, as yet, and according to conventional Economics, in 'the economy' in terms of what they get, or pay, in money. Wealth of people, and of materials – and of some "intellectual property" (rights) - is put in terms of money; in "balance sheets" and "accounts". Though trading in people, and in "trafficking" them, is now a criminal offence.

Broadly there is a problem in Trade: - that it is done in, and for, money; not for social objectives. Awkwardly there is an illegal part of the economy. But, though not in conventional Economics, much of the 'work' in actual economies is done without involving money; eg the topic of "women's work" - that Feminists have long struggled to get accepted – and measured. Here the whole of the licit part of the 'non-money part of an economy' is included and considered; much of it being basic to 'social' – but is left out of what is now conventional Economics as it is not done for money. So, how to 'account' – describe – the 'non-money part of an economy'? And how much should be done for money; how much outside the money part of the economies?

Sustainable economies – and Economics for them – a 'Social' requirement
The word "social" implies the existence of 'society' – of humans; and "justice" implies all the humans are to be 'comfortable'; not some in luxury, many struggling and others in poverty. To have SJ - the people continuing to exist - the economies have to be 'sustainable' and the Economics used (should) cover design and practice of sustainable economies – as some have tried to cover. But, as stated in the BIS Report of 2012 titled "The Future of Food and Farming", sustainability is not described in the Economics now in use. Instead, in what is still 'conventional' Economics; the phrase, assertion or command is, "we all want growth" - of GDP. Very different those who take 'GDP' as a rough metric of 'Gross Damage to Planet'; and to those who look to 'degrowth.'

System Design – the whole before the parts. Problems of complexity.
One difficulty in almost all present academia, politics and media is that they approach problems by dividing them up into 'subjects', 'faculties', 'stories', etc.; and by limiting responses to "what is your top priority". So that they bar system design – considering the whole before the parts. Whereas the whole, not only the parts, is described in Capra and Luisi "The Systems View of Life, a Unifying Vision" (CUP 2014). Which book does state most of the errors of Economics but, being a work of Science, does not describe the design (engineering) of systems of Economics avoiding those errors.

One widespread problem, even in the green movement, is restricting concern to the topic of Energy - as in "A Renewable World, Girardet & Mendonca (Green Books 2009 - for the World Future Council). Energy, resulting in 'carbon' (CO2e), is the most urgent (and much denied) problem; but it is not the largest problem. For far more energy than we now use comes from the sun; it is our habit of getting our energy from the 'cheaper' fossil sources that is polluting the world, leading to climate change.

Sustainability of Materials - Green Economics of Natural Capital.
A much larger (but longer term) problem, so far hidden, is that the materials we now take from geological stocks, are from unsustainable sources as there are no inputs of materials to the planet (Cox, GEI 2010). Specifically our present use of metals and other elements, eg phosphorous, is by taking 'ores' that are ancient geological concentrations of them. Then mixing up the materials into waste, which is often pollution, from which only some can be recycled. Note that mining has its own form of Economics, that provides for profit over the 'life' of a mine – but this is for 'exploitation' of geological stocks; away from preserving the stocks – of 'ores', of natural capital (a much confused term).

Life evolved to cope with the severe limitations of the availability of elements, and we could and should follow the sustainable methods of life. And also limit our numbers by just methods; not follow the practice of the various animals, eg aphids and rats, that have fluctuating populations. For some history and practice of growing plants on land for food see Cox in Chap 1.4 in GEI book "Food, Farming and Agriculture", 2013; which includes the problem that the now usual – mechanised – farming is unsustainable, whereas manual cultivation systems can, and often are sustainable. but are almost all in the non-money part of the economy. Hence, by excluding non-money work, conventional Economics states that unsustainable methods are to be used to "Feed the World" - but the Economics denies this quandary.

Work – in conventional Economics; or in social contexts. Two additional Sectors in 'the economy'.
Present Economics assumes that even materials can be measured in terms of their price – despite Physics ruling out creation of matter; and stating that mixing up the elements increases entropy – and money cannot override thermodynamics. This was written up by Roegen, and his work is described by Anca Gheorghica in GEI 2012 and elsewhere. In contrast, money is an artefact that can be, and is, created by 'central banks' and by banks that make loans by writing debt into their ledgers.(Robinson J in "Future Money", Green Books 2012; Positive Money (web site)).
Economics using money (the prices that are current) as the metric is now usual; with several attributes of 'markets' asserted. This is away from SJ; and also avoids considering sustainability. Unfortunately the current assumption is that all 'work' is paid work (and so that unpaid work is NOT work). So 'work' is determined by firms, by the jobs they provide, (or by 'the (labour) market'), and the workers should go to where the firm has the work – mobility of labour being put as desirable – not as breaking up families and societies.
What people do, within families (households) and within societies (tiny communities), is, in conventional Economics, assumed not to be 'work'; as it it is not done for money, not done for firms.. Whereas, in most of my Papers eg Cox 2015, I

117

include domestic ('household') work by adding two Sectors of the economy to the usual 3 (State, Trade, Voluntary) that are of work for firms, for money (as jobs). I include a Sector 4 of 'gift work between households'; and a Sector 5 of 'work within and for a household'. Whereas present Economics asserts that, to get enough work (assumed as jobs), firms must 'grow' – do more (and use more resources) so as to have more jobs (hopefully enough).

Also 'the economy' must grow, so that the (historical and future) borrowing (for 'investment' - debt) can be cleared away. But such economic growth involves much more being made – and so more materials (natural capital) being converted into waste. And it depends on it being sold – and so much goes to the rich (firms and individuals). Hence how inequality leads to social injustice is complicated and disguised. One snag being that the State, including LAs, is one form of 'firms' – but they depend on more taxes, or more borrowing (from firms such as banks) if they are to provide more jobs.

Digression on difficulties of changing practice – when stuck in a hard place'

There is a huge difficulty for (academic) Economics to include non-money ('domestic') work; in that there is no data on it. I grow food and eat it, but it is not in statistics of 'production' that Defra and ONS make. So it appears not to be "produce", though I eat it – and avoid buying such food from shops. Governments can understand it, sometimes, as the UK government supported us in "Dig for Victory" in the 1940s. The UN and FAO make some assessment, and allow the existence of "subsistence agriculture", but there are no adequate descriptions.

It seems we have gone into a hard place – the government having taken to support low pay, and also support firms in various ways. Shifting to accepting that non-money work exists, is useful, and is towards economies being sustainable should reduce the total amount of money turnover – which will appear as degrowth, and firms will howl. Part of this should come from small local communities doing more within them, avoiding much of the present 'work' done by (the paid staff) of the state. Eg why pay for childcare so that people can take paid work (which is not there)? This is that much now done appears to be a way of increasing the 'supply of labour', so that the 'price (pay) of labour' falls due to 'market forces'. Serious problems coming from breaking up local communities, so as to have 'mobility of labour' for the benefit if firms.

For many people have to move their locality when they move to another firm – or the firm moves them.Problems of taxation, of productivity, and export led growth

Awkwardly taxes are now mainly on labour (wages, VAT), little tax is on resources and pollution; as described in Robertson "Benefits & Taxes (NEF 1984). Tax on the wrong things might making difficulties if non-money useful work was recognised – for governments might then try to tax it. But the major error is in taxing useful work, instead of taxing using up finite resources. There is now much hope for LVT (or SVR) that was proposed some 100 years ago by Henry George – but the establishment avoided it; and it may be too late to introduce it now that land prices have been pushed up as the 'last' resort for 'investment'. .

A present problem in Economics is that the 'productivity' of the UK (firms) has not risen, as was expected in the 'recovery' (of employment in terms of the number of jobs) that has now occurred after the crash of 2008. It appears that 'productivity' is a troubled metric, and has long been poor in the UK. The non-money part of economy, if included in 'the economy', will be a further complication.

A further problem of present economies is that they have a strategy of 'export led growth'. But, on a finite planet, this is not practical – and is complicated by some countries having exported bits of their land, eg oil, got paid in return, and now have "sovereign wealth funds", which are 'invested' in various firms – and can control much of what is done – or not done. This seems to be one problem of competition; all want to be 'winners', but few can be. A crude view is that we are to struggle to put the others down.

From altering Economics, to altering economies – policies and then practices

Here the topic is about altering Economics, which is relatively simple, and proper to academia. But making this new economics practice – globally - would be a huge change. Though the "Transition Towns" are amongst those attempting to do so. And a very few communities have, at least some remanent of subsistence agriculture, fewer of gathering. I, and many others in the UK, grow some or much of our food, in gardens or allotments (Cox GEI 2014, & Chap 1.4 in GEI book, Food, Farming & Ag). Much has been written, and some done, in a Feminist context; attempting to get acceptance that Women Work – in their house and elsewhere. But this tends to leave out (non-money) work by men (the man in his shed as well as the woman in the/her kitchen). And 'paying' for the work women do might get it into Economics – but the economies have not the money to pay for it (hence citizens incomes seem impractical). But such proposals to pay for household work are distinct from recognising, in Economics, that non-money work exists, is useful and is often more efficient than such work done as jobs.

Some branches of economics : Transport, Education, TNCs, Caring

To change to sustainable economies there needs to be a huge reduction in mechanised transport. Most work done within walking distance in local communities would avoid work done as jobs for firms, and so would avoid much of commuting (andof the present assumption of 'investing' in much more infrastructure for transport). And shifting much work to be done in an around housing would help local social life - for going out to work breaks up communities as well as adding the unproductive 'working' time of commuting. I put the – initial - changes, for changing to sustainable economies, as reducing energy used by 5 to 1; and transport used by 10 to 1. Then continue reductions in resources used until the economies are actually sustainable (with an adequate safety margin). But this would appear as 'degrowth' - of the money part of the economy. But, and a portent of the future, much of the recent and praised 'growth' in the UK has been in the manufacturing of large cars, diggers; and 'investment' in more roads and railways is desired – to have cities grow. Put another way, cities depend on transport, and so infrastructure, to bring supplies into them, eg food, take wastes away. Whereas very many, very small societies (how small? Perhaps max 900 people) can avoid transport – mainly by avoiding Trade.

This gets to the present vast cost of Education systems, the commuting of staff and pupils to and from them; and the serious lack of the 'educated' to be able to do many jobs well (leading to immigration). Whereas if much work is manual, is done in or local to the housing, the children can, mostly, be there (avoiding the now huge 'taking in of each other's childcare') and so they can watch, then help, then do much of the work. Education is needed as we have huge brains. Having schools that do schooling uses resources, including buildings, and does provide jobs – but how is the money for this to be provided? Two problems; one of costs, the other of relevance.

TNCs – firms larger than States; Oligarchies

Another problem we have reached is of TNCs – of trading firms that are larger than States. And huge firms are very different to the concepts of 'markets' that seem to apply only to trade where there are over 1000 firms in a 'market'; and no firm has more than 1% of the market. Oligarchies have become prevalent, as in many aspects of energy. And TNCs may be beyond nationalisation; as well as registered in other countries or tax havens. For one effect of Trade, and "growth", is to have more imported. TTIP is another current development, see FoE view.

Caring: for the young, the old, the less able – and should much of 'education' be in 'caring'

Caring done within very local communities avoids much transport, keeps those communities together; avoids the vast expense of it done for money by firms of Sector 1 or 2. Put another way "economy of scale" rarely applies to caring. Though specialised care, eg medical, is proper for those with difficult or new problems. Some "Local Authorities" (now less local) are trying to shift to very local voluntary groups doing much of the caring; but local people helping each other without involving an 'authority' (firm) avoids most of the "overheads" - and avoids strangers coming in to care for the lonely.

Sociology and Politics– veering away from Economics.

"Social", and "Justice", imply the 'subjects' of Sociology and Politics; away from Economics. One question, or topic, is what sizes and types of communities can be 'pleasant' and just? One recent metric is "well being", but it tends to record the results, not help to guide design of economies and societies. Strife and war are huge problems, and Economics (GDP, etc.) has been used to run an economy to fight a war. There are, in the above, various thoughts and assumptions about economies that would be pleasant, mostly assumptions that small groups suit our species, huge groups are difficult. Are they true and practical?

It seems that much, including Management theory, is affected by what humans (and machines) can do – when in groups from few to many. As is Ergonomics which is (should be) the branch of Engineering connecting humans and machines. But is there an equivalent in Politics? Awkwardly much seems to confuse (writer and reader?) by taking properties of humans that apply only in groups of specific numbers (and geographical area of spread); then assume or assert that they will apply in what is proposed.

Sustainability – eg zero CO2e emitted – would be much easier to attain if transport was avoided. Yet transport is mostly put as desirable – it does lead to 'economic growth'. So one major topic is whether cities can be sustainable – I think not. That people do, or want to, live in cities is of minor importance: brute nature, and thermodynamics, include death and birth.

Confusion in the terminology of 'community' and other social metrics
Further confusion comes from "community" now being used for large numbers of people, far larger than those who can know each other and so be an actual community. For politics, etc., calls parliamentary constituencies, even the EU, 'communities'. This seems the now common way a word implying a desired property gets used to apply a desirable sheen to what is outside the range it can apply. Concepts such as society, community, friend, are limited by what individuals can do. Generally advertising, media and politics seem to thrive on the misuse of words and concepts. Elsewhere (Cox 2014, 2) I have tried to distinguish what is practical in social groups, but is this acceptable? Using the numbers of individuals in a group, in 10 to 1 steps, from 1 to 9 for household, 10 to 99 for 'band', up to 1 to 9G for the population of the planet. Much of "social" being limited by the limitations of humans. The only written description that I have seen of a solution in practice, is of the Zapatista movement, in the Chiapas region of Mexico, where the people have got their aboriginal rights to their land (back) and changed to independent local communities. Esteva described a study tour he was invited to – that they had organised - in "Liberators of Hope" in Resurgence 285 , p38 (2014). Starting from a declaration in 1997 "The school has been the main tool of the State to destroy the culture of Indigenous people".

4:4 Promoting social justice through local empowerment and the promotion of social cohesion

By Dr Susan Canney

One of the major causes of local environmental degradation in the Gourma region of Mali is the rapidly increasing numbers of cattle using the resources of the elephant range. It had been assumed that these increases were related to the increasing human population of the area but a study at one of the two lakes that still hold water at the end of the dry season revealed a different story.

One of these lakes is surrounded by a town and gardens. The other, Lake Banzena, is used by pastoralists, although these were becoming increasingly sedentary, and it had been assumed that the increasing numbers of cattle using this lake were related to this increasing sedentarisation. The levels of water in the lake at the end of the dry season were becoming lower each year and in years of poor rains it was increasingly threatening to dry completely. This would spell disaster for an iconic population of elephants, for whom this was the only source of water at this time of year, and also increase the potential for conflict with local people and their cattle as they tried to access the diminishing water.

In 2009 this very nearly happened. It was difficult to know how to resolve the situation, and so the Mali Elephant project conducted a survey of all the people living within 10km of the lake to gain a better idea of how this population used the resources of the area. Transhumant herders present during the 3 months of the data collection were also surveyed.

The local population comprised 730 people belonging to 161 households and 12 clans (of which 311 were children); while 95 migratory herders were surveyed. Surprise findings were that 96% of the cattle using the lake were not owned by the local people but belonged to wealthy individuals living in distant towns, who amassed huge herds as a sign of prestige, and then hired impoverished herders to find water and pasture for their cattle. In addition, over 50% of the women and children suffered from water-borne disease, while 37% of the women had miscarried during the previous 2 years.

The project used these data as a basis for discussion with the local community so that a shared perception of the problem developed. The next step was to ask for solutions and after several days of meetings, a plan was devised whereby the community would leave the lake if a place could be found for them outside the elephant range with clean water and good pasture. The project worked with them to find a new location and raised money for 3 boreholes.

Mali's decentralisation legislation makes provision for local communities to manage their own natural resources, and so to avoid a "tragedy of the commons" the clans came together to create a representative system of resource management to which all would clans and ethnicities would subscribe. This countered a common problem in this ethnically diverse region of Mali: that each ethnicity has its own system of resource management but each is reluctant to respect that of another ethnicity. A management committee of elders was created and "brigades de surveillance" of young men to patrol and detect infringements. Government foresters helped with the enforcement.

The systems of resource management also involved setting aside Lake Banzena and its critical elephant habitats for elephant use only and this agreement was also policed by the brigades.

The management committee's first act was to set aside an area of reserve pasture of nearly 100,000 hectares. The project helped the community protect this area with firebreaks and when it was the only part of the northern elephant range not to lose its pasture to fire, other communities asked for help to do the same thing. These communities began to charge the large migratory herds for access to their water and pasture to limit their impact on the resources of the area.

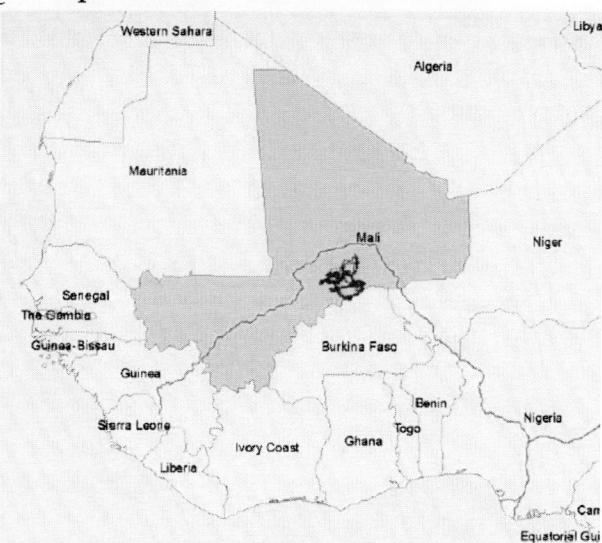

Map showing the location of the area of intervention (elephant migration route shown in brown

Unfortunately during the conflict of 2012, the solar panels were sabotaged but other communities who were not reliant on boreholes created similar systems. Three years later and local communities are receiving positive benefits from wise resource management that promotes ecosystem integrity (including elephant conservation).

Studies have shown that livestock from communities protecting their water, pasture and forests are worth 50% more than those from communities that don't have functioning resource management systems. At the same time, those managing their pasture are able to sell hay and charge outsiders for access to water and pasture. One family makes an additional ☐ 320/year from charging outsiders for access and another ☐ 530 from selling hay, significant additional income for these populations. As they say, *"we benefit twice: we have more pasture for ourselves and we raise money from others;"* and in doing so they control the destructive impact of the large herds from outside the elephant range that belong to wealthy urban-dwellers.

In addition to protecting pasture, those communities managing their resources collectively are closely protecting their forest resources and preventing the illegal cutting of trees and hunting of game species, including the near threatened Dorcas gazelle and Nubian bustard. They value forests for game and wildlife; firewood (and construction wood in the south); wild foods, medicinal plants, and commodities such as incense (*Commiphora africana*) and gum arabic (*Acacia seyal*). Protecting the forests protects the water holes at their centre from siltation and evaporation, and provides forage for fattening animals. The elephants help in the harvest of these benefits as they shake leaves, seeds and fruits down from inaccessible branches. Sheep and goats feed around their feet, and the women follow them to gather up a harvest of wild foods and forage that can be sold in the local markets. Local people associate forests with rain and wildlife: for them it is the same, as they regard all those things as connected.

Photos on following page show parts of the umbrella thorn tree (Acacia radiana) harvested by the women, with the help of the elephants whose browsing in the trees knocks the pods down for the goats to eat and women to collect

As well as potential sources of income from well managed resources, there is improved environmental security as "healthy" diverse environments are more productive and better able to withstand climatic variation.

Parts of the umbrella thorn tree (Acacia radiana) harvested by the women, with the help of the elephants whose browsing in the trees knocks the pods down for the goats to eat and women to collect

4.5 Global Food Security – Analysis and Solutions

By Bianca Madison-Vuleta

Addressing the challenge of global food security through the twenty first century is linked with other global issues, most notably climate change, population growth and the need to sustainably manage the world's rapidly growing demand for energy and water. Our progress in ensuring a sustainable and equitable food supply chain will be determined by how coherently these long term challenges are tackled.

This will also determine our progress in reducing global poverty and achieving the Millennium Development Goals. The challenge is to deliver nutritious, safe and affordable food to a global population of over 9 million in coming decades, using less land, fewer inputs, with less waste and a lower environmental impact. All this has to be done in ways that are socially and economically sustainable. It is clear that research is vital to meeting this challenge.

Global food security is fast becoming one of the most pressing challenges facing states today. The scope and the breadth of the issue encompass all the peoples and the governments of the world and demography is the driving factor pushing it to the top of the agenda. The human population is set to surpass the 9 billion mark midway through the century, with the attendant cost of ever greater pressure applied to the Earth's finite resources.

The World Bank has predicted that wheat production will have to increase by 50% and meat production by 85% over the next 20 years if we are to meet the demand.

The challenge facing us is to be able to feed the great mass of humanity in a sustainable manner and one that does not threaten the precarious balance of our ecosystems. Climate change is the other defining source of stress with its manifold repercussions upon water access and supply, the spread of pests and disease and the potential for ever more extreme and unpredictable weather patterns.

The UN estimated that almost one billion people are chronically hungry and malnourished in the world and over 6 million children die each year due to starvation. Judging by current trends this number is set to rise in the near future. Recent climactic developments have also given both humanitarians and policy-makers alike more serious cause for concern. At a time when the recession is biting in many parts of the world, and where booming populations have already made food scarce and prices high, this crisis could have extremely severe humanitarian, and indeed strategic, implications.

Global food security is, obviously, one of the key issues for the future of humanity, along with water, climate, and peace and security. The UN has a commitment to supporting governments as they work towards the millennium development goals (MDG) that were agreed in 2000 and that require us all to achieve some significant outcomes by 2015.

The first of these goals is to halve the number of people living in hunger from 860 million to 500 million, but it looks as though by 2015 we will be looking at well over 1 billion living in hunger. If we look at the bigger picture, the situation of poverty and hunger seems to be similar around the globe.

We have resistant poverty in sub-Saharan Africa, similar figures to 1990. In South Asia we have achieved reductions in the percentage of the poor; but given that there are so many people living in South Asia, the ratios are still too high.

Poverty in Sub-Saharan Africa has proved itself to be very resilient and hunger has remained disturbingly high, with more than 25% of the population hungry at any one time. There are still 29 countries across the globe where levels of malnutrition are life threatening.

There is a pressing need to ensure adequate nutrition, including not only calories but all necessary macro and micro nutrients for healthy and balanced diets and for deprived populations throughout the world.

At the same time as increasing numbers of people globally are inadequately fed, the over- consumption of high calorie diets adds to the rising demand for food; with all the associated economic, social and environmental impacts.

The most important challenges arising are:

The world will need to produce more food in the future using less water, land, fertiliser, energy and other key resources, and distribute that food more efficiently and equitably.

There is a need to reduce losses and waste, greenhouse gas emissions and other adverse environmental impacts throughout the entire food supply chain; from production to consumption and waste management.

Food must be safe, nutritious and affordable, yet be supplied and distributed in ways that meet the needs and aspirations of consumers in different economic, social and cultural contexts around the world. People need to be well informed and guided to make healthy choices.

There is a need to balance different uses of land and seas, often with competing priorities, such as sustainably increasing food production while maintaining ecosystem services on which food production critically depends.

There is a need to balance increased productivity from food producing animals with their welfare, recognising that absence of disease and high productivity do not always equate with high welfare standards and outcomes.

The complex and inter-related problems outlined above can only be tackled through coordinated and integrated interdisciplinary research, coupled with its effective translation into practice and policy. Our aim is to help improve the sustainability and security of UK and global food supplies.

The challenges range from those with a local or UK national focus to more wideranging European and global issues. Food security for the UK is inextricably linked to global production, demand and supply and must be considered in this broader context. There is clearly a key role for UK led research in helping to address the global challenges, especially those in developing countries.

Is the global market the solution to the contemporary food crisis?
Some economists argue that the food crisis is an aberration of capitalism and that the markets will right themselves in time. In particular, some predict that price rises will lead to increased investment in agriculture, leading to increased food stocks and therefore lower prices again.
We have been told for generations that the market responds to demand. People of the Global South have been told by economists, academics, world institutions and the governments of the West that the free market is the way to enrich their countries and lift their people out of poverty. This has, sadly, been proven to be wrong.
Despite embracing of the market-mentality, poverty and hunger remain virulent. Small farmers are killing themselves in huge numbers across the Global South. In India around 250.000 farmers have been driven to suicide in the last few decades. Jeffrey Sachs, an advisor to the UN general secretary, has warned against relying on the market to help when the people in need have no money to pay!
It is likely that food prices will begin to stabilise to a degree. However, most economists - including those who think the market can solve the crisis, predict that prices will remain at high levels for the next decade. THE ECONOMIST warned last year that we face an *"end to the era of cheap food"*.

One thing is for certain: the demand for the market to 'solve' he problem is a demand for more of the policies that have led to the current crisis. Some commentators have suggested that price rises might hit the urban poor but at least they will help subsistence farmers by pushing up the value of their crops. Unfortunately, it is not as simple as that. Poor farmers, often already severely in debt, are being squeezed badly by rising input costs such as fertilisers, seeds, pesticides and transport costs.
These prices are forcing thousands off the land as they simply can't afford to work it any longer. Heart-breaking after generations have worked and prospered.
Another problem facing small farmers and agricultural labourers is their position at the bottom of a global agricultural chain. Whereas, the real power is fully concentrated in the food processing corporations, grain traders and supermarket suppliers. Rising food prices exacerbate this problem by pushing up the value of farm land. This means many small farmers and landholders who are already deep in debt or on the poverty line can't afford to expand production.
The only people who can afford to expand in these circumstances are those with access to major capital or large amounts of credit - the big farm corporations and agribusinesses.
The Food and Agriculture Organisation (FAO) has shown that in most countries the majority of rural households are net buyers of food, not sellers. On average across the countries surveyed they found that only 31 percent of rural households are not sellers of food. Unsurprisingly, the FAO's research concluded that the poorest households and the landless are always the most badly hit.

Are small farms the answer?
It is becoming increasingly obvious that the industrialisation of food production and

the centralisation and concentration of agriculture have failed to give food security to millions around the globe. Some postulate that a return to small farms is the answer. Writer and campaigner George Monbiot argued this in the GUARDIAN in June 2008, pointing out that small farms are actually more productive than large ones. There is much research to back this up.

Large farms are invariably run by multinational agribusinesses seeking to maximise their profits fast. This leads to a short-term view of farming; where soil, water and chemicals are overused without regard for the erosion of the soil or damage to the environment.

Larger farms are more likely to grow a single crop rather than a mix of crops, depending on what is profitable. This depletes the nutrients in the soil and erodes the fertility of the land over time.

Large farms are often owned by companies with many other investments and sources of income. They do not have the same incentive to maintain sustainable farming methods as small farmers do. If larger farms over-exploit their land they have the resources to move on to new land. Smaller farmers don't.

It is widely believed that the effects of climate change - floods, droughts, extremes of temperature and other events are directly responsible for the food crisis.

Blaming climate change for the current food crisis is politically convenient. It implies that we are powerless to act in the face of extreme weather conditions and disasters. In reality, there is much that could be done to both deal with climate change and minimise its effects.

Sadly, many poor countries do not have the resources to deal with the impact of climate change. Every year ten million deprived people face flooding because the necessary investments have not been made.

Other countries have the resources but lack the political will to prepare for the effects of climate change - shown to devastating effect by Hurricane Katrina in New Orleans in 2005.

None of this is to say that climate change is not important or that it does not have an impact on food production or prices. But there is no reason for it to result in famine and hunger.

To simply blame climate change for these things hides the political, economic and social policies and structures that determine the impact the climate change has.

Food and the global market

The recent sharp rises in food prices can only be explained by referring to specific short term factors - such as the price of oil, increased speculation on food commodities, on global markets and the weakened dollar. But there are also long term factors shaping

food production. They act to make sudden crisis much worse.

A major factor is the changing nature of global food production. Poorer countries, in particular, have seen huge changes in land use, resulting in less food being produced for domestic consumption. As capitalism expanded its reach across the world, it pulled more countries into the world market and transformed them.

The power is concentrated in the hands of fewer and fewer people, as small units are eaten by the bigger ones. The concentration and centralisation of capital have naturally increased over time. This can be seen today in US agriculture. Since the Second World

Whilst the average farm size in the US has more than doubled, while the number of farms has fallen by two thirds.

The concentration of agriculture means that production can be undertaken on larger farms by fewer people. Sophisticated machinery has developed with the aim of cutting the number of workers needed. Impoverished small farmers are pushed from rural areas towards cities in search of work.

A similar dynamic is taking place in many parts of the Global South where many people are being driven off their land and forced to look for work in the cities.

The "liberalisation" of trade (removing restrictions on trade between countries) is a key part of the neo-liberal agenda of the world's most powerful governments today. In India, as well as many other developing countries, the impact of "trade liberalisation" has been to reduce food production, productivity and efficiency, undermine food security and sustainability, and increase the power of multinational food corporations.

Poorer countries are also often hampered by debt. Debt acts to make poorer countries beholden on richer ones. It forces them to produce cash crops for export rather than food for domestic consumption, as this is more profitable.

Bodies like International Monetary Fund (IMF) have been fundamental in shaping the agriculture of developing countries through Structural Adjustment Programmes (SAPs).

SAPs were agreements that poorer countries signed up to in order to receive aid or loans, or to "restructure" existing debts. Key elements of the agreements included cutting government spending, increasing privatisation, and opening up the economy to global markets. They have devastated agriculture in poorer countries.

The policies included in the SAPs lead to a decrease in food production in the countries that signed up to them. They increased the dependence of millions of people on the world food market - which, in the long term, pushes up global prices and makes poor people especially susceptible to fluctuations in global prices. SAPs have now been cynically renamed "Poverty Reduction Strategies" but the policies remain essentially the same.

The development of the food industry has been marked by the concentration of profits and power in the hands of multinational agribusiness. Neo-liberal policies have eroded support for small farmers, making it virtually impossible for them to survive.

A food industry based on 'competition and profit' has failed to meet people's most basic needs, despite the advances in production that have taken place.

Genetically modified crops

The current food crisis has sparked a demand for Genetically Modified (GM) crops to 'stop people starving'. These are crops which are modified in ways which make them resistant to diseases, pests and the effects of climate change. As such, it is said, they have the potential to produce higher yields.

But there are several question marks over GM crops. They pose a threat to wildlife by killing certain insects and so destabilising ecosystems. Crops which have been modified to contain insecticide, threaten to lead to resistant strains of insects developing. The long term effects of GM foods are completely unknown.

If GM crops pose such a potential threat to our health and the environment, why are they touted as the solution to global food insecurity? Major chemical and pharmaceutical multinational companies have patented them and have a vested interest in promoting them to make profits.

One should not, of course, be opposed to using science to improve food production, nor oppose GM crops on the grounds that they are not "natural". The problem with GM crops is that they have increased the power of multinational biotechnology companies over the global food industry and increased the dependence of poor countries on richer ones.

Also, there is growing evidence that GM crops do not actually increase yields. What GM has done is to radically increase inequality but has not solved world hunger. Those who present GM crops as the solution to the food crisis start from the wrong explanation for hunger. People do not go hungry because not enough food is produced - they go hungry because they don't have the means (i.e. money) to access it.

Specultation, oil and bio-fuels

The increased incorporation of agriculture and food production into the world market over recent decades has laid the basis for the current price rises, but it doesn't explain the dramatic increases of the past few years.

The single starkest factor is the growth of speculation on food and agricultural products on the world market. This explains how "spring wheat prices", as measured on the US markets, could jump by 25 percent in just one day at the beginning of 2008. Commodity speculation is based on gambling on the future prices of food, agricultural goods, metals or oil.

The credit crunch and accompanying panic in the financial and property markets have driven investors to look for safer investments in commodities. With food prices rising, this is seen as a sure way of making money quickly.

This link to the market means that domestic policies have a big impact on food prices. As a crisis in rice prices hit the world stage a few years ago, most rice exporting countries rushed to impose export bans. These temporarily protected domestic supplies but caused sudden extreme shortages on the international markets and led to panic buying and hoarding. This pushed the prices up even further.

The rising price of oil has also helped to drive up food prices. As farming becomes increasingly intensive in much of the world, it requires larger amounts of oil and other fuels to produce fertilisers, to power farm machinery and to transport and process crops.

According to FAO, the cost of many fertilisers nearly doubled in one year.

Many of the poorest countries are net importers, not only of food but also of oil, and are thus hit doubly by the rising prices imposed on them.

The rise in oil prices has been one of the factors causing a rush to invest in biofuels over the past decade or so. Biofuels were hailed as the new "green solution" to the financial and environmental costs of fossil fuels - but their green credentials have turned out to be a gross misconception.

In the rush to cash in on the profits to be made from biofuels, a great deal of land and grain has been diverted away from making food to producing fuel. In the US, the government funds the biofuel industry heavily, with federal subsidies, alone amounting to more than $7 billion per year (on average).

The IMF has estimated that 20 to 30 percent of the food price increases in the last few years is accounted for by biofuels. The central dynamic causing soaring food prices is the way the market transforms food from a basic human need to a tradable source of profit. This creates the situation in which it is possible to have an abundance of food, but hundreds of millions of people who cannot afford to buy it. This is the root of the current food crisis!

"This is the new face of hunger... There is food on the shelves but people are priced out of the market. There is vulnerability in urban areas we have not seen before."

- Josette Sheeran, head of the UN World Food Programme, quoted in the Guardian

"When circumstances refer, it impossible to feed their hungry children, normally passive citizens can quickly become militants with nothing to lose. "

- Tony Karon: "How hunger can topple regimes"

Food price rises have plunged millions into hunger and created food insecurity in a very short space of time. The "new hungry" have been fighting back through protests and strikes that have shaken governments and world institutions.

Since the first wave of major protests in Mexico in January 2007, there have been angry protests, riots and strikes in many countries, including Bangladesh, Cameroon, Egypt, Haiti, Ivory Coast, Yemen, Indonesia, Morocco, Senegal, Mauritania, Jordan, Uzbekistan, Honduras, Mozambique and India.

In some countries, resistance has meant the hungry pouring onto the streets in an upsurge of anger and desperation. In others the issue of food has fuelled wider workers' struggles.

Some protesters have demanded an end to "free trade" policies that have impoverished much of the Global South.

Others have demanded subsidies on food and fuel, or distribution of food aid to the hungry. Many have fought for higher wages to match the rising food costs. Rising food prices have created a crisis across the globe and brought the issue of food production onto the centre stage of food politics.

In the poorest countries of the world the price rises have been catastrophic- plunging millions into a state of hunger and malnutrition.In richer countries, such as Great Britain and the United States, the situation is not so acute but many millions of people are finding it an increasing struggle just to feed their families. The price rises have also focused the minds of governments and global trade and finance bodies around the world, which fear the growing resistance and instability caused by millions of newly hungry people fighting back.

Yet the international organisations and governments have no lasting solutions to the crisis. They all see the world market as part of the way to solve the crisis. Both the IMF and the UN Food and Agricultural Organisation have emphasised the role that business and the market should play in addressing the problem.

Sadly, more of the market-trading will not solve these enormous problems, as it was the global market that brought us to this crisis in the first place. As we have seen, over the last fifty years, world food production has been rapidly, and often violently, transformed as it has been incorporated into the global market. This process has turned agriculture into a massive global business and dramatically altered how food is produced, processed and sold.

Food has become a valuable commodity to be speculated on in the futures markets.

The drive to produce more food for less money has also created massive health problems worldwide and dependency on monocultures and chemical fertilisers and pesticides that harm the environment and threaten the basis of future agriculture. Even what we eat has changed - with world markets creating a dependence on a smaller number of key crops to feed the majority of the world. However, as mentioned before, there has been massive resistance every step of the way.

People have fought back against the impact of IMF and World Bank policies, and free trade agreements have been implemented across the Global South.

This new Anti-Globalization Movement has taken up these protests to the global summits of the rich and powerful; from the World Trade Organisation to the G8 group of the leading nations.

We must continue to fight to drive back the market's control of food production around the globe. We should build solidarity with the others who are fighting back and make connections amongst the different struggles. But it is clear that much more undamental change is needed to secure access to food for those who need it.

Capitalism is the most dynamic economic system the world has ever seen, yet even at "normal" times of supposed relative stability, hundreds of millions of people around the world starve because they cannot afford food.

Resistance towards gross injustice around the world shows that those hit by the price rises are not just victims: they have the power to force change. And this is true not just of those who eat the food but of those who work to produce, process and distribute it.

Food production is the single largest industry in the world. It involves huge numbers of people, including 2.5 billion *directly* involved in food production in the Global South.

Changes in how food is produced have created hundreds of thousands who are employed to work on the land or in the processing and transporting food and who have the collective interest and power to change the way things are organised.

Food is fundamental to all human life! Surely there can be no bigger indictment of a system run for profit than the fact people are starving in a world of such abundance of resources.

References

Food and Agriculture Organization of the UN (FAO): "The state of food insecurity in the world", 2012.

FAO, "The state of Food and Agriculture 2012- investing in agriculture for a better future", fao.org/doc rep./017/13028e/13028e.pdf

Fisher G. at al: "Socio- economic and climate change impacts on agriculture: an integrated assessment, 1990-2080, Philosophical Transactions of the Royal Society, Biological Sciences, 2005.

Intergovernmental Panel on Climate Change

Parrott N. & T. Marsden: "The Real Green Revolution", Greenpeace Environmental Trust, London 2012.

"Prioritising climate change adaption needs for food security in 2030", "Programme on Food Security and the Environment Policy Brief", 2008.

World Food Programme, www.wfp.org

4:6 Governance of Health Care in Green Economy: The Egyptian Drama

By Mohammad El – Naghi and Manal El Batrn (Egypt)

Abstract
This chapter is a study which investigates the new trends of Egypt health care future. It is an attempt to assess the impact of 25 January Revolution on future health care in Egypt and the challenges it poses to doctors and policy makers. For this purpose, a three-fold methodology was adopted.
Part one discusses the Egyptian Overview. The aim of part one is to describe in more details the health care sector and the economic factors that influence the health care sector.
Part two and three provide the basis for an understanding of the recent policy shift that took place in Egypt in response to Revolution of 25 January 2011. Part two provides insights in the phenomenon of doctors' struggle to meet their needs. The 25 January Revolution was a turning point not only from a historical, political and social perspective, but also for health care sector. Especially, Egyptian doctors went on a nationwide 'administrative' strike started May 2011 and continued till 2014.
Part three examines the main impacts of 25 January Revolution, including Political will & Leadership. This examination will allow us to identify possible new directions for government intervention regarding green economy and sustainability of future health care sector in Egypt.
Finally, the current challenge for Egypt is to find the rules and institutions for stronger governance – local, national and regional – to provide enough space for human, community and environmental resources to ensure that Green Health Care Sector works for people at large not just for select groups.

1- Egyptian Overview
The World Health Organization has categorized world countries into groups according to mortality as a consequence of climate change. Egypt was ranked in the third worst group amongst four. The estimated number of deaths as a result of climate change is between 40 – 80 deaths per million residents. [1] All of the above leads to a greater need for solutions, especially on the governance scale. This would change the society's attitude and behaviour towards unhealthy habits.

1.1 Health Care Sector
Egypt has variety of competitive Strengths and capabilities; the largest trained workforce in the Region, with an annual average of 10,000 graduates from medical schools, Egypt produces more doctors and pharmacists than any other country in the Middle East. At 26.839 million as of Q1 2012, Egypt's workforce is the largest in the Arab world and the second largest in the MENA region, after Iran. High Doctor to

Patient Ratio: In 2014, Egypt recorded 8.3 physicians and 14.85 nursing staff, in addition to 1.68 dentists, and 2.44 pharmacists per ten thousand citizens. Salaries in Egypt are considered amongst the lowest in the MENA region. The average wage in the health sector is comparatively low at US$ 15.4 per week. In contrast, the reputation of Egypt's healthcare workforce is excellent; which acts as a unique opportunity to minimize costs while offering high-quality services. [2] The health indicators in Egypt of the past decade show mild improvement in many aspects of public health, where the average life expectancy for males/ females had reached 69/74 years. Child mortality rates decreased, reaching 28 per 1000 for those below the age of five, and 25 per 1000 for infants in their first year of life. [3, 4]

Health care services in Egypt are offered by three main sectors, the government, the public sector, and the private sector. The government is considered the major provider in terms of capacity, size of expenditures and the different kinds of services offered. Approximately 50% of the populations are covered by basic government health insurance, a further 30% are enrolled in private health insurance schemes and 20% of Egyptians have no health insurance. [5]

Health sector faces significant challenges in caring for a rapidly growing population of 84.3 M; using a system held back by structural weaknesses. [6] Additional suffering from the double burden of infectious and chronic diseases such as Viral Hepatitis B & C, epidemics of influenza viruses, and increased mortality rate due to cardiovascular diseases.

Health care facility activities have been estimated to represent 3–8% of the climate change footprint in developed-country settings such as UK NHS and the USA. [7, 8] While no such health sector estimates exist elsewhere at a national level. This will therefore increase in Egypt; due to the vulnerability of the social, economic and environmental characteristics of the population. Effects are expected to affect children, the elderly, the poor, and people inhabiting rural areas the most. [1]

1.2 Influencing Economic Factors for the Health Care Sector

The Ministry of Finance declared that it had referred the fiscal year (FY) 2014/2015 general budget to the presidency for approval on May 26th 2014. The budget witnessed some significant changes in public spending, health, education, electricity and petroleum product subsidies. According to the fiscal year (FY) 2014/2015 budget, the public spending increased by EGP 65bn, around 10% compared to the current year's budget, to register EGP 807bn. Figure 1 shows the steady increase in Per Capita total health expenditure in Egypt since 1995. The healthcare budget increased by EGP 9.5 bn, surging from EGP 42.1 bn in the FY 2013/2014 budget to EGP 51.6bn in the 2015 fiscal year's budget. Minister of Finance said that the government plans to increase the expenditure on healthcare, education and scientific research to reach 10% of the GDP by 2017, what would require an additional EGP 100bn. [9] Figure 2 shows Per Capita total expenditures on health.

Figure 1 Source: World Health Organization, Contry Profile (WHO)

The budget stated that expenditure on wages have increased by 13%, rising from the current year's EGP 184bn to EGP 209bn.According to the International

Monetary Fund (IMF), Egypt's inflation rate is expected to be 10.4% during 2014 and 11.2% in 2015. [9]

e World Bank Group WBG is preparing a Country Partnership Framework (CPF) jointly with the International Finance Corporation (IFC) and the Multi- Lateral Investment Guarantee Agency (MIGA), for Egypt FY15-19. One element of the Framework focuses on ensuring equitable opportunities by supporting delivery of education, health and targeted safety nets. [10]

2. The Egyptian Drama

In January 2011, Egypt erupted in large-scale anti-regime revolution, resulting in the resignation of President Mubarak and the collapse of the regime that had been in power for 30 years. Then, a stage of political wallow ended with the Presidential elections held on June 8, 2014, and led to the victory of Abdel Fattah El-Sisi. [11]

One of the main objectives of the Egyptian Revolution in 2011 was to achieve social justice making the provision of good quality primary healthcare service a corner stone towards this target. In addition to the limited resources in the public sector, in some cases there is even misuse of these resources, due to lack of monitoring and accountability, leading to more corruption in the public health sector. Corruption damages the ability to deliver high quality service, and increases inequality. [12]

Egyptian doctors went on a nationwide 'administrative' strike started May 2011and continued till 2014 as shown below in figure (2). Mass resignations; as an escalatory step to bring pressure on the authorities and restate demands for applying the medical professions cadre law, health care reforms and better pay. [13]

Figure 2: Egyptian doctors went on a nationwide 'administrative' strike in May 2011

In its 2014 constitution, in article 13 the Egyptian government was committed to ensure that conditions for professional security, safety and health are met. The 18th article of the constitution stated that "Every citizen has the right for integrated health care according to quality standards; the Government shall ensure the preservation of public health services. The Government is committed to allocating a percentage of government spending for health of not less than 3% of GDP gradually escalates even consistent with global averages. Government is committed to the establishment of a comprehensive health insurance for all Egyptians covers all diseases system, and law regulates the contribution of citizens or their exemption according to their income levels. Government is committed to improving the conditions of workforce in the health sector. The Government encourages participation of the private sector and civil society in the health care services in accordance with the law." [14]

Environmental article 46 stated that "Every individual has the right to live in a healthy, sound and balanced environment. Its protection is a national duty. The Government is committed to taking the necessary measures to preserve it, avoid harming it, rationally use its natural resources to ensure that sustainable development is achieved, and guarantee the rights of future generations thereto. [15]

3. Egypt Post-Revolution

The experiences of countries with sustained advancement in healthcare reform and poverty reduction point to two key policy components. First, better make use of the poor's labor. Second, supply basic social services to the deprived population, including primary health care, family planning, nutrition, and primary education. [16] After the January 25th revolution, the Government of Egypt passed two laws to expand social health insurance (SHI) coverage to female headed households and children under five years of age. These laws were indicative of the government's commitment to the improvement of social justice and inclusion, although the extent of their effectiveness is debatable. In addition, a draft law for inclusion of informal farmers under the umbrella of HIO is being considered. [17]

The direct impact of January 25 Revolution and the doctors administrative strikes on healthcare sector; was the development of reform plan for the national healthcare system drafted by the government, which would drive new traffic to more than 1607 hospitals and will create further opportunities for investment, principally through the PPP program. Private investments in health care amounted of EGP 3.16 Billion in 2013/2014. [5]

3.1. Political will & Leadership

President, Abdel Fattah El Sisi stated on is letter to Egypt Economic Development Conference (EEDC) in Sharm El-Sheikh on the 13-15th March 2015 "With a sensible macroeconomic policy framework, persistent structural reform, and the welcome participation of the investor community; our ultimate goal is to generate sustainable high growth economy that is balanced and inclusive in order to build prosperity for the Egyptian people". [18]

On July 5, 2014, the President announced a wide range of reforms, introducing new taxes, increasing selected taxes, and reducing energy subsidies. Energy subsidies reached LE128bn ($17.9bn) in 2013/14 – representing about 7% of GDP from a targeted LE99bn and equal to over 22% of the government's budget. The implementation of reforms is starting to have a positive impact on the economy. Economic growth in Fiscal Year (FY) 14 of 2.5% is expected to increase 3.3% in FY15, and the budget deficit is projected at 10% for FY15, lower than the deficit of 12% in FY14. [11]

Suez Canal project is an $8bn project to widen and deepen the Suez Canal; aims to cut average transit times from 18 to 11 hours while quadrupling traffic. The government estimates the improvements in the canal will more than double annual revenues, which currently stand at more than $5bn. The project is considered the Cornerstone of the government's plan to kick-start the economy, and stimulates growth

in labour-intensive sectors, and to lower the unemployment rate of 13.1%. The enlarged transit route is part of a development plan for the whole Suez Canal Zone (SCZ), which comprises 75,000 sq km of land on either side of the canal that is earmarked for industry. [19]

After his three-day visit on Jan 2015, the UK Middle East minister said "Egypt's economic reform 'impressive' but more political steps needed". [20]

4. Proposed Framework towards Governance of Health care in Green Economy in Egypt.

Aims to enable Healthcare in Egypt to take advantage of the anticipated benefits of green economy investment and policy decisions that enhance outcomes in an integrated way and in accordance with national circumstances and priorities. The mitigation measures relevant to health care facilities have been examined in terms of; Direct impacts on the delivery of health care services; on environmental and occupational health for health workers, patients and communities; and indirect benefits such as improved resilience of health care facilities and more reliable energy provision.

There is an opportunity within 2015 to ensure appropriate representation of health within the international agenda as on Green Economy and climate change, sustainable development, and disaster risk reduction. By the end of 2015, countries are aiming to reach agreement on a new international framework for disaster risk reduction, definition of Sustainable Development Goals, and a new international agreement to address climate change. Each of these processes makes reference to the others, and to health. This presents a rare chance to ensure coherence in the way that health is represented in critical development agendas. [21]

The questions that are included in Governance level framework are; where we are now? Where are we going? What do we want to achieve? How do we do things? What are the values that guide our actions?

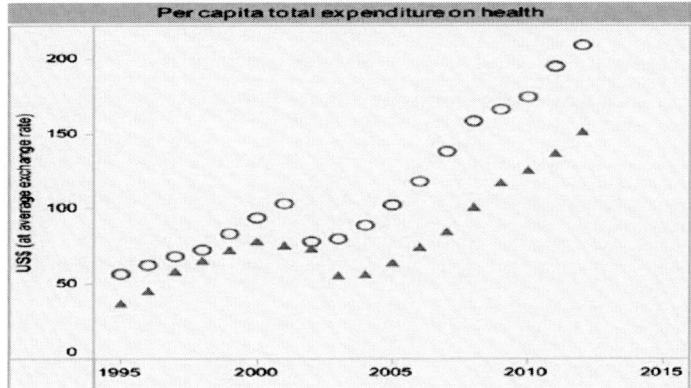

Figure 1 Source: World Health Organization, Contry Profile (WHO)

Eliminate	Raise
Overutilization Use of paper documentation Hospital Acquired Infections Avoidable Readmission Service fragmentation Poor communication	Green Practices education & training for Healthcare Workforce. Corporate Social Responsibility Accountability workforce engagement Safety and quality standards Patient outcomes & engagement Performance metrics Home monitoring Morale & Ethics Health promotion, Reimbursements Screenings financial gains
Reduce	**Create**
Environmental impact Energy / water Operating costs Fragmented approach to care Workforce shortages Overall hospital admissions Face to face provider visit Use phone/ fax Noncompliant health maintenance	Multi-organizational health care partnership. National Environmental health information Management system Patient care teams Patient registries, portals Virtual visits Multiple access points

Table 1.Green Healthcare Four Action Framework [28, 29, 30]

4.1 Where are we now? (Situation Analysis Stage)

4.1.1 Opportunities: Hospitals can take advantages within existing renewable energy sector in Egypt, the sunny weather and high wind speeds made Egypt the highest Wind Electricity Generator in Region, High-Intensity Solar Radiation, Long Hours of Sun and a prime resource of biomass. Additional chance is the Renewable Energy Investor-Friendly Government Incentive System. [22] Egypt Green Buildings Council & Green Pyramid Rating System can develop hospitals rating system. [23] Existence of the National SWM Programme (NSWMP). "Egyptian Integrated SWM Sector (ISWMS)", a separate sector, under the Ministry of State for Environmental Affairs (MSEA). [24] Available studies and data, and information gaps can be collected from MOH - The Central Agency for Public Mobilization And Statistics (CAPMAS).

4.1.2 Challenges include; Lack of awareness, Expected resistance to change habits, Myth of Greening costs more than conventional, limited supply of trained professionals, and lack of experience.

4.1.3 Nominating national, regional and international stakeholders; Internal stakeholders; patients, employees, pharmacy, owner/organization, suppliers, and visitors. External Stakeholders include; health insurance companies, admitting doctors, care services, voluntary helpers, sponsors, network partners, legislature, regional authorities, communities, regional media, and neighbors. [25]

4.2 Where we want to be? (Goal setting stage)

4.2.1 Quantitative goals and objectives to determine the investment priorities required for the medium and short terms include; Recruiting advantages, Better treatment outcomes, Risk mitigation, improved public perceptions and opportunities for philanthropic funding, Increase annual recycling rate, and Increase savings from single-use device reprocessing. Implement Pilot projects to lead by example, and Focus on incremental change.

4.2.2 Long-term regional vision for a shift towards a green economy include; Improved Health (Level & Equity), Responsiveness, Social & Financial Risk protection, and Improved Efficiency

4.2.3 Secure political commitment; important to set a timeframe for each goal.

4.3 How we get there?

4.3.1 We should have a Strategy.

Blue Ocean strategy (BOS) is a view beyond the current industry boundaries; offering a set of systematic and reproducible methodologies and tools to create new, wider potential of market space that is huge, deep, demand creative, highly profitable growth and not yet explored. **[26, 27]** BOS frameworks and tools include; strategy canvas, value curve, four actions framework, six paths, buyer experience cycle, buyer utility map, and blue ocean idea index. [26] BOS may be the tool which can expand the healthcare sector boundaries and impede it into an inclusive Green Economy.

Applying the BOS Four action framework which consists of 4 major items; Eliminate, Reduce, Raise, and Create. Each component has its own criteria to be achieved as shown below in

Green Healthcare Four Action Framework [28, 29, 30]

4.3.2 Analytical studies on Healthcare and environmental impacts of a shift towards a green economy. Identify the baseline and develop multiple scenarios (including the Business as Usual scenario). Execute successful financial strategy and funding mechanism. Publish a Green healthcare toolbox to guide Egypt and a capacity building program for decision-makers. Create subcommittees for specific projects, and finally report and celebrate successes to promote ongoing leadership and staff enthusiasm.

4.4 What are the values that guide our actions? (The Triple Bottom line)
The new breed of business uses additional criteria for success. They still want to make a profit, but they're also concerned about how they treat the environment, their employees and other stakeholders. Healthcare as a cornerstone society sector has to measure success not just on the bottom line of profits, but also on the bottom lines of people and planet;
When integrating healthcare as a social service, with the economy components to benefit from environment and to preserve it, this would lead to Sustainability

Figure 2: Egyptian doctors went on a nationwide 'administrative' strike in May 2011

5. Conclusion & Recommendations

Development of the *Egyptian Green Healthcare High Council* with specific responsibilities include; providing corporate governance and accountability, ensuring Green Healthcare Key Performance Indicators are managed appropriately and undertaking periodic reviews, Evaluation and agreement of the annual strategy for Healthcare, Supporting the development of strategic direction through identifying and reviewing target markets and considering whether Healthcare will be proactive or reactive in those markets, Advising on resource levels and expenditure, Assistance in identifying and advising on major issues of concern relating to trade in healthcare green goods and services, Ensure there is a healthcare component to a country's National Adaptation Plan (H-NAP) and to national communications to the UN Framework Convention on Green Economy & Climate Change (UNFCCC). Formation of the council may include other ministries, Parliaments and their committees, other levels of government, independent statutory bodies such as professional councils, inspectorates and audit commissions, NGOs and a free media.

Egypt should also designate a national focal point for Green healthcare within the Ministry of Health, encourage Inter-ministerial policy dialogue, and health sector strong engagement in the international and national policy processes on climate change.

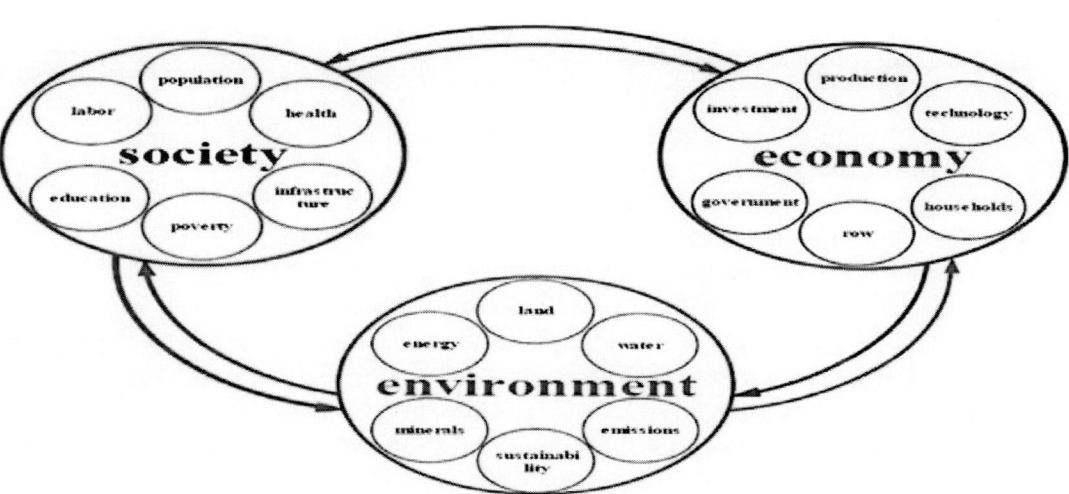

Figure 4: Source: (UNEP 2014) A Guidance Manual for Green Economy Policy Assessment.

References

1. Egypt's Cabinet Information and Decision Support Centre (IDSC), UNDP, Egypt's National Strategy for Adaptation to Climate Change and Disaster Risk Reduction, December 2011. P.34. http://cairoclimatetalks.net/sites/default/files/Adaptation%20Strategy%20-%20Final%20-%20E.pdf [Accessed 18 February, 2015]

2. Healthcare Master Plan 2013/2014, Invest in Egypt, http://www.gafi.gov.eg/content/invsectorsdocs/Healthcarevalueproposition.pdf [Accessed 14 February, 2015]

3. World health statistics 2013. World Health Organisation. Egypt. http://www.who.int/gho/publications/world_health_statistics/EN_WHS2013_Full.pdf [Accessed 10 February, 2015]

4. UNFPA, Population and Development in Egypt, 2014. http://egypt.unfpa.org/english/Staticpage/54790f72-6e8b-4f77-99e2-4c5b78c20d5c/indicators.aspx [Accessed 12 February, 2015]

5. General Authority for Investment and Free Zones (GAFI), The Arab Republic of Egypt, Egypt for a Brighter Future, Investment & Sector snapshots, 2013, P.79 http://www.gafi.gov.eg/content/EN/macro/EgyBrightFuture_Dec_2013.pdf [Accessed 10 February, 2015]

6. The Report: Egypt 2014, OXFORD BUSINESS GROUP, Health & Education. http://www.oxfordbusinessgroup.com/egypt-2014/health-education. [Accessed 12 February, 2015]

7. World Health Organization, Health in the green economy, Co-benefits to health of climate change mitigation, http://www.who.int/hia/hgebrief_health.pdf [Accessed 15 February, 2015]

8. NHS England Carbon Footprinting, Report. London, National Health Service, Sustainable Development Unit, 2008. http://www.seiinternational. org/mediamanager/documents/Publications/Future/nhs_carbon_emissions_modellingoct08.pdf. [Accessed 17 February, 2015]

9. Sara Aggour, FY 2014/2015 state budget announced, analysts weigh in, DAILY NEWS Egypt. http://www.dailynewsegypt.com/2014/05/26/fy-20142015-statebudget-announced-analysts-weight/ [Accessed 10 February, 2015]

10. The World Bank, Egypt: Country Partnership Framework 2015-2019, https://consultations.worldbank.org/consultation/egypt-country-partnershipframework-
2015-2019 [Accessed 14 February, 2015]

11. THE WORLD BANK, Egypt Overview, Context, http://www.worldbank.org/en/country/egypt/overview [Accessed 16 February, 2015]

12. Amira Abdel Latif, Quality of public health services in lower income areas in Cairo, Egypt. http://www.aucegypt.edu/research/ebhrc/publications/Documents/Chronicles2

014/Chronicles2014_QualityofHealthService_AabdelLatif.pdf. [Accessed 25 February 2015]

13. Ahram-online, Egypt doctors to go on 'administrative' strike, http://english.ahram.org.eg/NewsContent/1/64/99001/Egypt/Politics-/Egyptdoctors
-
to-go-on-administrative-strike.aspx [Accessed 10 February, 2015]

14. Arab Republic of Egypt. (2014). Constitution of Arab Republic of Egypt. Cairo, Egypt. Article 18: Health care, P.15.
https://www.constituteproject.org/constitution/Egypt_2014.pdf [Accessed 10 February, 2015]

15. Arab Republic of Egypt. (2014). Constitution of Arab Republic of Egypt. Cairo, Egypt. Article 46: Environment, P.20.
https://www.constituteproject.org/constitution/Egypt_2014.pdf [Accessed 11 February, 2015]

16. The World Bank, Global Economic Prospects, What Does Weak Growth Mean for Poverty in the Future? 2014.
http://www.worldbank.org/en/publication/global-economic-prospects/globaloutlook/
what-does-weak-growth-mean-for-poverty-in-the-future [Accessed 17 February, 2015]

17. The World Bank, A Roadmap to Achieve Social Justice in Health Care in Egypt, 2015. http://www.worldbank.org/content/dam/Worldbank/Feature
%20Story/mena/Egypt/Egypt-Doc/egy-roadmap-sj-health.pdf. [Accessed 25 February 2015]

18. A Letter from The President, Egypt's Blueprint for Stability, Investment and Growth, 2015. http://www.egyptthefuture.com/egypt-economic-developmentconference-
eedc/word-president/ [Accessed 11 February, 2015]

19. Daily News Egypt, Egypt's year in review 2014. January 13, 2015.
http://www.dailynewsegypt.com/2015/01/13/egypts-year-review-2014/
[Accessed 12 February, 2015]

20. Marwan Sultan, ahramonline, Egypt's economic reform 'impressive' but more political steps needed: UK minister.
http://english.ahram.org.eg/NewsContent/1/64/120435/Egypt/Politics-/Egypt
%E2%80%99s-economic-reform-impressive-but-more-politi.aspx [Accessed 14 February, 2015]

21. World Health Organization, Health in the green economy, Co-benefits to health of climate change mitigation. http://www.who.int/hia/hgebrief_health.pdf [Accessed 10 February, 2015]

22. General Authority for Investment and Free Zones (GAFI), The Arab Republic of Egypt, Invest in Egypt, 2014.
http://www.gafi.gov.eg/content/invsectorsdocs/RenewableEnergyvalue.pdf [Accessed 15 February, 2015]

23. Egyptian Green Building Council, Establishment, 2010, http://www.egyptgbc.

gov.eg/about/egypt-gbc.html [Accessed 13 February, 2015]

24. The National Solid Waste Management Programme Egypt (NSWMP), Main Report,December 22, 2011. http://www.eeaa.gov.eg/english/reports/NSWMP/1_P0122721_NSWMP_Main%20Report_December2011.pdf [Accessed 12 February, 2015]

25. Reller A., Greener Hospitals, Improving Environmental Performance, Environment Science Center, Augsburg, Germany, With support from: Bristol-Myers Squibb Company, ISBN 3-00-012582-5. [Accessed 14 July 2014]

26. Kim, W.C., Mauborgne, R. (2005a). "Blue Ocean Strategy: from theory to practice", California Management Review, Vol.47 No.3, pp.105-121. [Accessed 14 July 2014]

27. P. Auerbach, Competition: The Economics of Industrial Change (Cambridge: Basil Blackwell, 1988); G.S. Day and D.J. Reibstein, with R. Gunther, eds., Wharton on Dynamic Competitive Strategy (New York, NY: John Wiley, 1997). [Accessed 16 July 2014]

28. Kabir C, Potty A, Sharma R. Current opportunities for the development of leadership skills for doctors. Int J of Clin Leadersh. 2008;16:115–119. [Accessed 13 July 2014]

29. Stoller JK. Developing physician-leaders: key competencies and available programs. J Health Adm Educ. 2008;25(4):307–328. [Accessed 14 July 2014]

30. The Governance Institute. Leadership in Healthcare Org. Joint Commission, 2009. [Accessed 15 July 2014]

31. Freddy J. Nager , The Triple Bottom Line, 2012. [Accessed 14 July 2012]

Photo by Lea Seeberg and Miriam Kennet. Home Grown Blackcurrants from the Green Economics Institute's own garden

4.7 Silent Voices: An Emerging Women Power in Ethiopia

Photo by Paul Kennet. Women construction workers in Ethiopia.

By Mahelet Alemayehu Mekonnen

Much has been said about successful stories of many 'men' and their achievements but not many stories have been told that signifies women's achievements. Even though the role played by women is highly undoubtedly the most valuable and cradle of all in most cases the hard work of women is sadly left aside.

Ethiopia is a nation known for drought, famine, poverty and hunger. However, the current globalised world has not only shown the emergence of growth for this country but particularly the role of women in field of economics and particularly within the field of agriculture.

This chapter hopes to address the untold story of women in power, in a nation that have fought to become united not only in terms of democratic right but particularly in the sphere of economic progress. Thus, I will look at the establishment of the Ethiopian Commodity Exchange (ECX) and a brief over view of the Ethiopian agricultural sector.

One can only hope to address the fact that the 'works' and 'silent voices' of many women is yet to be told and thus for a nation at its infancy in terms of 'growth and transformation' it is imperative and absolutely necessary that the role of women is expressed and used to the to its fullest.

Ethiopian economy is composed of three kinds of sectors. The agriculture sector accounts for nearly 49% of the countries over all GDP whereas the remaining 39% and 11% account for the service and industry sector respectively (CIA Fact Book, 2011). Despite the huge share agriculture holds the growth rate for the economy in terms of agriculture is very small. The service sector accounts for 14.5%, followed by industry at 10.2% and agriculture at the rate of only 6% (Reference). Agriculture however has been a growing challenge due to the fact that nearly 85% of the population working within this sector are small-scale farmers using one or two hectares of land and in most cases using traditional means of agricultural techniques. Thus production in many cases to decreases accordingly.

Another major and challenging problem for most of agricultural production is the lack of export market due to stringent export standards and quality assurance that are negatively affect the small-scale farmer. Furthermore, the private sector within the commercial and seed industry is extremely small. For instance only about 26 private companies licensed to produce, 19 to import, 33 to retail and 4 to export seed operate within the country (Ethiopian Seed Association, 2010). The increasingly stringent market constantly creates a battle for survival for this sector. In many cases because of lack of standardized system the private industry becomes discouraged to enter such industry. Nonetheless, the past 5 years have seen a progressive change, one that has allowed many private individuals to enter the seed and grain industry.

One of the many establishments and one that is helping many market actors and thus far has shown a great progress is the start of the Ethiopian Commodity Exchange (ECX). Launched in 2008 ECX aims to revolutionize Ethiopia's traditional agriculture to a more thorough and modern system where all actors; the small-scale farmer, buyer and consumer are all linked in a chain of events that benefits all involved. Founded by women and former World Bank agricultural economist the ECX is the brightest hope for the Ethiopia's growth. It's CEO, Dr. Eline Gebre Medhin amongst the many talented businesswomen in Ethiopia is a cradle of hope for the transformation and progression of economic growth.

The values and goals of ECX is to enforce a commodity sector that links industries like transport, logistics, banking and others to create a link of partners in an exchange for the nations agricultural products. It allows producers, small-scale farmers, private industries, buyers and consumers to trust each other and work in a transparent, professional and market oriented environment. ECX is one of its kind in Ethiopia and in Africa as of its establishment in 2008 it has increased trade by 128% (Conway. 2011).

Another recent development in light of the current steady growth is the Ethiopian government new economic plan known as 'The Growth and Transformation Plan'. The plan is set out in five years from 2010-2015. It covers the most important sectors such as Agriculture, Education, Healthcare, Industry to name just few. The goal is to make a drastic and substantially aggressive change that can help the economic barriers of growth. The government's aim is to push the agricultural sector to be a major source of economic growth.

Thus far however, the progress in the past two years has been relatively slow. Nonetheless, there have been changes especially within the Agricultural sector. The agricultural sector in Ethiopia did not have a set regulatory body that clearly signifies the roles of agricultural related concerns. Particular problem within the agricultural policy and decision making is that not many within in this field are fully aware of the concerns and problems of the many problems faced in the field of agriculture. Thus policy makers fail to fulfill the needs of those involved within the sector. Thus, as a result the Ethiopian Transformation Agency (ETA) has been established to avail such discrepancy of lack of 'knowledge' based understanding between the decision maker i.e. the politician and the agriculturalist hence allowing all that are involved to establish a smooth transition (Ethiopian Agricultural Transformation Agency, 2011) . Our changing world today needs more food to fed its growing population and this food will depend on the ability to availability of resources. It is clear that Africa particularly emerging economies like Ethiopia are at the verge of growth but the constant battle for survival between the gender gap is an on-going and yet unresolved problem that hinders the potentially strong leaderships of women in the field of Agriculture. It is thus not only important but essential to empower these silent but yet strong hopes of Ethiopia and the many African countries that are bound to make a significant difference for this nation.

References:
CIA, Fact Book, Ethiopia. 2011. *"Government and Economy" Accessed [January 20,2012]* Available at <http://www.ciafactbook.com/country/Ethiopia
Conway G and Ibrahim M., 2011 "From Food Security to Wealth Creation:Why African Agriculture Matters. The Huffington Post, Available at http://www.huffingtonpost.co.uk/professor-sir-gordon-conway/from-foodsecurity-to-wea_b_1120042.html> Accessed on [1 January 2012].
"Ethiopian Commodity Exchange" 2011 Company profile, Accessed [January 20,2012]
Ethiopian Agricultural Transformation Agency, 2011. "Origin of the Agency" Accessed on [January 20, 2012]. Available at <http://www.ata.gov.et/about/>
Moyo, D. (2010). Dead Aid, Penguin Books, Rowland Phototypesetting, Ltd, England.Available at <http://www.ecx.com.et/CompanyProfile.aspx>

4.8 Social-ecological transformation and Green Economics: New perspectives for solutions to the most pressing problems of today

By Miriam Kennet

Introduction

This chapter will examine why we need a socio-ecological transformation and introduce some of the global scale problems we are facing. These include climate change, species extinction and threats to the natural systems upon which we depend. It then discusses neo – classical economics roots and causes of this situation, and what kind of economics transformations are needed. The contributions of Rosa Luxemburg are discussed including her work on international production, consumption, property rights and enclosure of the commons which are important elements today.

Finally there is a discussion of the characteristics of an economics which could produce such a socio – ecological transformation, which the chapter suggests could be a Green Economics with different attitudes to nature, inclusive of feminist perspectives and compatible with modern science, with a long term perspective. A focus on equity is in keeping with sharing the planet's resources with each other and with other.

Why we need a socio-ecological transformation in order to solve the most pressing problems of today

The world is currently experiencing crises of a magnitude and a type unseen in the 10,000 years of "civilisation." Our "civilisation" arose after the last ice age and was founded upon the particular climactic conditions of the Quaternary interglacial period. We now have the challenges of human induced climate change with sea level rise, and millions of environmental refugees predicted Lohachara Island was the world's first populated island, to be lost to climate change 5 years ago and left 7,000 people homeless. Sagar the largest island, houses 20,000 refugees from other islands along with many rare species and is also disappearing fast. This illustrates how people, planet and biosphere are intricately connected.

One fifth of humankind is in life threatening poverty, and three quarters of mammal species are predicted to be extinct by the end of this century, according to the IUCN Red List report (Barker 2007). There has never been a more pressing need for a saimultaneous social and ecological transformation, which needs to now take on board that poverty is an environmental issue and the environment is a poverty issue.

Dr Rajendra Pachauri, the chair of the Intergovernmental Panel on Climate Change,

warns that " the very survival of the human species is at risk," (Lean, 2005).
The polar ice caps are contracting and sea level rise could permanently displace up to 200 million people, (Stern 2006). With predicted global warming of between +2 to +4.5 % or up to + 6C by 2100, (Lynas 2007), extinctions, desertification and reduction in agricultural yields are anticipated. The Millennium Ecosystem Services Assessment, (2005) found that ecosystem services are being degraded and an increase in 'non-linear events' brings increased disease, collapse of fisheries and other threats, in particular to fragile ecosystems which are also hosts to rapidly growing human populations.

These changes make our task urgent and compelling. Further, our current economic system perpetuates poverty, inequality and social injustice. The economic system fails to meet even many wealthy people's needs. A UNICEF report, (2007) about the well – being of young people in the UK, shows that a country which has the fifth largest economy in the world, simultaneously has the worst rankings among the 25 richest nations, in terms of the well- being and happiness of its young people when analysing indicators such as relative poverty and deprivation, relationships with family and peers, health and safety and feelings of well being. The report raises significant questions about how the pursuit of economic wealth, as current attained and measured, may actually detract from broader measures of well being. Seventy per cent of the world's 1.2 billion people in life threatening poverty, according to a UN Report, (UN 2006) are women and children. Every day 6,000 children in developing countries die for lack of acess to clean water (Sullivan 2000, Crisis in water). Only 1 per cent of the world's titled land belongs to women (Firth ,2006).

Gendered domestic violence is the single largest global cause of female morbidity, more than war, traffic accidents, and cancer (Smith, 2006). It is therefore vital to redress the balance of poverty and power between men and women on the planet. Wangari Maathai, likens the things that matter in society to an African stool, *"The three legs represent three critical pillars of a just and stable society. The first leg stands for democratic space, where rights are respected, whether they are human rights, women's rights, children's rights, or environmental rights. The second represents sustainable and equitable management of resources. The third represents cultures of peace. The seat represents society and its prospects for development."*
These three pillars have got lost in the drive for global economic success defined as ever increasing profit, industrial productivity and trade flows which has brought the risk of destruction of much of our habitat.

Neo–classical economics roots and causes of this situation and what kind of economic transformation do we need?

Today's economics discourse has become almost unrecognisable from its origins as provisioning for the needs of the household or the estate. Its root is the word *oikia*, ancient Greek for a house. The root of the word, Eco-nomics is the same as that of ecology.
Green Economics reverts it to its original and useful beginnings: the provisioning of needs for all of us and the biosphere within the household we all share, which is actually the earth.

Neo-classical economics has come to mean the exact opposite, which is, everything formal, mathematical and external to the household sphere which has assumed superiority over the earth believing itself to be some how outside its systems and limitations. Examining our resource needs and working out how to share them fairly among the people of the world is a major task. In 1890 Marshall described economics as "it examines the part of individual and social action which is most closely connected with the attainment and with the use of the material requisites of well-being." (2005:57.Hogdson). However Samuelson (1948) the father of neo-classical economics, argued that "economics is the allocation of scarce means between alterative uses, as a universal matter of choice for every individual in a world of scarcity. Instead of the whole system of production and allocation of the means of life, the choosing individual alone became the foundation stone of economic theory (2005:57) in Hogdson. Economics which purports to be value free science, is in fact practised in the main by white middle class men and outside the home sphere. The discipline of economics has to some extent been subsumed by business schools which aim to "grow" companies. There are very few women economics professors, just 23 in the UK in 2003(RES Report: Humphries). Economics has become mathematically oriented and exclusive with a fixation on " economic growth" as the key indicator of progress, conceived as more important than indicators relating to the health of people, well being or ecosystem integrity.

Economics, the provisioning for needs, is done by all of us. Every creature and every ecosystem has an "economic" or resource need and impact. We need to broaden the scope of economics in order for it to helpful in solving today's socio – and ecological problems. The emerging discourse of Green Economics reclaims economics for all people everywhere, aiming for all people and the biosphere to be beneficiaries rather than inputs. Green Economics rejects the short term timescales of business cycles in favour of geological lengths of time as only archaeological and palaeontological explanations can illuminate what is happening.

Green Economics has arisen from the need for an framework which can encompass social and environmental insights and does not factor out "life- world" evidence but instead embraces the complexities of people, nature and their dynamic interrelationships.

Green economics logic is built upon an interdisciplinary range of philosophies and methodologies from human learning, from the economics of Aristotle and Xenophon, through the enlightenment to post-modern illustrations of difference and power relationships. Its world view is that everything happens within the earth's boundaries and so no longer theorises economics as being separate from but rather within the earth's systems. There are no resources which don't come from nature.

Socio-ecological transformations and Revolutions: The relevance of Rosa Luxembourg's analysis for today's solutions

Luxemburg made a number of analytical observations which are useful in starting us on the path to transformation. An updated environmental definition of such transformation is given by Olsson, Folke and Hahn (2004). They define it as resilience, in social – ecological systems, the ability to cope with environmental variability and disturbance events. Characteristics of such a system might include property rights, environmental ethics, public accountability and reciprocal exchange systems. These are all pertinent to learning to live with change and uncertainty and elements can be found in the ideology of indigenous peoples. The industrial revolution brought benefits according to mainstream economics definition s. However Luxemburg correctly predicted some of the drawbacks.

Enclosure and the transformation of property rights

Concurrent with the industrial revolution, the commons began to be enclosed for the benefit of the few who made money out of them and prevented the rest of humanity or other species from accessing them. This has been followed most recently by the enclosure of knowledge with intellectual property rights and patents. (Shiva in Biopiracy). Luxemburg argued that three things were aimed for: to coerce labour power into service, to impose a commodity economy and to separate agriculture and trade and drive farmers off the land and into towns. She showed how colonizers created a fiction that land had always belonged to the political ruler- rather than being owned in common.(Luxemburg 1913 :352.).

These ideas have largely been implemented. Everything has been commodified including, including land, knowledge and ecosystems services which are a new way of defining the role of nature.

Capitalism and the transformation of wealth and power A new system of economics, capitalism, emerged, whereby the rich could increase their wealth or capital. In theory the poor would benefit as wealth trickled down. There was a theoretical justification for periods of enduring hardship with the Kuznets curve which showed that theoretically less developed countries could take off into an accelerated growth, after a period of hardship. The view that more development along capitalist lines will provide the socioeconomic transformation required has pervaded development theories such as sustainable development. It became accepted that the rich should enjoy so-called free trade with no constraints or trade barriers for the good of society, as the invisible hand of the market would ensure their decisions ultimately benefited everyone.

Corporations grew in this laissez faire environment into huge monoliths and many of them are larger and more powerful than governments. Luxemburg argued that it was the very dispossession of the peasants of their common land which provided both the property, and also the labour **with which to keep this system going, and hence that** poverty is part of the engine of the capitalist system. She foresaw that this system needed previously non industrialised areas, beyond the spatial scope of the capitalist consumption or democratic area, to provide cheap international production but that this would ultimately reach limits of expansion. Encroachment for international production is a little explored area but is extremely pertinent to the issue of democracy.

Corporations find an area of potential cheap labour and then set about creating favourable market conditions before entry, being complicit in combinations of civil instability, displacement of people, regime change, economic instability and military action.

Luxemburg realised that expanding capitalism would need new markets, and that there was ultimately a limit to them. Advanced capitalism's requirement of ever expanding rich consumer markets for its products and lower and lower paid, poor workers for its production must eventually must reach a saturation of possibilities, including finite physical limits of resources. Consumption is a battle ground. People are manipulated to consume more by government including infrastructure for global trade corridors and demand is artificially stimulated by activities such as corporate advertising.

Transformations in attitudes to nature, civilisation and agriculture

Luxembourg identified a struggle against the natural economy. Just when humans thought they had tamed nature, largely by means of economics and technology, climate change has forced a rethink of our position in the universe and our role as stewards of nature. We are beginning to realise that rather than using science to control nature, we are going to have to use our knowledge to live within and respect it. The power of nature was pivotal to elements of early belief systems and religions which we can learn from.

Transforming the limits of civilisation- 10,000 years of town dwelling-An audit. We need to assess the viability of agriculture, and urbanisation during this period of rapid global environmental change and to establish the best course of action. The issues of population growth, people displacement and scarce resources raise important economic questions. Agriculture enabled cities to develop, but the project of "civilisation" itself is under threat. Civilisation derives from c*ivis*, the Latin word for townsman or citizen, *civis*, adjectival, *civilis,* which implies urbanisation. Mega-cities surpass human-scale communities, their own local ecosystem services and the carrying capacity of their immediate hinterland. There is an urgent task, fundamental to Green Economics, to reanalyse "civilisation" and to develop strategies for how human living and economic patterns can adapt for survival.

Transforming the human habitat and ecosystem services crisis and the current mass extinction. This is affecting the ability of our habitat to sustain us all, as a species. It is becoming clear that our economics is running into limits of expansion and we need therefore to re-think the whole premise of our economics to limit further human induced global environmental damage. If the consumption rate of the rich countries continues and is adopted by poorer countries we would require the resource of three planets, so we have reached the limits of possible ecological footprints within this earth and the natural world.

Transformations in international production

The internationalisation of production in globalisation is little understood, but is one of the most pertinent phenomena identified by Luxemburg. Large TNCs outsource production across sectors, firms and countries, (Ietto –Gillies 2005 :48) and workers rights are eroded by casualisation. The arms trade has grown rapidly and everything and everyone is commoditized and a growing slave trade including even in children.

Three quarters of world trade originates with multinationals and over a third is internal to the firm precluding regulation or scrutiny or competition from other companies. (Ietto -Gillies UNCTAD 1996).

The globalisation of international production and effects on national and local economies has been described by Dicken (2007). "There has been a huge transformation in the nature and the degree of interconnection in the world economy, and especially in the speed with which such connectivity occurs, involving both the stretching and the intensification of economic relationships. There is today a deep integration organised primarily within and between geographically extensive and complex transnational production networks and through a diversity of mechanisms. There are changes are not so much in volume as in **composition**. There has been a huge increase in intraindustry and intra – firm trade. Both of which are indicators of a more functionally fragmented and geographically dispersed production processes. Dicken (2007: 7)

Flows of material and non material processes are organised into relational structures and processes in which the power relationships between key actors such as firms, states, individuals, and social groups are uneven. (Dicken 2007: 8). States, labour unions and even NGO's compete to attract TNC's. Vertical dimensions of transnational production networks, intersect with territorially defined political and economic systems and horizontal dimensions of territorial systems of different geographical scales. Firms have global reach according to Ohmae,in The end of the nation state. According to the World Trade Report (2005a) 4/5ths of global manufacturing and 2/3rds of agriculture are concentrated in 15 countries, and outward FDI is similarly concentrated with 30% emanating from the US and the UK.

The Surmounting of democracy and government by TNCs and the transformation of existing power structures

Gillies explains that "*transnational companies can and do play governments of different countries or regions against each other with the objective of raising the offer of financial incentives for the location of inward investment FDI . Thus the TNC has a strong element of bargaining power towards both governments and labour force in that it canrelocate to different countries with relatively low costs of change."*. (2005:293 Ietto-Gillies)

This is a concern as there are several countries where democracy is under serious threat. Large MNC's can influence government. For example Shell is widely suspected of this in Nigeria, and Burma Oil in Burma, both of which are repressive regimes. In many cases corporate regulations are created in the same department that ought to be regulating their activity. Regulation has become the subject of lobbying at extra national level in order to resist the impositions and limitations governments place on corporate activity.

Differing currency and taxation laws give firms the opportunity of developing location and intra firm transfer strategies that give them the benefit of transfer pricing manipulation and therefore higher profits. With outsourcing and the transfer of rules and regulations environmental dumping is facilitated.

New markets reflecting environmental and other concerns are hijacked by larger firms buying up more ethical trading houses, for example the Body Shop was bought by L'Oreal. Large family owned organic dairies are bought up by global firms who retain the family name and marketing.

Large firms use their market power to avoid complying with usual labour standards. Lidl has been investigated as a firm with geographical variation in working conditions. In the case of Lidl this affects workers' human dignity such as very limited toilet breaks and pressure on women not to have children to discouraging unions. The economics system needs to be fed by increasing consumption, and according to Rostow the final state of economies must be a stage of "high mass consumption." Here it has come up against the limits to growth (Meadows et al). Furthermore, production is concentrated into large scale operations to create "efficiency," or " lean supply" with a consequent reduction in diversity of suppliers.

Inequalities are widening between and within countries, with key indicators of infant mortality and life expectancy becoming increasingly divergent. Dicken points out that the benefits of trade, are limited in the poorest countries. This is due to dependence on a narrow economics base and exacerbated by downward pressure and lack of stability in the price of traded goods. Combined with a market mechanism that fails to share the benefits equitably (Dicken 2007: 519) this has resulted in the terms of trade worsening considerably between 1990 and 2000.

The characteristics and scope of an economics for socio – ecological transformation
a) Moral and Spiritual aspects of economics for transformation
Satish Kumar, (2007) suggests that we need a transformation in our attitudes to each other, and to other living things on the Earth. He suggests that we have lost the idea of spirit and become wedded to materialism," identifying the roots of this in the views of Descartes and Newton who looked upon the Earth as an object of human dominance. He reminds us that Nature rights are equal to human rights, Kumar suggests we need a *"geo centric world view"*- which is in fact how green economics is constructed with the earth at the center or foot of all activity and observations. Kumar says that we cannot solve a problem in the mindset that caused the problem in the first place and "we need to realise the subservience of economics to ecology."(Kumar 2007:33).

Green Economics recognizes poverty as a moral issue, yet the application of neo-liberal logic appears to be making matters worse for the world's poor. Neo-classical economics views world poverty as offering opportunities for further exploitation as a vast untapped market offering cheap resources and labour for revenue growth (Prahalad and Hammond, 2003, p.1). In Green Economics wealth and power are recognised as inextricably intertwined, so an appropriate level of decision-making is encouraged, which allows access and transparency for everyone. New indicators, rather than just GDP (which only measures the activity, throughput and quantity as monetary value of goods exchanged) show what the social and environmental justice targets could be, analysing trends and identifying risks such as in education, work, consumption, relative distribution of wealth and health of people, species and ecosystems (Anderson, 1991) .

b) Eco – ecological/economic transformation
It is recognised that all these elements need to be reworked, and particularly that power structures need to be changed as economic power is often concentrated in the same hands as political power. Lack of democracy appears to be a factor in several parts of the world where there is unrest or extreme poverty where a small ruling class hold the economic power and control the government.

c) Economics objectives for transformation
The objectives of Green Economics are indivisible from its methodoloy:
i) To create economic conditions where social and environmental justice thrives and benefits all people everywhere, non human species, the planet and its systems.
ii) To reform mainstream economics into a discipline which no longer supports or accepts that only a minority can be wealthy, but which works towards a fair and equitable society which lives within its means in all senses. Further Green Economics seeks to re-examine broader versions of reality, beyond the views of the rich and powerful, rejecting the idea of rational economic man "homoeconomicus" as a benchmark in order to hear different voices, as proposed for example by feminist theory (Ghilligan,1982).
A key reason for mainstream economics' failure is its lack of influences and learning from other areas. Green Economics attempts to combine trans- and inter-disciplinary studies to counteract this narrow thinking, As Welford exhorts, "*if we were to emphasize moderation and sufficiency rather than maximisation of output, consumption, incomes and profits, this would have a radical and fundamental impact on the way we lead our lives and the way we treat the environment.*"
(Welford, 2007)
iii)To enable all people everywhere to participate in the economy with equal power, equal rights and with equal access to decision making. Green Economics methodology brings new perspectives to conventional economics tools and enables it to reveal the power relationships and vested interests in the global economy. It also reincorporates political economy and the moral and transformational aspects of the economics of Smith (1776). It offers new solutions to 'managing the commons', which has been restricted to theoretical models (von Neumann and Morgenstern), and exercises based on the prisoner's dilemma (Arrow, 1951) which perpetuate assumptions of self interest as the key motivation of human activity.
Learning from this broad range of wisdom is essential to enable our economic systems to adapt to operating within a 'carrying capacity' of the earth. Pegging the level of that capacity should be a pressing subject for economic debate. Green Economics reembeds the economy within ecological and social structures. Economic growth, progress and development are measured by indicators that aim towards 'creation' mimicking the abundance of nature, not 'annihilation' of resources (Goldsmith, 2005). Profit, prices and markets are regarded as incidental, rather than drivers of the economic system. Green Economics treats people, the planet, nature, non-human

species, and the biosphere as beneficiaries, not just resources or economic factors of production.

This new discipline operates on the principle that the needs of people and natural systems must be satisfied simultaneously. The purpose of economic activity is to satisfy needs, not to enhance the power of people, corporations or states. Global industrialism, according to Dobson (2000, p.27), is regarded with suspicion. The welfare value of products is questioned, as well as their transformation into forms of identity through marketing.

The concept of equilibrium is reclaimed from price concerns to encompass impacts and effects in political, social, moral and ecological terms reflecting concern for people, society, non-human species, nature and the biosphere as a holistic whole. In this way, Green Economics acts as a filter for other systems as it is does not seek to impose one system globally, as in capitalism or socialism, but rather advocates diversity using a Green Economics analysis for each situation. Many practitioners of conventional economics are critical of their own discipline, according to Medena and Samuels (1996) and Ormerod (1994). "The subject has become so obscure that even orthodox economists are bemoaning its intellectual poverty," says Kitson (2005). Mainstream economists observe that their work has little bearing on the real 'life-world' or on important concerns such as ending poverty (Kitson, 2005). However, disciplinary insurgence is rare because of the limited professional progress that usually follows. Unfortunately, many well-known economists, for example, Pasinetti (2005) continue to advocate a more intensified business as usual approach, fixated on growth, more profit, which entails increasing economic hegemony of global corporations and is framed by increasingly elaborate theory,. Green economists argue that these blinkered and alienating positivist dogmas cannot solve the problems of today.

d) Transformation in attitudes to economics and its relationship to science and earth science

Mainstream economics employs a set of positivist, modern tools to produce the desired simplified logic that is vital for the picture of the world that is its basis. It produces results that contradict insights from other sciences such as the urgency of human induced climate change. It is focused on an infinite growth assumption and supposedly innate individual preferences in our prescribed role as passive consumers.

Green Economics can integrate the world's big ideas, such as those presented by The Big Bang, Evolution, Quantum Mechanics, Risk Theory, New System Theory, Relativity and Climate Change. Green Economics incorporates the ideas of progress in scientific thinking and in scientific methodology such as natural science, ecology and social science rather than econometrics.

Economics therefore challenges the reductionism and supposed objectivity of mainstream economics which is based on the supremacy of unadjusted market solutions at the expense of people and the planet.

e) An Holist transformation

Leonardo da Vinci (1452–1519) believed that it was important to understand the connections between the 'art of science' and the 'science of art'. Science in the late 20th century realised that everything was interconnected. As Harrison (1992, p.365) has argued, "The demands of the environment will present humanity with the challenge of breaking down the compartmentalisation of knowledge". Green Economics "could well become the science overarching all the others. As part of this, we desperately need anoverarching science of human interactions, both with each other through an economic system and with the environment, combining socio-economic and technological studies with dynamic analysisof the physical environment". Green Economics fosters the realisation of Harrison's vision.

f) A Transformation from short termism to long termism

Green Economics takes a view that is much longer-term than the short business cycles of neoclassical and economics. Due to its consideration of the effects of a transaction on the 200 000th generation and beyond (Myers, 1985), Green Economics can draw from history, paleontology and archaeology. As a consequence, Green Economics does not simply discount the future. Intergenerational equity is investigated by such writers as Alderson (2006) who is greatly influenced by Chong (2006). Instead of mobilising the resources of the planet in support of human kind, we must surely mobilise the resources of human kind in support of the planet. This postulates a revision of our value systems, social paradigms and consumption culture (Myers, 1985).

g) An inclusive transformation including women and men together, using a feminist economics discourse

There are two realms of economic activity, that of competitive production and exchange in markets and that of direct production such as subsistence agriculture, care and reciprocity. Feminist economics contributes the notion that production does indeed occur in the home or 'okia'. Mies (1994) concentrates on methodology in economics and has been in integral influence on the development of green economics along with Mellor (1992) and Henderson (1983). Their approaches warn against

theories that legitimise a single-gendered *homo economics* (rational economic man) version or 'story' of reality that excludes *gynaika oikonomika, (economic woman)* from the public economic sphere. Feminist methodologies allow us to dig into the foundations of a discipline and expose them as particular and contingent. It reveals the placing of boundaries in economics as an intensely political act.

Feminist economics has opened debate about the role of women in the global economy (Mies, 1994) and found evidence of patriarchy and exploitation. Women have provided unpaid, nonvalued, invisible work and the discipline of economics has excluded their experience. There has, been a recognition of the power of nature, due to human induced climate change and this has challenged the belief of man's domination over nature, which is embodied in patriarchal culture.

There is an urgent need to design an economics which helps to limit further ecological devastation, and to design an economics which can work under some of the radically changed environmental conditions predicted in some scenarios, such as agriculture being limited to smaller regions of the world. Major climatic and other shifts could bring a lack of availability and viability of natural resources impacting on our basic needs such as food and water and the likelihood of major displacement of people. Our economics must be able to deal with such severe problems and the inherent uncertainty of climate change.

Conclusion

Humanity has come to a crossroads where we have reached the limits to the economic logic on which its agrarian, industrial, and technological revolutions were based. Economic growth sustained by resources in furtherance of this aim have been discovered to be finite. Yet supply chains have become more globalised and wasteful of resources. Furthermore, the natural world has turned out to be extremely complex and fragile whilst at the same time enjoying the ultimate power to wipe us out as along with many other species. In order to preserve a natural world which we could reasonably call home- and an economics based in that home- or oikia, we need to undertake a rapid socio-ecological transformation and to re-align our entire economics systems. Luxemburg also pointed out the need for grassroots democracy and co-operation. Recent primate studies indicate that co-operation is an important aspect of society, De Wal (2005), contradicting economic theories like the prisoner's dilemma and the tragedy of the commons. De Waal suggests that reciprocity arose from sharing of food within the group, in prehistoric times. This, he suggests involves keeping a balance of good deeds which we expect them to be roughly equal and reciprocal.

Mainstream neo-classical economics has been based on inequalty between rich and poor, between men and women, between man and other species, between man and the planets natural systems. Our economic system has allowed for one fifth of humankind to go to bed hungry at night and there is no justification for this. If we want to call ourselves *civilised,* it's time to transform in a peaceful and positive way to a caring and sharing culture where everyone and everything counts, and into a Green Economics system of abundance and growth in nature shared by all and richly embedded in the natural world.

References:

Alderson P., (2008). Childhood Poverty, in International Journal of Green Economics vol 2 no1.Inderscience Publishers.

Anderson V., (1991). Alternative Economic Indicators. London: Routledge

Arrow K., (1951). Social Choice and Individual Values. Yale: University Press.

Barker, A.S., (2006). Rhinoptera bonasus. In: IUCN 2007. 2007 IUCN Red List of Threatened Species. <www.iucnredlist.org>. Downloaded on 15 January 2008.

Broswimmer F., (2002). Ecocide. Pluto Press

Chong C., (2006). Restoring the Rights of Future Generations In International Journal of Green Economics Inderscience Vol. 1. Issue 1/2.

De Waal F., (2005) Our inner ape, Granta Books.

Dicken P., (2007). Global Shift. Sage Publications.

Dobson A. (2000). Green Political Thought. Routledge Abingdon.

Hodgson G., (2005) Can Economics Start from the Individual Alone? P. 56 -67 in A Guide to What'wrong with Wconomics, Fullbrook E. (2005) Anthem Press. London.

Firth M., (2006). UN Report Women Denied Representation, Making the War on Poverty Hard to Win. Independent 8th March p.2

Hodgson, (2001) How Economics Forgot History. London: Routledge.

Ghilligan, (1982). In a Different Voice, Cambridge MA.Harvard University Press.

Goldsmith E., (2005) Rewriting Economics www.greeneconomics.org.uk accessed 17.January 2006.

Ietto – Gillies G., (2005) The Study of Transnational Companies in A guide to what's wrong with economics. P. 288- 29) .

Ietto -Gillies G. (2005)Transnational Corporations and International Production Edward Elgar

Ietto Gillies G UNCTAD 1996 in Ietto -Gillies G. (2005)Transnational Corporations and International Production Edward Elgar

IUCN Red List Report of Threatened Species UN (2007)World Conservation Union

Hammer E. (2007 Dec/Jan)Corporate Organics, Organic Dilemmas, The Ecologist p. 39-42

Harrison P (1992) The third revolution. In Nelissen,Van der Straaten and Klinkers, Classics in Environmentalism (1997)The Netherlands International Books.

Henderson H (2006) Growing the Green Economy- globally, -in International Journal of Green Economics Vol 1 3 /4 Inderscience.

Hermann A. (2006) Schwarz-Buch Lidl Europa; Berlin 2006, German edition, ca. 140 pages. ver.digmbh medien buchhandel verlag, Paula Thiede Ufer 10, D 10179 Berlin.9.90 Euro plus shipping,ISBN-number 3-932349-21-0. In English, The Black Book on Lidl in Europe; Berlin 2006, English edition:14,90 Euro plus shipping, ISBN-Nummer 3-932349-22-9 (English).

Humphries J. (2003) first published (1995) Gender and Economics:

Kennet M and Heinemann V. (2006) Green Economics Setting the Scene.in International Journal of Green Economics. Vol. Issue 1.

Kennet M., (2008) Ietto – Gilies Transnational Corporations and International Production, Book review in International Journal of Green Economics Vol 2 n.2

Kennet M., (2007) Editorial, Putting Back the Forgotten Factor of Reality into Economics.in International Journal of Green Economics volume 2 no 1

Kitson M., (2005) Economics for the future in Cambridge Journal of Economics Vol 29 .no 6 Dec (2005).

Scot Cato and Kennet M (1999) Green Economics:Beyond Supply and Demand to meeting people's needs.Green Audit.

Kumar S. (2007) Earth I love, Spiritual Economy. Nature is the real source of our wealth. Resurgence Magazine, No 245 November/December 2007.

Lean G. (2005)Global warming approaching point of no return, warns leading climate expert, Independent 23rd January 2005.

Luxembourg R. (1906) The Mass Strike.The Political Party and the Trade Unions. Merlin Press London

Luxemburg R.(1913) The Accumulation of Capital(2003) Routledge.

Lynas M (2007) The hellish vision of life on a hotter planet, Independent 3 February p.3

Marshall A. (1890) Principles of Economics. 8th Ed. London Macmillan 1920.

McDougall D. (2007)Stemming the Tide, rising Seas. Dec Jan The Ecologist, P.28-30.

Meadows D.Randers J. and Meadows (2006) The limits to growth: a thirty year update Earthscan

Medina S.G and Samuels W.J. Foundations of research in economics (1996)Edward Elgar

Mellor M (2006) Ecofeminist political economy in International Journal of Green Economics. Vol 1no 1/ 2

Mies M. (2006) Patriarchy and Accumulation on a world scale revisited, The Iceberg Model of Sustainable Economics in International Journal of Green Economics Vol 1 no 3/ 4

Myers N (1985) The Gaia Atlas of Planet Management: Good Books

OlssonP, Folke C. and Hahn T.(2004) Ecological Transformation Social-Ecological Transformation for Ecosystem Management: the Development of Adaptive Comanagement of a Wetland Landscape in Southern Sweden:Center for Transdisciplinary Environmental Research Formatiert

Omerod P. (1994) The end of Economics. London. Faber

Passinetti L. (2005)Cambridge school of Keynsian economics,Cambridge Journal of Economics, Oxford University Press, December Vol.29.No 6

Prahalad C.K. and Hammond A. (2003)Serving the world's poor profitably,Harvard Business Review on Corporate Social Responsibility,Harvard Business School Publishing.

Rostow W (1990)Theorists of economic growth from David Hume to the Present, Oxford University Press.

Samuelson P. (1948)in (1964) ed Paul Samuelson Economics, International Student Edition.

Scot Cato and Kennet M. (1999) Green Economics:Beyond Supply and Demand to meeting people'sneeds.Green Audit.

Shiva V. (1997) Biopiracy The Plunder of Nature and Knowledge Smith J (2006) Watchout Patriarchy is making a comeback,Independent 8th February p.29

Sullivan C (2000) Do Interventions and Policy Interventions Reach the Poorest of the Poor: The Crisis in Water Paper from the author

UN Millenium Ecosystem Assessment (2005) and United Nations Foundation, www.unfoundation.org/features/millennium_ecosystem_assessment.asp

UNICEF Report (2007) Childhood well being in industrialised countries acessed 14th February 2007.

Stern N. (2006)The Economics of Climate Change The Stern Report.Cambridge University Press 2007

Welford R.(2007) Examining discussing and suggesting possible contribution and role of Buddhist Economics for corporate social responsibility in International Journal of Green Economics Vol 1 no 3/ 4

World Trade Report (2005a) in Dicken P (2007) Global Shift.Sage Publications.

Part 5: Climate Justice

5:1 Solar Panels and renewable energy in Mexico

By Jose G. Vargas-Hernandez (Mexico)

Mexico has a great opportunity for the use of renewable energy RE), regardless of type energy is concerned, solar, geothermal, hydro, etc.., Because it is a country with diverse climate sea world, though little explored sparsely and it is necessary to identify the most suitable for promoting public policies and find the absolute advantage, given the international theories, we can use the same basis for rethinking the development of the sector, using as a guide the absolute advantage that Mexico has in its natural resources and climate types. We also see that international experience shows that it is possible to establish markets "green energy" where end users cover their costs and is a highly profitable emerging market, for both sides, provider and consumer, we also see as government programs exist that support the same, a fact that makes it tempting for the investment of national and international firms.

1. Introduction
Renewable energy (RE) currently occupies an increasing space in the energy landscape, and global economics. All developed countries and developing countries are changing their energy policies for the development of technologies that provide economic growth, and can meet the demands of its population. The technologies that use renewable energy are currently experiencing the highest growth rate in the world. Mexico is no exception. Over the last decade and currently the energy reform led to the development of the energy sector, currently there are 10 major private companies engaged in the production of renewable energy, who sell both CFE (Federal Electricity Commission) as direct producers, and production equipment to businesses and individuals. Mexico has initiated a way to diversify fuels used in electricity generation. The intensive use of fossil fuels has impacts on energy security by the volatility of prices and availability of fuels, the environment by the emission of greenhouse gases and health.
It is for this reason that in Mexico recently, legislators and government have developed various policies, laws, rules and regulations to promote the rational use of nonrenewable resources and increase the implementation of energy sources that cause less environmental impact, such as renewable energy. In the latter context, the use of solar energy could play an important role.

Various energy planning documents developed and / or supported by several national and international organizations and actors such as the Ministry of Energy (Secretaria de Energia), bilateral cooperation agencies, research centres, NGOs, associations and representatives of civil society and private industry, have highlighted the enormous potential for Mexico to take advantage of the solar resource, both for thermal applications such as electricity generation.

In the case of electricity generation, international experience shows that PV systems require some form of intervention by the authorities conducting energy policy to overcome the obstacles and create a market that will accelerate their development.

2. Objective

This chapter analyses the renewable energy industry, specifically solar and photovoltaic (PV) panels. While a new industry and an emerging market in Mexico, it is also a potentially growing market niche, making it a sector of business potential which is economically viable. The period of analysis oscillates between 2000 and 2013. This work is focused on the review and analysis of the renewable energy sector since the operation of the technology, its application, its current market, and chronological development, immersing foreign and national investment as well as the sale and production of PV equipment. The present study investigates these aspects using techniques such as Herfindal-Hirshman Concentration Index (HHI) and Pascual concentration indices, also game theory.

The research questions are: What are the main features of the RE market in Mexico? What is the industry outlook both in development and production? And who are major investment companies in the photovoltaic industry in Mexico.

3. Background

According to the National Association of Solar Energy (ANES), until 2006, virtually all PV systems installed in Mexico, were in isolated applications of the grid and electrical network, rural electrification, communications, signage, water pumping and cooling. However, from the year 2007 there are records of applications connected to the grid and electrical network. This trend has continued in subsequent years so that in 2011, of 3.5 MWp installed in that year, about 94% were connected to the electricity grid systems. The annual installed capacity, systems isolated and connected to the network, has shown a fluctuating behavior in the period 2005 -. 2011 In cumulative terms, the increased capacity of 16.5 MWp to 32 MWp. Regarding the annual electricity generation of 23,235 MWh is increased in the year 2005 to 44.974 MWh in 2010.

4. Description of technology

Although until the middle of last century, the use of solar energy to generate electricity materialized its first applications, mainly during the early space race between the U.S. and the former Soviet Union, the phenomenon that gave origin was observed by first time over 100 years ago. This phenomenon, called "photovoltaic effect," generally speaking, can be explained as follows:

A. When sunlight shines on two layers of semiconductor material, that is, those that conduct electricity only under certain conditions, this causes the release of electrons which flow from the bottom layer toward the top of the semiconductor;

B. On passing the electrons (electricity) through one or more electrical loads (e.g. a lamp) then they give up their energy;

C. Finally, the process is repeated to re-combine the electrons with the semiconductor material of the top layer .

Today this phenomenon is exploited by using small plates, called photovoltaic cells, which are made primarily of silicon, one of the most abundant elements on earth. The arrangement comprises a number of these cells encapsulated and electrically connected in series and / or parallel, mounted on a support structure, is called photovoltaic module or panel. A set of these panels are usually mounted on stands or structures, but today can be integrated as elements of shade, or even as part of the facades of some buildings.

A special feature of PV is that electricity is delivered as a direct (or continuous) stream, so that connection to the main electrical networks is still necessary to transform in alternating current, the form how the CFE delivers electricity in in homes. It is for this reason that in order to harness solar energy, in most cases, it requires an inverter, which along with other electric components form what is called a photovoltaic system. One of the main advantages of PV systems is that maintenance costs are low throughout life, approximately 20 years for PV modules. However, their initial investment costs are still high compared with other technologies; although the costs of operation and maintenance are virtually null compared to the costs of generating electricity. It is expected that both their investment and generation costs continue to decline significantly over the next few years.

There are two markets that can harness solar energy for electricity generation: the interconnected electric systems and network or autonomous isolated systems.

A. Interconnected systems to the electricity network

They are found mainly in urban or rural areas, which are interconnected to the National Electricity System (SEN). These systems consist of the following components:

1) Panel or PV array
2) Current inverter
3) Interconnecting devices, protection and measurement, switches, protection system and bidirectional meter.

B. Isolated systems

Isolated systems are characteristic of rural or isolated areas, where it is not

economically feasible to construct a grid interconnection with SEN. These systems consist of the following components :
1) Panel or PV array
2) Bank and battery charger
3) Interconnecting and protection devices.
4) Current invertor. Rev. Optional, for alternating current loads.

C. PV isolated system Unlike the SEN interconnected systems, these do not require a measurement device. However, additionally require a battery bank and a controller to store the electricity that will be used at other times in the photovoltaic system cannot generate, for example, at night.

 PV isolated system Source: alternativas nuestras invest in PV projector, still behind China and Singapore, because it is part of the Sun Belt. These are countries with latitude + -35 with respect to Equator and exhibit higher levels of solar and sunlight radiation of the planet. For Mexico, there are areas where there is a greater 5kWh per m2 radiation. Attraction also includes other factors such as market potential, politics, business environment, financial stability and renewable energy policies. The size of the electricity market, its projected growth in electricity consumption in the next 2 decades and its competitive cost of PV technology also cover electrical networks and their ease of distribution, among others .

Mexico currently has an installed capacity of 33 MW in solar PV projects, mainly in applications of rural and industrial electrification. Currently there are several construction and development projects of this kind that would have an installed capacity of 39.1 MW. In late 2011, a Spanish company called Siliken invested in a photovoltaic power project in Durango called La Manzana del Sol. The ame project has 100MW of installed capacity now in its first stage and who estimates that this would to have a total of 400MW in the five years after its initiation.

6. Market structure

A. Major PV companies in Mexico
Mexico is the leading supplier of photovoltaic modules in Latin America, with an annual production capacity exceeding 276 MW still above countries such as Chile, Brazil and Argentina. Among the leading developers of photovoltaic are: Abengoa, Abener, Del Sol Systems, Microm, Iberdrola and Silken.
1). Solar Thermo high concentration
Today in Mexico there are no operating plants using such technologies harnessing solar energy. However, in the state of Sonora is developing the project 171 CC Agua Prieta II, by CFE same that consists of a combined cycle hybrid system, 477 Mwe, and a thermal solar field trough parabolic channels with a power of 14 MWe. It is expected that this central enter into operations in 2014-2015 .
Growth potential of solar thermal energy in Mexico Source IIE
 The national energy sector has grown since early 2000 to late 2013 and can be seen as the sector photo voltaic energy barely appeared in the outlook in mid-2012 producing

only 0.01 of energy and being less 1% of its development potential .

B. Share of renewable energy companies in Mexico

The following table shows the number of companies participating in the market for 2009, according to INEGI. IT can be appreciated that for this year are 65 companies involved in this market segment. Gross production for 2009 amounted to a total of 450,968,876 units, with a total investment of 29,504,562 bp generated a total income of 522 313 705 million, and given the figures we also see that there are 27 companies that dominate this market goes to 77.07% of it.

C. Concentration index segment

In the table below it is shown the participation of companies in the renewable energies sector, also there are calculations of the Herfindal-Hirshman Concentration Index (HHI). For 2009 were also calculated by size of enterprise, the data give an HHI of 0.60 that is a monopolistic competition because 27 of the 65 companies control the market hogging the 77.07% of the market, leaving only one 22.93% for all other companies.

Nonetheless, economic theory tells that the market tends to be from monopolistic to oligopoly due to the size of companies and the influence they have in the market competition.

This relatively new market and little taken into account is a tempting niche for the large firms because consumers are almost all the same, houses, apartment buildings, hospitals, businesses, hotels, sport clubs, government projects, solar parks and even the producers themselves would benefit because costs would be lowering. It is known that the solar energy market in Mexico ascents amount millions of dollars, of which 30 belong to photovoltaic.

Because it is an emerging market that is relatively new, turns out to be extremely profitable for all companies making the development and growth of this focus solely on their production costs, and market strategy.

7. Costs

Photovoltaic systems in network connection in Mexico differ in cost depending on its capacity. In late 2011 SENER and GTZ conducted a survey to stakeholders and actors in the country to determine these costs. For the residential sector where the average investment for PV systems with a capacity between 0.24kWp to 1.65kWp is U.S. $ 4.851 / kWp with leveled costs of U.S. □ 17.8/kWh. Meanwhile costs for systems with capacities between 2kWp to 10kWp are reduced U.S. $ 3,000 / kWp - 4,200 / kWp and leveled generation costs range from U.S. □ 10.9/kWh (Mx $ 1.3) and U.S. □ 15.4/kWh (Mx $ 1.8). By early 2014 these costs were reduced to 1100 dlls.

It is estimated that the average lifespan of photovoltaic panels is 25 years useful to 100% and up to 35 years total lifetime. And it is estimated that the initial investment is recovered in the medium term between 3 and 6 years after purchase.

8 Regulatory frameworks for renewable energy

Currently the following legal and regulatory instruments allow the use of solar

PV grid connection

A. General Law on Climate Change

On June 6, 2012 this law was published in the Official Gazette Diario Oficial de la Federacion, which has among its purpose to ensure the right to a healthy environment and to establish the occurrence of powers of the three branches of government in the development and implementation of public policy on two guiding themes: Climate change adaptation and mitigation of emissions and greenhouse compounds.

B. Law on the Use of Renewable Energies and Financing of Energy Transition (LAERFTE) and its regulations.

In late 2008 this law was published in the Official Gazette Diario Oficial de la Federacion, which has the purpose to regulate the use of renewable energy for electricity generation for purposes other than the provision of public service. Its regulation was published in the Official Gazette of September 2, 2009, including more specific areas for compensation of renewable energy projects.

C. Interconnection Agreement for Renewable Energy and Power Cogeneration System in Small and Medium Scale.

On April 8, 2010, the Energy Regulatory Commission (CRE) published these model contracts in the Official Gazette, and is intended to establish the rights and obligations of a user that connects a source of renewable energy to SEN. These interconnection agreements are based on the principle of "net metering".

Interconnection Agreement for Renewable Energy of Collective Source or Collective System Small Scale Cogeneration contract (to be published by the CRE)

This type of contract applies to everything related to Small Scale generation described in the previous paragraph. With the characteristic that the collective source of electricity generation belongs to a group of generators, besides, the energy generated by the collective source. It is divided, for billing purposes, between the owners depending on the percentage of investment made by each of the owners. Since PV systems can reduce or stop suddenly generate electricity, for example, partially cloudy days, it is also necessary to establish a series of technical rules to avoid discomfort or harm to other users. For this, the CRE and CFE have developed a specific regulatory framework for interconnection technologies based on renewable sources such as photovoltaic systems:

1) Specification for low voltage interconnection of photovoltaic systems with capacity up to 30 kW (CFE G0100-04).

2) Annexes to the Interconnection Agreement in Medium Scale: Characteristics of measuring equipment and communication (Annex E-RMT) and technical requirements for interconnection (Annex ERD-T).

3) General Rules for Interconnection to SEN or permit generators with renewable energy or efficient cogeneration (published in the Official Gazette by the CRE,

the May 22, 2012).

In more graphic form below is shown how is composed the regulatory and policy framework for PV in Mexico, which consists of the following legal structure

Legal structure. Source: PROSOLAR SENER

In addition to public institutions (CRE and CFE) there are private institutions for issuing standards in the electricity sector such as the National Association for Standardization and Certification of the electricity sector that have issued Mexican Standards.

9. Conclusions

In the present work it has been observed how has been growing this renewable energy market considering the potential as an emerging market. Mexico is considered one of the most attractive countries to invest in this sector being considered as the 5th country with more possibility of development. Also it is seen that the HHI for 2009 is . 60 which tells that it is a monopolistic competition with a tendency to be oligopoly. The profitability of the sector is abundant, generating profits of more than double the investment for businesses.

This being concluded it can also determine that the investment for consumers becomes profitable from the 3rd and 6th year, with costs ranging between 1000 and 10000 dollars according to their size. Within the regulatory framework also see the growing legislative restructuring encouraged to developing different ways for both the private sector and the public.

References

1. CRE Comision Regulatoria de Energia (2012) www.cre.gob.mx/documento/1770.pdf

2. CONUEE/ GTZ, (2009) *Deutsche Gesellschaft fur Internationale Zusammenarbeit* (GIZ). www.giz.de.

3. Ruiz Jaimes, E. (2014). Energias renovables, el rumbo para Mexico. *El Economista* (Nota periodistica) http://eleconomista.com.mx/entretenimiento/2014/03/12/energiasrenovables-rumbo-mexico

4. INEGI CENSOS 2009 (Mexico 2014) http://www.inegi.org.mx/est/contenidos/espanol/proyectos/censos/ce2009/default.asp?s=est&c=14220

5. LGCC, DOF, (2012) http://tinyurl.com/LGCC-DOF

6. LAERFTE, DOF, (2008) http://tinyurl.com/947pccg

7. PENG (2012). *Negocios Globales*, Queretaro, Mexico segunda edicion CENEAGE

8. PROSOLAR SENER (Mexico, 2012) *Programa de fomento de sistemas fotovoltaicos en Mexico* www.energia.gob.mx

9. RLAERFTE, DOF, (2 de Septiembre de 2009) http://tinyurl.com/947pccg

10. SENER Secretaria de energia (2014)
http://egob2.energia.gob.mx/portal/electricidad.html
11. Saenz, G. (2007). *La Regulacion, Clave Para El Desarrollo De Las Energias Renovables*. SENER (2014). Universidad Autonoma De Madrid,
http://www.renovables.gob.mx/
12. Secretaria De Economia (Mayo, 2013). ProMexico Inversion y Comercio; Energias renovables, *Unidad de inteligencia de negocios*
http://mim.promexico.gob.mx/work/sites/mim/resources/LocalContent/42/2/130726_DS_Energias_Renovables_ES.pdf
13. Secretaria De Economia (2014). *ProMexico Inversion y Comercio*
http://mim.promexico.gob.mx/wb/mim/energias_perfil_del_sector
14. Secretaria de energia (Mexico, 2013). *Prospectiva del Sector Electrico 2013-2027*
http://sener.gob.mx/res/PE_y_DT/pub/2013/Prospectiva_del_Sector_Electrico_2013-2027.pdf
15. SENER Secretaria de energia (Mexico, 2013). *Prospectiva del Sector Electrico* 2013-2027 www.energia.gob.mx
16. SENER (Mexico, 2009). *Energias Renovables para el Desarrollo Sustentable en Mexico.*
http://www.energia.gob.mx/res/0/ER_para_Desarrollo_Sustentable_Mx_2009.pdf
17. SENER (Mexico, 2012). *Energias Renovables para el Desarrollo Sustentable en Mexico*. www.energia.gob.mx
18. Secretaria de Energia (Mexico, 2013). *Prospectiva del Sector Electrico* 2012-2026 Tercera Edicion. Ed. Fondo de Cultura Economica. Mexico.
http://sener.gob.mx/res/PE_y_DT/pub/2012/PSE_2012_2026.pdf

5.2 Green Economics: 10 Key Points

By Miriam Kennet

1. Green economics is provisioning for the needs all people everywhere, other species, nature, the planet and its systems, all as beneficiaries of economics transactions, not as throw away inputs.

2. All under pinned by social and environmental justice, tolerance and no prejudice and creating quality of life for everyone including future generations and all the current generations, including older and younger people.

3. Ensuring and respecting other species and their rights. Ending the current mass extinction of species. Ensuring biodiversity.

4. Non violence and Inclusion of all people everywhere including people with special needs and special ability. Ensuring all nations have equal access to power and resources. Local people to have control over their own destiny and resources. Increasing life expectancy, human welfare and per capita GDP in the least developed countries.

5. Ensuring gender equity in all activities. Educating, respecting, empowering women and minorities.

6. Ending current high mass consumption and overshoot of the planet's resources and returning to live within the comfortable bounds of nature in the climatic conditions under which human's built their civilisation. Choosing life style changes over techno fixes and eco technology. Lowering each of our own carbon usage, and living lightly on the earth. Changing how economics is done: from being an abstract mathematical exercise to embracing realism and the real world we all live in and share and in which we are all concerned stakeholders.

7. All people valued and respected equally

8. Poverty prevention

9. Climate change prevention, adaptation, mitigation. Protecting the most vulnerable from risk. Ensuring the future of small island states. Quickly reducing carbon per capita globally to 2 tonnes in the next 5 years and zero soon after. Limiting and reversing climate change. Moving to renewable energy sources.

10. Building a future- proofing economics to solve the current economics uncertainty and downturn which is suitable for the 21st century. Creating and nurturing an economy based on sharing, rather than greed and profit. Completely reshaping and reforming current economics to do all the above.

5.3 Ten Key Points for reversing the Trend of Climate Change

By Davide Bottos

One of the goals that drive us is to imagine a sustainable future. Global warming is perhaps the most dangerous threat, and must be stopped if we want to build a future. Most of the actions that we know are effective in this regard, must certainly be taken by governments. The International conferences on climate, however, show that the path is not easy. With the hope that China and the U.S. finally move the important step in the fight against global warming, while we can identify some key points that describe climate change. Most of these are related with our daily lives, so that we have the opportunity, with our behaviour, to act in a sustainable manner.

1. Reducing CO2 emissions

People can act by using public transport, car sharing, bike sharing, etc. and governments should promote them. But the majority of the Co2 emissions in the world (approximately 80%) comes from industrial activities. For that reason we have to try to eradicate the problem at its root, for example by increasing the supply of electricity from renewable sources for industries.

2. Stopping deforestation and overbuilding of natural territory

Everyone knows that the only living being capable of capturing CO2 is the plant. In the idea that we have of sustainable future, the plants are a key element, to preserve and, it would be desirable, to increase. For that reason is necessary to stop the actual trends of deforestation and overbuilding. This last point is also the main cause of many recent floods in Europe, in the U.S. and Indonesia.

3. Recycling

Even today, when a product runs out of its life cycle, it is often discarded and replaced with a new one. In most countries, even advanced, is no longer treated and ends up in dump. Here we have devoted a lot of scarce natural resources (eg, iron, plastic, etc.) so that they can not be reused. By the time it is easy to imagine that they will run out, so it is essential to reverse the trend by recycling as much as possible. Nobody throws a gold ring just they don't use it anymore. We should begin to have the same perception of the preciousness that we have for the gold, for all the other scarse materials.

4. Reusing

One of the failure of the free market is that it allows each one to transform natural resources into products which, once exhausted their life cycle, become unusable and are destined to dump. In order not to transform our world into a big dump, we must ensure that the products we use in everyday life do not run out once their cycle of life, but can continue to maintain their usefulness over time. Regulating productive activities and placing particular restrictions on products are necessary to stop the loss of utility of materials, such as iron and copper, but especially plastic products.

5. Promoting research

The man has always discovered new innovations and many of these have proved incredible in the past. It started with the fire, passing through the wheel and the language, up to the DNA. Each generation has the feeling that it can not go over the level of knowledge acquired. This impression, however, is significantly wrong and we must be confident that many current problems will be solved by future discoveries.

6. Promoting freedom of information

Some developing countries may not be aware of the trend of global warming and therefore not to adopt all the behaviors to prevent it. For this reason is fundamental, and this is one of the main goal of Green Economics Institute, promulgate the knowledge of these topics around the world. Nowadays we have internet, a powerful instrument that gives to everyone the opportunity to get in touch with anyone around the world. Therefore, each of us may contribute inquiring first, and then informing.

7. Banning and regulating economic activities that pollute and destroy natural resources

There are products for which the packaging needs more materials (paper, plastic, etc.) than the products themself. By reducing the amount of packaging products, where they are not strictly necessary, we could preserve a significant amount of materials and natural resources (eg plants). Today we see that in the Mediterranean Sea the presence of fish products has been steadily declining. This is mainly due to unregulated exploitation and destruction of the seabed by boats. Without a law that preserves the marine ecosystem, it is threatened in its natural play.

8. Promoting renewable energy and energy efficiency

This point regards both states that people: governments can provide incentives to the production of electricity from renewable sources. They can also reduce energy inefficiency, for example by controlling the level of heating of the public locals. Nowadays anyone can install a solar panel on his roof (of course this has to be convenient). Moreover, in everyday life we can significantly reduce energy consumption (for example by using energy-saving bulbs, completely turning off appliances when not in use, etc.).#

9.Promoting investments in green economy

This point regards both states that people: governments can act creating laws to promote investment in «green» activities (for example by reducing taxes on green banks) and people can act in this way as well, such as choosing where to allocate their personal investments.

10. Controlling the growth of world population

In 1798, Thomas Robert Malthus assumed that «food production would increase in arithmetic progression against population's geometric progression, keeping us on the brink of insufficiency». This theory has been much discussed and it still is today. What we can be sure of, is that the earth is a finished place, so that the production of natural resources could grow up in the future, thanks to scientific discoveries, but can never reach infinity.

All these points are interrelated and should be considered together. They (or their absence) represent the current reasons of climate change and, at the same time, they suggest us how to act to stop global warming, biodiversity loss, waste of natural resources, pollution and all the other threats that make up the «climate change». For this reason we think that this historical period is both a period of serious crisis for our planet and a great opportunity to build for the first time a sustainable future.

Truly sustainable markets, those dedicated to the discovery, trading and distribution of *real value* would therefore, naturally:

Value thermodynamically optimisation – such that their use of energy and materials would be in alignment with the physical characteristics and limits of the planet with a focus upon 'entropic efficiency'.

Value abundance rather than scarcity – prioritising technologies and behaviours which deliver either *natural* (e.g. biologically-based) or *managed* (e.g. through closed loop stewardship) abundance.

Enhance natural vitality – valuing technologies and processes which make use of the planet's natural rejuvenative and productive abilities, learning from and utilising natural production techniques as the basis for their technological and industrial models.

Balance their interdependence – recognising and balancing the web of social interdependencies they exist within, seeking mutual equity within all relationships.

It is time for real value. It is time to value the abundance, vitality and interdependence of all that exists on this precious, irreplaceable planet. To move beyond the surface, sensational value of current market price and start to define and trade the real value which sustains us all.

Part 6: Young People and Education for Social Justice

6:1 Young people and the lost generation. An economics perspective from young people

By Adam Saleh

A symptom of the global economic downturn and global economic crisis of 2008 has been an ever increasing number of young people out of work; this is supported by the figures presented by the International Labour Organization (ILO 2012) which said in its report that out of some 620 million young people aged between 15 and 24 about 81 million were unemployed. This is the highest level in two decades of record-keeping by the organization (ILO 2012). Over the past year, movements of mass protest have taken hold all over the world, led largely by young people who felt as if their futures were being stolen from them. The "Occupy Now" slogan has become synonymous with the youth's rejection of a system which no longer seems able to guarantee them employment in a society plagued by financial scandals, bankruptcies, and crippling debts.

With almost one in four young people unemployed in developed countries, and the majority of young people from developing countries working in the informal economy, or the black market, the world is facing a serious youth unemployment crisis. This could eventually lead to greater social instability and unrest and may cause even greater resentment between the older and younger generations who already live in disharmony. There is a strong chance that instead of improving from generation to generation, living standards could in fact drop for the first time in centuries, condemning the next generation to experience a lesser quality of life than that enjoyed by the generation which preceded them.

Recently, Martina Milburn, chief executive of the youth charity, The Prince's Trust, said: "Young people are facing the bleakest jobs market for decades, which is crushing self-esteem and derailing ambition. We need to act now to ensure an unemployed generation does not become an unemployable one" (Operation Black Vote 2012). This quote exemplifies how a large number of young people around the world feel today, as they realize that the opportunities which were once available in the job market are now diminished due to a lack of investment and a slow economic growth in the world, particularly in the West. "Even in East Asia, perhaps the most economically dynamic region, the unemployment rate was 2.8 times higher for young people than for adults."

(Operation Black Vote 2012).

However, as the ILO report reveals, the true picture of youth unemployment is even more worrying as prospects look bleaker. Many young people are extending their time in higher education because they cannot find jobs, and sadly they are accumulating debts which they will spend years paying back, if they are lucky enough to find a job (ILO 2012).

Finding solutions to the problem of youth unemployment is crucial, and governments should put it at the top of their priorities, because as the worst hit group, young people are more likely to become involved in criminal activities or adopt anti-social behaviour, either out of despair or frustration. The Work Foundation based in the UK says more than 450,000 'NEETS' - youngsters Not In Education, Employment or Training – have never had a regular job. Simon Cox of BBC News said this word is "the latest buzzword for teenage drop-outs". He adds: "'NEETS' are 20 times more likely to commit a crime and 22 times more likely to be a teenage mum"(Cox 2005). It is not just a UK problem, because according to recent figures, unemployment among Europe's young people has soared by 50% since the financial crisis of 2008. It is rising faster than overall jobless rates, and almost half of young people in work across the EU do not have permanent jobs, according to the European Commission Department for Work and Pensions (2012).

In the case of most countries, the task of finding solutions to these global problems will not be an easy one. We now have a disaffected youth which is becoming more restless and is gradually sliding towards the extreme. We saw the first warning signs in London last year as the capital grappled with widespread rioting and looting.
The education system has, by all accounts, failed many young people. One of the ironies of the present education system is that all too often it neither prepares young people for work nor does it give them the right tools to help them navigate through unemployment. Studies tells us that the so-called 'soft skills', social and emotional literacy, knowing how to engage with others, showing initiative, tenacity, selfdiscipline, a sense of enterprise, can all make a difference, sometimes achieving more than the simple application of a high IQ (BBC 2012).
Innovative solutions are needed to address the problems across the world. In Germany, about 60% of the country's youth choose an apprenticeship over an academic education and most get paid doing it, effectively lowering the unemployment rate. Each year, 1.5 million youths in Germany are in an apprenticeship with a 90% success rate. A full time job is available after completion, with about half of them taking jobs from the company that trained them. This is a possible solution which is being considered in other EU member states but the problem it presents for many is the cost. Germany alone spends $1 billion per annum on the scheme (Mortimer 2012). However, governments face a political quagmire when trying to introduce these schemes. Across the European continent, the recession has caused a surplus of unemployed adult workers who are skilled and experienced, unlike the youth where the majority are less skilled and have little to no experience. In the UK companies like

TESCO faced significant public scrutiny after they were encouraged to adopt a government training scheme which allowed them to take on young people on benefits without paying them for 6 weeks and no guarantee of a job at the end of it. These where mainly unskilled jobs which did little to enhance the CV's of prospective candidates, and meant they ended up doing hours of shelf stacking for a 6 week period with no recompense (Department for Work and Pensions 2012).

Promoting labour-intensive sectors, such as green jobs, is key to generating employment opportunities for young persons, particularly in transition economies but the problem of funding and investment crops up again, because the money is just not there. Most countries have introduced, or were forced to introduce, as was the case for Greece, Spain, and Italy among others, tough austerity programmes to reduce their deficit. Does it mean that these countries need to wait for growth to improve before they embark upon new green projects which could create jobs? And does this also mean that a whole generation will need to be sacrificed to the vagaries of the stock markets and actions of profiteering multinational companies and banks? For the sake of posterity governments across the globe need to act quickly to ensure a generation of young people do not lose faith in democracy (Mortimer 2012). Governments must realise the importance of the green economy and green jobs and capitalise on the many advantages they will bring in the future. They most stop thinking about short term solutions and make sacrifices to ensure the youth of today are ensured a bright and fulfilling future (BBC 2012).

References
Department for Work and Pensions (2012) Boost for unemployed young people as Youth Contract opens for business. Last accessed 25.06.2012 at: http://www.dwp.gov.uk/newsroom/press-releases/2012/apr-2012/dwp031a-12.shtml
Mortimer, C. (2012) Young people are sick of being pushed around. Last accessed 26.06.2012 at: http://blogs.independent.co.uk/2012/06/25/young-people-aresick-of-being-pushed-around/
ILO (2012) Invest in youth or lose a generation, ILO says. Last accessed 25.06.2012 at: http://www.ilo.org/global/topics/youth-employment/lang--en/index.htm
BBC (2012) ILO warns of youth unemployment 'crisis' . Last accessed 26.06.2012 at: http://www.bbc.co.uk/news/world-europe-18155938
Operation Black Vote (2012) Unemployment figures rise again. Last accessed 25.06.2012 at: http://www.obv.org.uk/news-blogs/unemployment-figuresrise-again
Cox, S. (2005) "A 'Neet' solution". BBC News. Last accessed 25.06.2012 at: http://news.bbc.co.uk/1/hi/magazine/4158696.stm

6:2 Young Brazilians and Unemployment

By Professor Maria Madi (Brazil)

In the aftermath of the global financial crisis, the labour market has become a key variable in macroeconomic policies based on austerity programs. In addition, as a result of the business management actions, the labor market dynamics turend out to be subordinated to economic efficiency targets, that shape employment relationsoverwhelmed by longer working hours, job destruction, turnover and outsourcing.

Workforce displacement and loss of rights could also be part of the spectrum of management alternatives aimed at cost reduction (Goncalves and Madi, 2011). This scenario, characterized by precarious jobs mainly based on short-term contracts, has been enhancings the vulnerability of workers, mainly young people. In the current global context, in truth, many youth employment challenges could be thought as expressions of systemic tensions, both in the social and economic spheres, that have been deepen by the management of the financial crisis (The Economist, 2011).
As a matter of fact, the impacts of the 2008 global crisis in the Brazilian economy and society have also been affecting the access to work conditions of young people -between 15 and 24 years old - that amounted 33,433.710 persons in 2009. By analyzing the recent employment trends by age conditions, our aim is to highlight the specific trends of youth employment regarding the challenges for job creation and social inclusion.

Section one will briefly describe the Brazilian economic scenario and present the government responses to manage the impact of the international crisis. Section 2 will identify the current youth people employment trends and challenges. Finally, youth employment alternative policies are emphasized.

1. Aftermath of the global crisis and policies oriented to growth
Brazil is worldwide known not only for being one of the biggest world's emerging countries but also for having one of the world's highest income inequality levels. After the 1990s, social changes were driven by economic reforms and macroeconomic policies that promoted price stabilization and deepened the financial and trade integration into the world economy (Madi, 2004). In the last decade, policies related to credit access conditions, minimum wage and poverty reduction (mainly based on cash transfers) fostered higher economic growth rates in the 2000s. In this scenario, changes in the consumption structure were noted, particularly in lower income households. Regarding the labor market, lower unemployment rates were observed in a context where the government was enhancing further informal labour combat and the expansion of aggregate demand.
Considering the immediate impacts of the global crisis, the deterioration of private

expectations in Brazil provoked a fall in the levels of production and employment; an increase in the levels of stocks, a fall in the investment levels and liquidity constraints in the domestic credit and capital markets. The first signs of the global crisis on the Brazilian labour market appear to have been felt in October 2008, when there was an increase in the rate of expansion of employment. According to data from six main metropolitan areas in the seven months following the crisis - October 2008 to April 2009 - the proportion of workers unemployed rose from 7.5% to 8.9%, that is to say, an increase 1.4 percentage point. The first effects on formal employment were felt in the manufacturing industry and also in civil construction. Regarding the level of occupation soon after the global crisis, negative variations were observed for both men and women (OBIG, 2011). The highest level of unemployment turned out to be observed among young people when compared to adult labor force. In addition, the burden of unemployment was also more intense among women between September 2008 and May 2009.

These tensions shifted to the political sphere and led to economic policy responses in order to support economic growth. As a result, the levels of investment, production, consumption and employment were stimulated by a reorientation of monetary and fiscal government policies and actions. In this scenario, the government decided to stimulate the levels of domestic demand and supported the continuity of the process of income redistribution (Goncalves and Madi, 2011). The redefinition of credit strategies- oriented to households and corporations- was centered on the expansion of domestic credit flows by the operations of public banks (Banco do Brasil, Caixa Economica Federal and BNDES (National Bank of Economic and Social Development). In addition, policies implemented to support the domestic investment included: i) the maintenance of the investment path outlined in the Growth Acceleration Program (mainly infrastructure); ii) the expansion of Petrobras investments in the oil sector; iii) the launch/expansion of the housing program "Minha casa minha vida" (My house my life) oriented to civil construction and lower income classes (Sicsu, 2011). In this context, the government also stimulated capital inflows and Mergers and acquisitions turned out to be instrumental to the strategy to improve competitiveness.

Considering the people unemployed, the government extended the period of granting unemployment benefit and increased its value. Specific programs oriented to youth unemployment – such as the First Job- were expanded all over the country. In addition, the coverage of the cash transfer program – Bolsa Familia- was enlarged and the number of families involved achieved almost 2 million - in 2009 reached 12.4 million people (Sicsu, 2011). In this setting, the increase in the real minimum wage levels has been considered an important instrument of income distribution since it also impacts the income of a little more than two thirds of those receiving Social Security benefits (about 27 million people). As a result, soon after the global crisis, positive rates of households' aggregate consumption and government consumption supported the macroeconomic growth. Besides, the performance of the investment in civil construction contributed to face the impacts of the global crisis on the economic performance.

In the last two years, particularly after the worsening of the European financial situation, the Brazilian government has been enlarging the set of protectionist and anti-cyclical actions centered on the management of the domestic aggregate demand. Nevertheless, signs of internal stagnation in 2012 have turned out to be more clear while a wave of strikes all over the country have revealed social and economic tensions in the labor market.

2. Current youth employment trends and challenges
Green economics takes into account a "long-term, earth-wide and holistic context", where equity and inclusiveness could be understood within a multidisciplinary range of knowledge (Kennet and Heinemann, 2006) In fact, the importance of integrating population dynamics into this approach is crucial to promote effective government policies that requires the apprehension of the recent trends of the youth labor force participation and job creation.

According to ILO data, the labor force participation of young people in Brazil (14-25 years old), that is to say, the share of young people population that is actively engaged in the labour market by either being employed or looking for work, increased between 2000 and 2009, from 20,812.200 to 20,963.960, respectively. Beyond this soft quantitative growth, some important qualitative changes could be highlighted. The young female labor force increased from 52.1 per cent of the total young labor force in 1999 to 55.6 in 2009.

Nevertheless, when considering the male workers, the young male labor force participation decreased from 75.2 per cent the total young labor force in 1999 to 72.0 in 2009. This decline could be explained by better access to education. As a matter of fact, the effect of the educational level on the monthly earnings of male workers seems to be more relevant to characterize the distribution of earnings among men occupied. Consequently, more young men have been postponing their entry into the labour market in order to pursue their studies. In this scenario, the cash transfer program -Bolsa Familia - could have contributed to shape this new scenario.
Positive rates of job creation (formal contracts) were observed, particularly in the tertiary sector (trade and services), as the result of the domestic aggregate demand policies that, in fact, turned out to dampen the impacts of the global crisis on the Brazilian economy and society, Besides, the public policies oriented to support the expansion of investments in civil construction also enhanced a process of job creation with some displacement of men by women (OBIG, 2011).
Between 2008 and 2009, there was a decrease in the absolute number of young labour force (Table 1). Nevertheless, the rate of youth unemployment and the number of young people unemployed increased in that period. In this scenario, where there was an increase in the share of youth unemployed in youth population, the young female employment rate continued to be higher than the young male rate. In this context, the expansion of the cash transfer program- the Bolsa Familia- might have been decisive to

reduce young women's vulnerability since the cash transfers contribute to support minimum levels of their consumption basket. According to DIEESE (2011a), the number of women that benefit from the program reached almost 27 million people in 2010.

In spite of the increase in the youth unemployment rate, the trend to reduce the share of youth unemployed in total unemployment does not seem to have been changed between 2008 and 2009 (Table 1). This trend reveals that the Brazilian population has been aging. In fact, the growing rate of the population decreased from 3.04% per year in the period 1950-1960, to 1.05% in 2008. According to IBGE (2008) projections, the median age of the population could change from 20.20 years to 39.90 years, between 1980 and 2035, and may reach 46.20 years, in 2050. In the last decade, although young women increased their participation rate in the labor market, the female youth employment rate has been higher than the male youth rate. Young women challenges in the labor market could also be reinforced by the trend associated to a sex ratio that has been constantly falling after the 1970s (IBGE 2008).

In addition to the employment rate gap, young women are also facing a wage gap and increasing turnover. In truth, their participation is stronger as domestic workers, or even in services and trade occupations, where working hours are longer and wages lower. In spite of the highest educational levels of women compared to men (DIEESE, 2011a), the average nominal wages among women represented 72.3% of the average nominal wages of men in May 2009. The distribution of the female monthly earnings reveals the predominance of a situation where more than 80% of women -without education and with at least 14 years of education- earn up to two minimum wages. Evidences reinforce the wage gap since the effect of education on female monthly earnings are only significantly noticed when women study for more than 15 years. It is worth to highlight that in Brazil only 29% of women with more than 15 years of education earn up to two minimum wages DIEESE (2011a).

Table 1. Labor market in Brazil: indicators regarding young people (MF, 15-24 years old), 2000-2009

Year	Youth Labor force (1000s)	Youth unemployed (1000s)	Youth unemployment rate (%)	Adult unemployment rate (%)	Share of youth unemployed in youth population (%)	Share of youth unemployed in total unemployed(%)
2000	20,812.200	5,351.304	25.7	10.9	15.7	47.1
2001	20,755.810	3,713.021	17.9	6.4	11.1	48.6
2002	21,313.210	3,837.002	18.0	6.1	11.3	49.7
2003	21,489.400	4,084.612	19.0	6.7	11.9	48.4
2004	22,217,490	4,010,595	18.1	5.9	11.5	49.8
2005	22,846.880	4,419.598	19.3	6.1	12.6	50.8
2006	22,048.330	3,910,865	17.7	5.6	11.3	49.1
2007	21,490.590	3,605.026	16.8	5.6	10.7	46.4
2008	21,193.840	3,284.221	15.5	4.8	9.8	47.2
2009	20,963.960	3,736.011	17.8	5.7	11.2	45.3

Notes: Young people: 15-24 years old; Adults: +25 years old; MF; male and female; Labor force participation: the share of young people population that is actively engaged in the labour market by either being employed or looking for work.

Source: ILO

One relevant challenge that affects the level of earnings of the young working people is the increasing turnover in the Brazilian formal labor market where the short duration of a large share of employment contracts is one of the characteristics of the formal labour market. The total number of contracts with less than one year duration increased its participation in the formal labour market, representing 39.3% of total contracts in 2000 and 43.4% in 2009. Taking account a systemic approach, the high annual turnover rate is mainly the result of "workforce adjustments" that have promoted by business management actions in a labor market environment that reinforces contractual flexibility (DIEESE, 2011).

3. Alternative youth policies for social inclusion
The global crisis scenario seems to have increased the challenges for the elimination of the existing youth inequalities in the labor market. The Brazilian government responses to the international crisis were not able to overcome the gap

between the adult unemployment rate and the youth one, in spite of specific programs oriented to youth employment. Otherwise, the challenges to youth employment include precarious jobs, mainly based on short-term contracts. The employment and wage gender gap are also part of the inequalities among the youth labor force. In the aftermath of the global crisis, the minimum wage policy and the cash transfer program have been decisive to dampen social vulnerability among young people, both men and women.

The apprehension of the Brazilian political and social reality is decisive to enhance alternative government responses that could privilege youth issues in the formulation of investment and job creation policies particularly in the aftermath of the global crisis. For example, credit allocation policies could be combined to youth employment targeting. In this sense, central banks could shape asset based reserve requirements to stimulate more youth employment (Epstein, 2007); otherwise, central banks could give preferential access to the discount window for financial institutions that aim to invest in or lend to organizations which will generate "more and better" youth employment.

This effort is crucial since the task ahead is to shape institutions toward sustainable and inclusive growth for future generations.

References

Cardoso, G. et al. Aftermath as culturas economicas da crise em debate. Lisboa. Editora

Mundos Sociais. 2011.

Departamento Intersindical de Estatistica e Estudos Socieconomicos (DIEESE) Anuario das Mulheres Brasileiras 2011. Sao Paulo. 2011a (access on 24/11/2011).

Epstein, G. Central banks, inflation targeting and employment creation. Economic and Labour Market Papers. Geneve. International Labour Organization. 2007.

Foster, J. B. A Failed System.The World Crisis of Capitalist Globalization and its Impact on China. Monthly Review, march 2009.

Goncalves, J. R. B.; Madi, M. A. C. Private equity investment and labor: faceless capital and the challenges to trade unions in Brazil. In: Serrano, M. et al. (ed.) Trade unions and the global crisis: Labour´s visions, strategies and responses. Geneve, Intenational Labour Office, 2011.

IBGE Brazilian Institute of Geography and Statistics Population Projection of Brazil, Social Communication, Rio de Janeiro, http://www.ibge.gov.br/english/presidencia/noticias/noticia_impressao.php? id_noticia=1272, 2008.

Kaul, I; Conceicao, P.; Le Goulven, K. and Mendoza, R. (eds.) Providing public global goods: managing globalization. UNDP, New York, Oxford University Press. 2003.

Kennet, M. and Heinemann, V. (2006) Green Economics: setting the scene. Aims, context, and philosophical underpinning of the distinctive new solutions offered by Green Economics Int. J. of Green Economics, Vol. 1, No.1/2 pp. 68 – 102.

2006 Madi, M. A. C. Financial Liberalization and Economic Policy Options:

Brazil, 1994-2003. Texto para Discussao, IE/ UNICAMP. 2004.
Madi, M. A. C. and Goncalves, J. R. B. Stabilizing an Unstable Economy by Hyman Minsky, International Journal of Green Economics, Vol. 2, No. 3, 2008.
ILO http://kilm.ilo.org/KILMnet/view.asp?t=Table%2010.%20Youth %20unemployment%20(by%20sex)&I=K10&C=|BR|&Y=*&S=|1||2||3|
Observatorio Brasil da Igualdade de Genero (OBIG). A crise economica internacional e os (possiveis) impactos sobre a vida das mulheres. Nota Tecnica http://www.ipea.gov.br/sites/000/2/boletim_mercado_de_trabalho/mt40/04 _NT_crise.pdf. 2011 (acess on 24/11/2011).
Sicsu, J. Licoes da crise de 2008-2009: o que o Brasil deve fazer agora? http://www.diap.org.br/index.php/noticias/artigos/18845-licoes-da-crise-de-2008-2009-o-que-o-brasil-deve-fazer-agora. 2011. (access on 24/11/2011)

6:3 Youth's struggle for change

By Eleni Courea (Cyprus)

Introduction

In one of J. M. Barrie's lesser known plays, Ernest Crichton announces teasingly: "I am not young enough to know everything." And perhaps youth does know everything – or else it likes to think so. In a different context, George Bernard Shaw declares: "Youth is a wonderful thing. What a crime to waste it on children."

Indeed, the power of young people is often forgotten. Our unfaltering confidence in our opinions is dismissed as arrogance. We are deemed temperamental, inexperienced and ignorant until we reach our thirties, at least. It is important, therefore, to realise not only what green economics can do for young people, but what young people can do for green economics. As always, the world is plagued with problems. The international economy is flailing under the Great Recession—considered by many to be the worst financial crisis since the Wall Street Crash—which led to the crises in Portugal, Ireland, Greece and Spain.

In the Middle East, we have witnessed the uprising of thousands of people against the oppressive dictatorial regimes which have governed the nations of Egypt, Tunisia, Libya, Yemen and Syria (among others) for decades. With these affairs in mind, many do not seem to realise the role young people have played, and how we are affected more than anyone else.

Financial Crisis

Within the last 60 years, the proportion of 16-to-19-year-olds with regular jobs remained consistent at around 40%. This figure even rose to a relatively high 45% in the year 2000. As a result, almost 7.3 million teenagers were employed, full- or parttime. But at the turn of the 21st century, something changed. The number of teenagers employed began dropping dramatically, with young people being expelled from the workforce. And although from 2000 to early 2008 overall employment rose by about 10 million jobs, teen employment dropped by more than 1.5 million. In this day and age, the job market is difficult for everyone, but the youngest workers are by far the hardest-hit. Half the young people aged 16 to 24 now seeking a job cannot find one.

"The numbers are incredible," according to Andrew Sum, a US expert on teen employment, "Proportionally, more kids have lost jobs in the last few years that the entire country lost in the Great Depression." Even darker is the revelation that, in the United States, there has been a sharp rise in youth suicide as a result of the recession.

Arab Spring

In this bleak financial situation, is it any wonder that the public—and especially youth —is discontented with the government? In the Middle East, financial hardship in combination with oppressive dictatorships set off the large-scale and ongoing revolution. It's no coincidence that the revolution was initiated by countries with little oil revenue (Egypt, Tunisia) and was most successful there, when compared with the struggle in oil-rich countries. In Libya, for example, Gaddafi can afford to bribe supporters and pay troops with money from his sources of "black gold".

What is surprising about the uprising is that it all began from one of the smallest Arab countries, Tunisia. Even more incredible is how—in essence—the entire uprising was sparked by one young man, a 26-year-old street vendor named Mohamed Bouazizi, who set himself on fire in protest of police corruption and ill-treatment. This set off multiple demonstrations which evolved into the Tunisian Revolution, and consequently the Arab Spring.

With the expulsion of President Ben Ali from Tunisia and President Mubarak from Egypt came the spread of the revolution throughout the Middle East. It is common knowledge that none of this would have been made possible without the internet and the emergence of modern-day social networks. It is wrong, however, to cite such websites as the reason why the revolution has spread—a gun does not fire a bullet of its own accord. It is young people in the Middle East who took the initiative and used Facebook, Twitter and Youtube as their medium to spread the fight for liberty and justice to neighbouring countries.

It is now undoubtable that youth played the key role in the Arab Spring. From 26-year old Mohamed Bouazizi, the first man to turn against the authorities, to the rapidly growing and disproportionately large population of young people (the "youth bulge") in the Arab world, it is the youngsters who are at the frontline of the fight for democracy.

Where Green Economics Comes In

Clearly, however cliched the phrase has become, young people are the future. We are hungry for change and we are the ones full of energy and determination to create a better world for ourselves and future generations to live in. What we need is a medium to help us make these changes, something beyond the biases of politics and the media. This is where Green Economics comes in. It can be used to tackle issues which conventional economics has so far failed to address. It could even find a solution to the major woes of the sovereign debt crisis, the depleting sources of fossil fuels, the rise of nuclear energy. It brings in a fresh perspective, seemingly providing us with a view of our planet through brand new eyes.

Likewise, Green Economics itself needs someone to advocate it, someone to use the means it provides us with to build a better future. Within the very first years of a new millennium, conventional economics has failed us. We can see with our own eyes the corruption and poverty which is widespread throughout the third world, crippling the entire continents of Africa, Asia and South America, and threatening to spread to

formerly prosperous countries such as Greece. The injustice is clear, with a gaping development gap which is only growing wider, with dictators in some countries basking in their riches while their own people are scavenging for food. Huge expanses of rainforests continue to be cleared incessantly; oil and toxic waste is constantly spewed into our oceans, polluting our water, the very essence of life. The time has come for green economics to make a stand: and young people are the ones who can initiate it.

Conclusion

Our generation was first defined by a more peaceful revolution: *Generation Z*, hit by a technological revolution which brought us modern touch-screen mobile phones, laptops and all sorts of gadgets, the newest of which all revolve around Internet access and Social Networking. This recent wave of young people has been heavily criticised for being fixated with technology, for doing nothing but sit at home in front of a widescreen TV, for spending hour after hour surfing the net, for never going out to change the world. But we have become the first to achieve a revolutionary change without leaving the house.

Thus today's youth will be able to take pride in its actions and tell it's children: "When I was your age, I found a job during the recession because of my knowledge with computers." "When I was your age, I created my own website from scratch and ended up earning thousands." "When I was your age, we used the internet to start a revolution."

References

The Admirable Crichton – J.M. Barrie http://books.google.co.uk/books?lr=&ei=5eYnTqnMG4PoUOC_gJkN&client=firefoxa&cd=1&as_brr=0&as_drrb_is=b&as_minm_is=0&as_miny_is=1800&as_maxm_is=0&as_maxy_is=1920&id=ulpJAAAAMAAJ&dq=%22not+young+enough+to+know+everything The Arab Spring http://www.guardian.co.uk/world/interactive/2011/mar/22/middle-east-protestinteractive- timeline
http://www.usip.org/publications/youth-and-the-arab-spring
http://www.lemonde.fr/cgi-bin/ACHATS/acheter.cgi?offre=ARCHIVES&type_item=ART_ARCH_30J&objet_id=1151265&clef=ARC-TRKD_ 01 The Arab Spring and Social Networks
http://www.miller-mccune.com/politics/the-cascading-effects-of-the-arab-spring-28575/ http://www.newsweek.com/2011/01/27/inside-egypt-s-facebook-revolt.html http://www.fastcompany.com/1720692/egypt-protests-mubarak-twitter-youtubefacebook-twitpic Generation Z
http://www.smh.com.au/news/parenting/children-of-the-techrevolution/2008/07/15/1215887601694.html George Bernard Shaw Quote
http://www.quotationspage.com/quote/30143.html
http://quotationsbook.com/quote/45094/
http://www.1-famous-quotes.com/quote/7528
Great Recession http://www.guardian.co.uk/business/2009/jan/26/road-ruinrecession-individuals-economy

http://www.mcclatchydc.com/2009/01/27/60822/congressional-budget-officecompares. Html Mohamed Bouazizi
http://www.nytimes.com/2011/01/23/weekinreview/23worth.html?_r=1&src=twrhp
Young People in Great Recession
http://www.time.com/time/magazine/article/0,9171,1952331,00.html
http://www.frumforum.com/how-will-great-recession-shape-youth
http://www.huliq.com/10282/recession-wake-finds-more-youth-suicide-and-othersputting-life-hold

6:4 Why Green Economics is Important for Young People

By Miriam Kennet and Miriam Prasse

Some young people today have a much better understanding than previous generations about the importance of protecting nature and stopping climate change. Other young people don´t really care, think that they personally won´t be affected and that it is only a problem for their children´s children. However, this generation of young people is actually going to be the one which experiences the strongest and sharpest effects of the links between the economic crises, the ecological crisis. This will be at the same time as current costly mass extinction of species and catastrophic climate change. This means today´s that young people will find it hard to get jobs. Because of the current economic crisis, there is huge uncertainty, massive swings between inflation, deflation and commodity prices are skyrocketing. This generation is the first one where the pension is not guaranteed.

There are fewer and fewer young people in Europe and more and more older people to support. The birthrate is declining in the west and older people are living longer, so each young person will need to actually do even more for the community. The benefits and proceeds of their work will need to be shared by the state much more widely and especially with older people. Due to the current mountains of debt and toxic assets in most countries, the underlying concept of a pension and the economic and financial viability of a pension as an instrument is now in question as many schemes are technically bankrupt and wont be able to pay out when the time comes anyway. Problems seem to be almost endemic within the conventional economic framework where huge infrastructure decisions have been placed in the hands of very few decision makers. This has led to corruption on a world scale and an unimaginable mess which this generation will have to sort out. This is the generation which will have to reinvent economics so that it becomes once again a useful tool to provision for everyone's needs, not just the wealthy few. What is needed is planning for the community and its needs and those of the poorest and most vulnerable. Economics is no longer just about wealthy western white educated males (homo economicus) deciding on their spending preferences according to some graphs and statistics well away from the real world.

A man in a business suit is no longer the pinnacle of human evolution. Economics has to be about access and benefit for all. Women form half the global population but are 70% of the worlds poor and own only 1% of world assets. The future will be mixed and diverse with access to economics for everyone and everything. The rhea bird laying its eggs, the women threshing corn to feed the community will have equal, if not greater weight than the man in a suit, fiddling with equilibrium graphs. Real world and real economies are what matter in this new world. Recent major reports on climate change (Stern 2006) show that the cost of climate change prevention are between one per cent and twenty per cent of global GDP, depending on whether or not we act in time. The cost of the current species loss is actually seven times higher still. (TEEB report UN: Sukhdev 2008)

Poor people are much more dependent on nature and much more vulnerable to global environmental change, to extinction events and to global warming. According to a recent article in the New Scientist magazine, much of the planet will become uninhabitable for people and useless for farming. We will all be squeezed into the temperate climate zones as well as into the UK, Scandinavia and into the north and south Polar regions. Sea level rise may be around 3 metres (currently whole countries like the Maldives are saving up money in order to buy new land on which to relocate). Courrier International no. 968 (Nossiter 2009) described a truly shocking and disturbing vision of the future for us all if we don't act to clean up our activities. This dangerous outcome results from a combination of climate change and poverty, a situation which we might all face, if we don´t find a solution to the combination challenges of the global economic downtown and the ecological crisis. In Dakar this week, little 7 years old Aba Dione died when he was playing at his hometown of Ville de Pikine, Senegal. This town is plaged by disastrous pollution. There is 4 metre thick foundation layer of toxic, plastic bottles, cloths, bags, sandals and mud, rubbish and human waste on which goats graze and little children play in the toxic and dangerous stench. All of this makes breeding grounds for swarms of flies. The waste foundation layer is vital to stop the regular flooding of peoples' houses and to lift the floors and rooms up out of the encroaching and rising waters which cause cholera, malaria, yellow fever and tuberculosis. A horrific choice. Nothing shows more clearly the absolute links between poverty, climate change and human activity and our absolute responsibility to each other. No one should have to live like that. Economics times of plenty in the west allowed such conditions to go unnoticed and unmitigated amongst the world's 1.5 billion global poor. This is a shocking legacy of the years of "plenty and global economic growth" In the current more frugal and less wealthy years to come, we need to sort out this kind of mess, where some have "everything" and others have nothing.

This generation is the one that is going to pay for the activities of previous generations without necessarily even experiencing those benefits. Ironically this generation has grown up in Europe as some of the richest ever in terms of conventional wealth. However they have now inherited tons of debt and the dwindling bundle of natural resources, they will receive with which to repay that debt, is now at a turning point and is starting to become exhausted.

Green economics has entered the picture as a ray of hope in this bleak landscape. It is a school of economics with proper solutions, and in which intergenerational and intra generational equity are at the very core. It takes a very long term view of what economics is. It uses long term environmental change data compiled from statistics, describing millions of years of earth cycles and thousands of years of global environmental change to inform its decision making. This is completely different from the current fashionable school of "business studies" which often runs economics at universities. Business studies uses periods as short as one month to decide on investment criteria, or politically only looks as far as the next election, which is usually held within 5 years.

Green economics explores benefits and costs for future generations and takes a precautionary view of uncertainty, never going beyond a tipping point or a point of irreversibility. It maintains safe minimum standards of natural resources and seeks to never exhaust natural capital. It maintains a balance between people and the planet so that natural capital can always be replenished safely. In terms of Sustainable Development Economics it seeks to be in the strong sustainability camp, in that it does not believe that human made products can substitute for natural ones in most cases. Humans cannot construct a rain forest or a tree, only nature can do that. We need to stop destroying what nature has grown for us and to stop destroying what it has provided us with to meet our own needs. We need to stop fouling our nest and to conserve, reuse, recycle and repair and if necessary not to use things we cannot replace. We need to harness the intrinsic value of sharing and of equity and the existence value of what we want on the earth; rather than totally human and short term centred ideas of use value and short term economic benefits. Nature is not simply there for our own ecosystem services. It has a deep and important intrinsic value of its own, much of which can't be measured. We should not only care for and not only save what we can measure or what this generation can use. We must adopt a more sophisticated attitude to the earth and its systems, not plunder everything just because we can.

Mainstream economics suggests that we use discounting as a methodology to allow us to disregard the future, as it might not happen. This allows cost benefit analysis and net present value to justify stealing from future generations. It means we can spend their natural resources without replacing them. It also accepts private and public financing initiatives for huge infrastructure projects, which mean that this current generation of young people will have to pay for not only what they themselves use but all the projects used by recent previous generations. However unfortunately we are now at that future cross roads as many of these large projects do now have to be paid for. All within a shrinking real economy and with depleted natural capital. The problem is that this continuous economic growth a) has stopped and b) for most people it did not lead to either happiness nor increases to well being. For example in a recent UN study, young people in the UK were once again amongst the most miserable in Europe but the were ironically, also amongst the richest. This shows that money does'nt buy anyone happiness.

In fact most increases to real wealth happen outside the formal economy. These include making new workers or people, making open source software, creating well being through human relationships, caring for older people, caring for younger people. Many of these happen well away from the formal economy today. Now Green Economics suggests that all of these should be shown as the factors of real world

economics and that they should be valued and resourced. Women s work, caring work and natural capital must be valued and resources not exhausted or depleted.
Green Economics helps young people to see themselves as part of a local and a global community and to implement a new vision for the future in which they themselves are starting to have a staring and a crucial role in shaping the future. They have an absolutely central role in preventing further poverty, in solving climate change and in helping themselves in their own future. Green Economics creates a common purpose to reach a common and global vision but it is a vision which is diverse and appropriate in its own way for each human community and for each natural community of the biosphere.

In fact now this generation of young people are going to play the most crucial, critical, fundamental and pivotal role in the very survival of our species. This is a massive responsibility for our young people but also a huge opportunity to be the generation that turned its back on repressive and destructive ideas and move towards something much more exiting and more positive. The green economics future is much more hi tech and much more interesting. Green Economics, the newly emerging school of economics, helps and equips young people in order to meet this historic challenge. By expanding the scope of what is included in economics and guiding us towards a better future, perhaps even the only future on offer, Green Economics is offering an exiting, high tech, progressive and a truly sustainable future, provisioning for all human needs and those of other species, the biosphere, the planet and its systems. Lets embrace it and move towards its sustainable economic agenda.

This chapter was originally published in "Ecosprinter,"the magazine of the Young European Greens, as part of a Green Economics Institute, training course in Berlin on green jobs.

6:5 A Young person's view from Asia

By Norfaryanti Kamaruddin

Green Economics and its implementation in Asia is a very topical subject as it concerns a very large and increasing number of people working in this area. It covers a wide range of topics, including dynamic innovation in greening business, information technology and communication, technology trends, gender equality in Asian economies, the green built environment, climate change and sustainability, social justice, and biodiversity.

Asia, being the largest continent has the largest population in the world and it had 4.1 billion in 2009, which constituted 60% of the total world population in 2009. Most of the Asian countries are still undergoing development. This is becoming more challenging as the world is facing triple-e crisis; economy, energy and environment, which Asian countries need to overcome at the same time.

China is trying to manage its economy sustainably by incorporating "Green Tech" approaches. This book highlights China's experience in trying to greening their economy as well as initiatives by other Asian countries such as India, Turkey, Malaysia, Bangladesh and Bhutan. Asian countries mostly have their own unique way of managing and developing their economies. This is due to the diverse cultural and political situations in each country. This diversity could be an advantage and disadvantage, depending on how each person might look at it.

There are many reports highlighting gender inequality in Asia. According to Helen Clark in the China Daily, achieving equality for women is not only a laudable goal but also a human right. It is also good Economics; it helps deepen democracy and enables genuine long-term stability. For example, the agricultural sector is a major sector in most of the Asian countries. Yet, very few women have any authority in it. Furthermore, according to the latest Human Development Report, almost half the adult women in South Asia are illiterate, a higher proportion than in any other region in the world.

On the other hand, Asia has some of the coldest and some of the hottest, some of the wettest and some of the driest places on earth. Asian countries are also among the biodiversity superstars – and are home to the majority of the Earth's species. Therefore, the effects of climate change have strong impacts all around Asia. For example severe effects of recent earthquakes, tsunamis, and floods are happening in Asian countries.

Therefore, Asian countries are in a position to benefit from the wider scope and innovation in adopting Green Economics approaches. Green Economics reclaims economics and provisioning for the needs of everyone and everything on the planet, other species, nature, the planet and its systems. It is used for progression and sharing.

6.6 The Pitfalls of Economic Modelling
An economics student's critique

By Max Basta

All economic models are reductive by nature. A model serves to explain the workings of the real world in a way economists can understand, and then to provide basis for claims about the future of the economy. If a model is desired to estimate the future price of car windshields, the model-maker might include past data about the price of car windshields, the cost of producing glass and the cost of the labour necessary to shape the glass into a flat, uniform sheet. The model-maker need not include the price of crude oil in her calculations as it is clearly irrelevant to her cause. She knows if she excluded the cost of producing glass her model would not yield a very good estimate of the price of car windshields. What she might not know is that the local sand quality affects the cost of producing glass, and causes less damage to car windshields on impact, thus consumers are willing to pay an increased price for car windshields in areas with higher sand quality because of their perceived longevity. Other model-makers sometimes make similar errors in their assumptions, and these assumptions bias their estimates in similar ways.

If the model assumes a value to be fixed, but in reality it is variable, the neglected variable may cause a different result in reality than predicted by the model. If a policy model mistakenly dismisses a negative externality as irrelevant, this negative externality will grow because of the lack of care taken by the state to prevent it.

If the model mistakenly dismisses a variable as irrelevant, the effects of this variable will become apparent when the model's estimate is found far from the true value.

If a model of GDP growth omits the environmental effects of concurrent greenhouse gas emissions, greenhouse gases will continue to accumulate so long as this model is pursued by policy makers.

If a model of consumer preferences fails to take into account the negative effects on quality of life of being bombarded by advertisements, the results will show that the consumer prefers certain goods and by inference prefers them to be advertised to her – even if she could and would prefer to live a life unsaturated by advertisements.

A model of preferences defines a consumption bundle as "a complete list of the goods and services that are involved in the choice..." (pp. 33 Varian) so that if the goods are (x1, x2) then x1 might be pineapples and x2 might be "a complete list of the goods and services" other than pineapples. Obviously, however, if 'breathable air' is included in this "complete" list then no sane consumer would consume pineapples. No sane consumer would consume anything if in doing so they would be knowingly substituting away from breathable air.

This alludes to a trans-economic assumption that priceless primary resources like breathable air are either a) excluded from models which excludes from policy consideration or b) included in models but given a financial or 'utility' value in order to make the model make sense when in fact their utility value is literally infinite. For this section Y stands for output, K for capital, L for labour and A for technological progress.

Blanchard's *Macroeconomics* pp. 248 defines technological progress as:

1) It can lead to larger quantities of output for given capital and labour. Think of a new type of lubricant that allows a machine to run at a higher speed and so produces more;

2) It can lead to better products. Think of the steady improvement in car safety and comfort over time;

3) It can lead to new products. Think of the introduction of the CD player, the fax machine, cell phones and flat-screen monitors;

4) It can lead to a larger variety of products. Think of the steady increase in the number of breakfast cereals available at your local supermarket.
A model of growth using a production function $Y = F(K,AL)$ assumes the growth rate of technological efficiency to be greater than zero. This implies an assumption that A has no upper bound.

Nowhere does the text examine the possibility of technological progress decreasing. It is simply assumed that A will continue increasing ad infinitum. However on pp. 260 Blanchard admits "The truth is that, despite a large amount of research, [the slow-down of technological progress in the mid-1970s] remains largely a mystery".

If it transpires that this assumption is flawed, and technological progress does stall, it follows that our estimated ability to tackle such devastating issues as climate change may be biased too.

References
Olivier J. Blanchard: Macroeconomics (4th edition) ISBN: 0-13-186026-7 234
Economics of Social Justice; A Handbook for Students
Hal R. Varian: Intermediate Microeconomics – A Modern Approach
(8th edition) ISBN: 978-81-7671-065-7

Part 7
7.1 The Philosophy of Social Justice in Nigeria's Green Economy Setting

By   Dr Chidi Magnus Onuoha

1 .Overview of the Nigerian Economy
Pre-Oil Era

During the pre- oil era, the non-oil sectors particularly agriculture, solid minerals and taxation were the main drivers of the Nigerian economy. In other words, the economy was dominated by primary products and solid minerals such as cocoa, groundnuts, palm oil, iron and tin, coal etc. These products had substantial shares of the world export market which kept the economy in good shape as it had capacity to generate financial resources required to fund the administrative cost of governance and developmental projects at both the centre and regions.

The Oil Economy

The discovery of oil and the subsequent oil boom of the 1970s led to the neglect and the ultimate collapse of the non oil sectors. Today, Nigeria is one of the striking examples of an undiversified and mono product economy in the world depending mainly on revenues from oil and gas despite her rich endowment in human and natural resources. Over the years, the Nigerian oil economy, has witnessed poor management and lost opportunities arising from wastage, loss of oil and gas revenue, poor governance structures, poor conservation planning, damage caused by oil spills, gas flaring, and the weak linkages between the upstream and downstream sectors of the industry.

It is a known fact that hydrocarbon is an exhaustible and non-renewable natural resource. It is also susceptible to vagaries of international market place whose price is volatile and can be influenced by external economic and political forces. The reserve-to-production(R/P) ratio based on some published data indicates about 43 years of crude oil proven reserves based on 2007 Wikipedia Report . With respects to natural gas, the R/P ratio is 236 years, based on proven reserves report of 2008(175 TCF). However, from technical stand point, only average of 30-40% of these reserves are recoverable under current technology, depending on natural characteristics of the crude, reservoir conditions and other factors, giving an effective R/P of approximately 15 years for crude oil and about 74 years for natural gas respectively.

Unfortunately, our oil and gas make only small contribution to GDP, despite generating the majority of export earnings, as it is a highly technology and capital intensive industry that employs few people. The materials and equipment used in the exploration and production are not produced in-country. There is minimal domestic manufacturing input in the oil sector, especially in the oil product refining. The local content makes up about 5% in goods and services.

2. The Inclusive Green Economy Approach and the Philosophy of Social Justice in Nigeria

According to the Central Bank of Nigeria (CBN), the oil sector had negative growth in the period between 2005 and 2007. Nigeria is endowed with all kinds of natural resources but is unable to translate it into secondary and tertiary production for domestic growth.

But inclusive growth as espoused by the philosophy of social justice is essential for three key reasons: to alleviate poverty, build livelihoods and improve quality of life. Nigeria became the largest economy in Africa, with a GDP of $510 billion as a result of the rebasing of her economy. The critical variables that influenced the new GDP were mainly within the domain of the non-oil sector particularly, agriculture, banking, telecommunication and entertainment.

Despite the economic and social progress which successive Governments announced, the country continues to face persistent, long term development challenges and poverty, as well as increasing negative impacts of economic activities on its resource base and natural environment. Similarly, unemployment and underemployment remain significant, especially among the youth and women. This evidence calls for re-appraisal and addressing the link between economic growth and poverty alleviation with a different approach. This is where **the Inclusive Green Economy Approach** comes in. This new approach is driven by three philosophies- social, economic and environmental justice and it seeks to overcome the ever deepening ecological and on- going development challenges. Most countries of the world are transiting to Green Economy and it has become imperative for Nigeria to follow suit.

For the purpose of this paper, we shall be looking at the philosophy of social justice in Nigeria's green economy setting, priority sectors that will expeditiously help drive it, and the critical factors that will enable these sectors achieve their targets. Before then let us understand what a green economy connotes and the building bloc underpinning it.

3. **What is Green Economy?**

Green Economy is defined as an economy that aims for sustainable development without degrading the environment and results in reducing environmental risks and ecological scarcity. This new economic vehicle holds much promise for Nigeria nay Africa. This is because mainstream (conventional) economics has provided no analytical framework to counter or even address numerous ecological problems such as climate change, deforestation, ocean surge, erosion, desertification, and depletion of biodiversity, as well as ending the age-long poverty scourge.

This new approach has also caught the attention of the United Nations whose definition of a Green Economy includes:

(i)   Ending market failure and the internalization of externalities;

(ii)   Systemic view of the economic structure and its impact on relevant aspect of sustainable development;

(iii)   Achieving social goals, for example job creation and examines ancillary policies needed to reconcile social goals with other objectives of economic policy; and

(iv)   Aligning macroeconomic framework and development strategy with the goal of identifying dynamic pathways towards sustainable development.

In other words, it is an approach that results in improved human well-being and social equity, while significantly reducing environmental risks and ecological scarcities. A green economy is low carbon, resource efficient and socially inclusive including by creating new jobs. Three economic sectors are the key to this effort: agriculture, energy and infrastructure.'

4. **The Building Bloc of the Philosophies of Social, Economic and Environmental Justice: The Ten Key Values in a Green Economy:**

The building bloc of the philosophies of social, economic and environmental justice are part and parcel of the ten key values in a green economy aptly identified and defined by the Green Economics Institute and are as follows:

i)   It aims to provide for the needs of all people everywhere, other species, nature, the planet and its systems, all as beneficiaries of economic transactions, not as throw away inputs.

ii)   This is underpinned by social and environmental justice, tolerance, no prejudice, and creating equality of life for everyone including future generations and all the current generations, including older and younger people.

iii)   Ensuring and respecting other species and their rights.

Ending the current mass extinction of species. Ensuring biodiversity.

iv) Ensuring non violence and inclusion of all people everywhere, including people with special needs and special abilities. Ensuring all nations has equal access to power and resources. Increasing life expectancy, human welfare, and per capita GDP in the least developed countries.

v) Ensuring gender equality in all activities. Educating, respecting, empowering women and minorities.

vi) Ending current high mass consumption and overshoot of the planet's resources and returning to live within the comfortable bounds of nature in the climatic conditions under which humans built their civilization. Choosing lifestyle changes over techno fixes and eco technology. Lowering our own carbon usage and living lightly on the earth. Changing how economics is done: from being an abstract mathematical exercise to embracing realism and the real world we all live in and share and in which we are all concerned stakeholders.

vii) Valuing and respecting all people equally.

viii) Poverty prevention. Climate change and instability prevention, adaptation, mitigation. Protecting the most vulnerable from risk. Ensuring the future of small Island States.

ix) Quickly reducing carbon per Capita globally to 2 tonnes in the next 5 years and zero soon after. Moving to renewable energy source.

x) Building a future-proofed to solve the current economic uncertainty and downturn which is suitable for the 21st century. Creating and nurturing an economic base on sharing, rather than greed and profit. Completely reshaping and reforming current economics to do all the above.

5. Targeted Priority Sectors to Drive the Philosophy of Social Justice Process in the Nigerian Green Economy Setting:

As stated earlier, the inclusive growth as espoused by the philosophy of social justice is essential for three reasons: it seeks to alleviate poverty, build livelihoods, and improve the quality of life. Much as all the sector of the economy has employment and improved standard of living prospects under the Nigerian green economy setting, however, there are targeted sectors that will drive the process and impact felt more and these include agriculture, energy and energy efficiency, infrastructure and procurement (control of corruption)

Agriculture:

The declared aims of Nigeria's national agricultural policy are to:

''attain food security; increase production and productivity; generate employment and income; and expand exports and reduce food imports thereby freeing resources for critical infrastructure development and delivery of social services''. Efforts of previous Federal Governments have been characterised as treating agriculture as a purely a development issue. The Jonathan administration attributed the unsatisfactory state of Nigeria's agriculture to a dominance of subsistence-orientation hence we witnessed a shift in policy concept, philosophy and approach to a business and commercial orientation.

Nigeria faces two central challenges to her agricultural sector and food security: population dynamics and climate change. With a population of 162 million people in 2011 and expected to increase between 230 and 430 million people in 2050. Urban population in 2011 grew by 51% and still growing, while the population of people earning less than US$2 per day in 2009 was 84%.

(a)Population Dynamics:

There are quite a number of lessons emerged from the current and projected future population dynamics of Nigeria with major implications for agriculture and food security and to be addressed by the philosophy of social justice in a green economy setting. These are:

(i)   Nigeria's population is growing, and the country's food security challenges will grow with it. At the current growth rate of domestic food production, Nigeria is unable to feed its growing population. Domestic food production will have to expand at a faster rate.

(ii)   Nigeria's urban population will soon outstrip the rural population. The population shift to urban centres is projected to become even more pronounced in the future. Despite its roots, the urban population is disconnected from production system and will rely on the market for food supply. This supply will have to come from domestic production or imported food.

(iii)   Youth make up a growing share of the population. They are the bulk of urban migrants and are thus unavailable for agricultural vocations. This raises the challenge of retaining and educating the next generation of farmers. As agricultural technology development and diffusion has stagnated, the sector continues to rely on human labour for farm power. This stagnation is due to lack of local innovation, especially the mechanization that is appropriate to the ecology. Farmers cannot afford equipment, and in turn there is lack of local maintenance capacity. Mechanization and labour saving devices are in urgent need and require the development of local capacity.

(iv)   Rural poverty will increase just as urban poverty has increased. Employment and income will have to be created for a large and growing youth population. With modern research and technology, agriculture provides a great opportunity to turn rural poverty and stagnation into development. At least in theory, the rural youth could produce the food the urban youth consume. However, this would assume that the urban youth have the required purchasing power. But a different scenario may play out in which the rural youth do not benefit, where big agribusiness produces the bulk of food for the urban centres. Can there be agricultural jobs without consumers? Can there be high demand for agricultural products without jobs for youth? Whatever way one looks at it, it is clear that agriculture as a development issue will remain a core challenge for Nigeria for the coming decades.

To address these challenges, Nigeria's agricultural and food security policy and programmes should adopt:

(i)   a twin-track approach, on one side encouraging commercial agribusiness, while on the other side supporting the huge population of subsistence producers, as this is critical to rural food security, social cohesion and poverty alleviation.

(ii)   The nature of these supports and encouragement should more than in the past consider the environmental challenges and remedy the consequences of past and present agricultural practices and management, which hinge on input support, and land resource utilization, management and conservation.

(iii)   The central role of women in the agricultural economy needs to finally be recognised and be reflected in the policies and measures that purport to buttress smallholders.

(b)Climate Change

The second challenge to Nigeria's agricultural sector and food security is climate change. It already has varying, mostly adverse effects on agriculture and, therefore, food security in various parts of the country. Consequently the National Adaptation Strategy and Plan of Action on Climate Change for Nigerian (NASPA-CCN), has identified a number of key measures with assigned roles to stakeholders at the national and sub-national levels. Higher temperatures results in decreased agricultural productivity and production, high evaporation rates and reduced soil moisture, lowering of the groundwater table and shrinking of surface water. Heat stress reduces human labour use on farms, lowers labour productivity and leads to rapid deterioration and wastage of farm produce.

Changes in the amount of rain, increased rainfall intensity and changes in rainfall patterns lead to decreased resource productivity and production (crops and livestock). Changing and erratic rainfall patterns make it difficult for farmers to plan their operations, may reduce the cropping season and can lead to low germination, reduced yield and crop failure. Erratic weather interferes with processing off produce (an example is sun-drying of crops and smoking of fish). Increased frequency of major storms causes damage to farmland, crop and livestock. Major storms can also cause road wash-outs, which make it difficult to access farms and to market products.

The NASPA adopted by the Ministry of Environment in November 2011 and approved by the Nigeria's Federal Executive Council, has two overall focuses with respect to agriculture and food security.

These are:

(i)Adoption of improved agricultural systems for both crops and livestock

For example, diversify livestock and improve range management; increase access to drought resistant crop and livestock feeds; adopt better soil management practices; and provide early warning/meteorological forecasts and related information.

(ii) Implementation of strategies for improved resources management

For example, increase use of irrigation systems that use   small amounts of water; increase rainwater and groundwater harvesting for use in agriculture; increase planting of native vegetation cover and promotion of re-greening efforts; and intensify crop and livestock production in place of slash-and-burn practices.

Energy and Energy Efficiency:

Energy supply in Nigeria can be classified two main categories: urban and rural. Urban areas are essentially on the grid while rural areas are largely off the grid. Nigeria's roadmap to power sector essentially focuses on the development of grid-based electricity and the sector reforms only extend the national grid to rural areas which are close to main urban areas. Rural areas that are remote and have a low demand density will have to depend on off-grid energy solutions as economies of on-grid deployment do not favour rural electrification. Off-grid areas will have to depend on alternative solutions and only recently critical stakeholders in the power sector came up with a coordinated, coherent and comprehensive renewable energy policy (REP) to drive hydropower, biomass, solar, and wind as energy sources.

In this regard, like existing sources of electricity, this alternative solutions-renewable energy can become a source of energy that may be traded and procured by the power industry as they would procure fossil or non-renewable energy sources. The REP document, no doubt, will serve as a blue print for sustainable supply and utilization of renewable energy sources within the economy for both on-grid and off-grid energy solutions.

The document also advances an energy efficiency policy (EEP). Energy Efficiency is a source of energy since it would reduce inefficient consumption, thereby providing greater access to electricity consumers.

In the light of the above, both renewable energy and energy efficiency can be viewed as part and parcel of a strategy to achieve a greener energy. Many countries around the globe are pursuing this approach to their energy future. It is therefore important that Nigeria joins the league of aspiring green economies.

But the tools necessary to drive renewable energy development and improve energy efficiency require important rule changes and coordinated actions among several ministries, departments and agencies (MDAs). Unfortunately these are yet to be actualized.

Nigeria will have a more potent renewable energy and energy efficiency policy if it is backed by law. This will boost access to energy services and ensure the sustainable growth of clean energy contribution to Nigeria's energy mix, by so doing ameliorate the electricity challenges in Nigeria by attracting investors to the sector. Let us look at two case study scenarios:

Case Study 1
The Pay As You Go Solar (PAYG Solar)

PAYG provides clean electricity to households, anytime anywhere. The solar panels provide between 1 and 5 kva to the household, enough to run a small business such as tailor or barber shop during 24 hours per day. Finance is provided a 100 per cent by the PAYG solar company, which commits to providing quality service through an MoU with government. Government regulates and rewards honest business with interest waivers and tax holidays. Customers pay on a monthly basis and own the panels after 2 years without having to pay a large sum upfront (no loan scheme required at consumer level). PAYG Solar is fast growing in East Africa, with companies such as MobiSol and M-KOPA installing many MW in Tanzania, Kenya. There is no limit as the business is built on quality service provided in small household and MSME units.

Policies and regulatory framework needed here to create the incentives to develop this green business (PAYG Solar) and mainstream sustainable consumption and production actions in include:

(a)Incentives from the Federal Government through the Standard Organization of Nigeria(SON),with support from Energy Commission of Nigeria overseeing the importation of quality solar products, with the National Electricity Regulatory Commission(NERC) and Distributing Companies(DisCos), providing regulatory framework for off-grid to protect the growth of off-grid solutions and the Nigerian Customs providing zero duty on solar as stipulated in Renewable Energy Policy and approved by Federal Executive Council in May 2015. In the medium term, Rural Electrification Agency (REA) is to reinvent itself as the Renewable Energy Development Agency to focus on promotion of off-grid, mini-grid and solar(and other renewable energy) solutions working with private sector investors to achieve fast rural electrification.

(b)There will be collaboration between the Federal and State Government to support the training and job creation provided by PAYG Solar companies for technicians, installers and artisans. Accordingly, NAPTINS, ECN Research Centres, and State Electricity Boards will collaborate in this regard.

(c)Incentives from the State Government through Tender process for PAYG Solar companies, with technical check by an ad-hoc panel of Nigerian renewable energy (RE) experts, afterwards there will be an MoU between State Government and selected PAYG Solar companies, holding companies responsible to provide quality installation and service. The State Electricity Boards will support and run training for technical staff.

(d) Loans/loan guarantees to PAYG Solar companies: It is likely that would- be investors will provide the pioneer funding. Loans by State Governments are a tool to reward honest business, as well-performing companies (abiding by/exceeding the terms of MoU or creating jobs) could be rewarded with interest rate rebate, waivers or tax holidays.

(e) Increased Publicity and Advocacy: It is recommended to start the roll-out with MSME in the main markets of state capitals and through SME business associations.

(f) PAYG Solar Companies can **predict their profits** because customers pay fixed charges on a monthly basis, in line with the technical capacity of the solar panels (usually 1kva or 3.5kva). The companies are held to provide **warranties, guarantees**, after sales support and training of staff by the MoU signed with State Government. Companies undergo **quality checks** by SON, the State Government's tender process and technical experts verifying the products they are installing before roll-out at state level. Company take out their own **insurance,** which Government can support indirectly if desired. **Remote monitoring** technology allows companies to detect tampering with the solar equipment. A 10% or 20% down payment by customers will belong to the companies in case of non-payment of monthly charges.

(g)Customers pay by **Mobile Money** and if they fail to pay for the service, they can be cut off. After two years of payment, the solar panels and kit become the **Customers Property.**

(h) **OUTCOMES:** Pay-as-you-go solar can bring affordable clean energy to small businesses and households everywhere. Customers no longer have to wait for the national grid to reach them. Solar power beats the noise of generators and can beat the costs too. Investing in PAYG Solar makes good business sense. An investment of between $1m and $2m will bring about the installation of about 1,000 to 2,000 PAYG Solar systems. This can be achieved within 6 to 8 months. A PAYG Solar company would typically reach-break-even around 5,000 installations. Compared to grid extension, this is a time and cost-efficient, private sector-driven and people-oriented solution. One kilometre of grid extension costs between $7,000 and $20,000 and takes years to be planned and delivered.

Case Study 2
Save80 Energy Efficient Stove

Another case study, this time under energy efficiency policy is the green innovation as represented by Save80 Energy Efficient Stove made from stainless steel for sustainability. The Save80 Cook Stove uses small wood sticks as fuel for cooking due to the high quality of the equipment. It has high power capacity of 1.5 kW and also highly efficient. Cooking is easier compared to the cooking with usual fire. The Save80 can change your life positively. It not only save your money, but also reduces harmful smoke and protects the environment. The durable heat retaining container "Wonderbox" innovation also ensures that cooking of nearly all dishes, like maize porridge, potatoes, rice and beans, etc completed in the box without further use of fuel wood only a short time of heating in the Save80 Cook Stove. This will not only save fuel, money and emissions, but you will not need to supervise the cooking process when using the Wonderbox. Operating on a principle of retained heat, the Wonderbox keeps food warm for several hours and can also be used to store hot water for a long time, such as overnight. The high quality cooking equipment consists of the Save80

Cook Stove, an 8-litre pot, a pan, both with lids and durable heat retaining container " Wonderbox" and an adapter for small pots .The Stove is suitable for cooking, heating and sterilizing water, frying and deep frying. But it is not suitable for baking, except for flat bread. The temperature produced by the Stove is too high for other baking products.

Since 2009, the Save80 Cook Stove has been registered as a CDM (Clean Development Mechanism) project 2711: "Efficient Fuel Woodstoves for Nigeria" under the Kyoto Protocol, by the UNFCCC (United Nations Framework Convention on Climate Change). After the first verification exercise by UNFCCC appointed auditors, the DOEs (Designated Operational Entities) in September 2010, a report on our project was published on the UNFCCC website as "one of 10 CDM projects worldwide that make a unique contribution towards improving people's lives and achieving sustainable development." Ever since, the Stove has gotten the homes of over 37,000 households in Nigeria.

The implication of this process in terms of carbon reduction emission, employment generation and income for the Nigerian population is enormous.

Infrastructure

Infrastructure is the key to sustainable development because of its capacity to enhance productivity and competitiveness. Nigeria's lack of competitiveness and low indices of development are often linked to general inadequacies in infrastructural developments in the transport sector (road network, aviation, railways, waterways, energy/power, telecommunications etc). A number of factors have contributed to poor delivery and deterioration of critical infrastructure in Nigeria. These include: under-investment, poor maintenance culture, pressure of population explosion, neglect of the urban and regional planning, etc. The transport sector remained largely underdeveloped and lacked intermodal linkage while the deterioration was most acute in the power sector with contributed to poor delivery and deterioration of critical infrastructure in Nigeria. These include: under-investment, poor maintenance culture, pressure of population explosion, neglect of the urban and regional planning, etc. The transport sector remained largely underdeveloped and lacked intermodal linkage while the deterioration was most acute in the power sector with perennial shortages in generation, transmission and distribution.

The provision of quality and affordable infrastructure is a major challenge in Nigeria. It is well known that past governments in Nigeria had developed sector-specific infrastructure Master Plans over the years. However, such plans in most cases were either not well articulated or poorly implemented to achieve the desired results. However, the Former President Jonathan's administration 30 –year National

Integrated Master Plan (NIIMP) covering all the sectors with the implementation strategy of using a 10-year and 5-year operational and medium term plans seem not to be sustainable and the review is imperative.

Besides, there is the need for public investment in sustainable infrastructure (including public transport, renewable energy and retrofitting of existing infrastructure and buildings for improved energy efficiency) and natural capital, to restore, maintain and, where possible, enhance the stock of natural capital.

Upfront investments in maintenance and conservation are almost always cheaper than trying to restore damaged ecosystems and the social benefits that flow from restoration can be several times higher than the costs. Potential rates of return can reach 40% for mangrove and woodland/shrub land, 50% for tropical forests and 79% for grasslands when multiple ecosystem services are taken into account. Investment in ecological infrastructure therefore, provides cost-effective opportunities to increase resilience to climate change, reduce risks from natural hazards, improve food and water security and contribute to poverty reduction.

Public Procurement

With growing complexity of modern projects and high cost value involved, the public procurement becomes a risk sharing and a collective responsibility of senior executives in an institution. The unavoidable use of human capital in the implementation of the processes brought about the inevitability of fraud. The need to control fraud and achieve effective implementation of public procurement goals brought about the establishment of Public Procurement Act in 2006. Ever since the adoption of the principles and standard governing Public Procurement has not received commendable result, hence the need to review the Act to strengthen it and also accommodate public procurement policies geared towards promoting greening of business and markets in Nigeria.

6.0 Critical Factors to be taken into account in addressing these Sectors

The following issues must be taken account: Energy efficiency, labelling and standards, water efficiency, eco-innovation, and sustainable trade.

(i)Energy efficiency:

It is identified as a major issue for MSMEs, emphasising the positive impacts such measures will have on the SMEs through cost reduction and material recovery thus supporting the move towards greening Nigerian economies. This includes the implementation of the Resource Efficient and Cleaner Production (RECP) programme to enhance energy efficiency in the manufacturing and tourism sectors. Energy

Efficiency is one of the deliverables under 2020 targets of the Africa-EU Energy Partnership and is a major component of the UN Secretary General Sustainable Energy for all (SE4ALL) initiative.

(ii) **Labelling and standards**:

Eco-labels provide an indication of how well a product or service is environmentally adapted. Most green products are niche products and consumer awareness and readiness to act are still low. For the products, there is an opportunity to expand market share or access new international markets for sustainable product within and beyond the Nigerian border. However, innovation capacity is limited, patchy and requires more support. Labelling and standards have been identified as a cross cutting area to develop local/product schemes also in view support by African countries to the Africa Eco-labelling Mechanism(AEM), Eco-Mark Africa(EMA) eco label and thus to secure recognition of sustainable African products in overseas markets. There is the need to support eco-labelling programmes in Nigeria, especially in the leather industry etc.

(iii)Water Efficiency:

Demand for fresh water has increased significantly during past two decades in Nigeria. The reason for the increase in demand are economic growth and development, improved standard of living , growing population and increasing consumption by those population and expanding industries of the priority sectors(agriculture, tourism, manufacturing and energy). Frequent droughts leading to water scarcity, decreasing rainfall and rising temperature further emphasize the need to promote water saving initiatives. Activities will build on experience secured in the African Beverages Industries Water Saving Initiative (ABIWSI) project, based on needs identified under the African regional roadmap for implementation of the 10 Year Framework Programmes on Sustainable Consumption and Production Patterns(the "10YFP" adopted at Rio+20. The current six programmes of 10YFP are: consumer information; sustainable building and construction; sustainable food systems; sustainable lifestyles and education; sustainable public procurement and sustainable tourism, including eco-tourism.

(iv)Eco-innovation:

Nigeria is facing deficiency in up-to-date and resource efficient technologies and often had to rely on industrialized and emerging economies to access knowledge expertise, acquire technologies and equipment to adopt and implement cleaner production techniques. Eco-innovation has been identified as an area to implement

RECP in order to promote an environmentally sustainable industrial growth.

(v)Sustainable trade:

In the priority sectors, green economy measures create opportunities for penetrating new markets and enhancing trade in the environmental goods and services. On the other hand, cross-sectoral discipline of identifying and harnessing trade opportunities feeds into the promotion of environmental sound production processes, improved resource efficiency, creating incentives for increased investments in green technologies and contributes to green job creation. In this way sustainable trade bolsters the transition to a green economy, while being enhanced by it.

7.0 Conclusion:

Green economy holds much promise for Nigeria. With effective policies and regulatory framework to create incentive for green business development, as well as urgent need to enact relevant laws that will drive green economy initiatives especially by Members of the 8th National Assembly. If relevant laws are in place, investors will be attracted, business will prosper, employment created, livelihoods built and in the long run poverty alleviated. By so doing, the goals of the social philosophy of a green economy will be achieved.

8.0 Cited References

1. Onuoha C.M(2014) Transiting to a Green Economy(From Economic Growth to Sustainable Development . Green Economics Initiative of Nigeria.
2. Kennet M et al (2011) Ten Key Values of Green Economics. In: Green Economics-Voice of Africa. Green Economics Institute, UK publication.
3. Green Deal Nigeria(2012) Henrich Boll Stiftung Nigeria(May)
4. Adaju Segun(2015) Pay As You Go Solar(PAYG). Henrich Boll Stiftung Nigeria.
5. Ahmed Yahaya(2012) Save 80 System. Developmental Association for Renewable Energy.
6. Draft National Renewable Energy and Energy Efficiency Policy (NREEEP, 2015) For Electricity. Ministry of Power. Federal Republic of Nigeria
7. Nwajiuba C. (2012) Nigeria's Agriculture and Food Security Challenges. In: Green Deal Nigeria. Henrich Boll Stiftung Nigeria.
8. UNOPS(2015) Switch Africa Green Projects. Kenya Operation Hub(KEOH) March 27

Part 8
8.1 Strategies For Social Justice Via Economic Theory

By Wendy Olsen, Daniel Neff, J. Rangaswamy, and Vincent Ortet

Introduction and Abstract:

Using transdisciplinary social theory, we reinterpret the social position and agency of some people working in rural India. We aim to transcend the classic polarity between choice-oriented economic theory and constraint-focused Marxist theory. We offer an innovative theory about the strategies that people (and more generally agents, such as couples) have for their economic and other fields of behaviour. A sociological theory encompassing agency along with economic resources and people's desires or 'visions' offers a fresh way forward. The chapter develops one chunk of such a theory by drawing upon Bourdieu's concepts of habitus and his integration of cultural factors, which he called cultural capital, along with social and economic factors. The strategies of the agents are listed for a series of 39 household 'cases' using a mixed-methods triangulated data set which we have created for two South Indian villages. A dialectic is represented through a longitudinal dataset consisting of both interviews and a survey – a useful data source, since strategies are not fixed, but instead are developed, deliberated, and changed in the light of events using judgemental rationality. The hypothesis that social class or human-capital assets determine the workers' degree of resistance to employers' control found no support. Instead strategies in the labour market could best be understood using qualitative data linking their visions with the current actions. Thus our agency-focused approach avoids the determinism of old forms of structuralism, not only by assumption, but also in practice through a qualitative research method. In concluding, we stress the local and particular nature of the findings, whilst also summarising the more general benefits of using this particular social theory framework. Specific benefits include (1) linkages with policy intervention; (2) pluralism of theory of social change i.e. transdisciplinarity; and (3) deep understanding of a local scene whilst having middle-range theoretical concepts that can be transposed to other scenes.

Introduction to the Strategies

This chapter offers a theory of labouring strategies and then broadens out the concept of strategies to enable a strategic structuralism in social science. One motivating factor is that individualistic neoliberal thinking dominates development decision-making. Methodological individualism is quite problematic. The neoclassical styles of economic theorising, which underpin neoliberal thinking, are also a problem. They are often used in ways that are dehumanising and dangerously a-cultural. It is important for an alternative style of analysis to be developed which can be used to create the conditions for more emergence of human flourishing. In other words, we argue, the expansion of good social theory can be part of a wave of development thinking that underpins and partly constitutes good development practice. In summary, we aim to present a theory of strategies that allows elements of other social theories to be embedded within a deliberately and explicitly moral approach to any issue. We define what we mean by 'ethical' and 'moral' strategies within the chapter.

This chapter thus claims to be humanist, pro-development (in the post-development sense), and supportive of good action in labour relations. It is on the one hand a path-breaking critical realist empirical study of labouring. A theory of labouring strategies, offered in this section and then fleshed out in the other sections along with the empirical basis from which it arose, offers an alternative to four main schools of socio-economic thinking: neoclassical; new institutionalist; Marxist; and feminist "Gender and Development" (GAD) thinking. We have built upon Marxist and feminist foundations and there are also numerous bridges between the theory of strategies and the institutionalist study of evolving contractual practices as well as with the neoclassical theory of labour supply and demand. Thus the conceptual elements from other theories are not dropped out completely, or 'opposed'. Instead an over-arching approach, usually known as moral economy (associated for example with Andrew Sayer's work, 2000a) is offered to help formulate each agent's normatively loaded strategic vision. Here, by 'agent', I mean either a researcher as agent or even a corporate agent such as an NGO's vision, and hence that NGO's strategy for dealing with a problem. The specific problem taken up in the paper is workers being coerced by employers to work for free, or under exploitative conditions, in rural South India. Workers have their own strategies, which we explore empirically; and some of the local residents had *ethical strategies* which went beyond one 'field' of endeavour to treat multiple fields and multiple agents; while a few also had *moral strategies* where they took up not only their own wellbeing, and their family's wellbeing, but wider issues of balancing the good of all against the good of oneself. We call the ethical strategies second-order strategies, and the moral strategies third-order strategies. We expect most scientists to be aiming to develop third-order moral strategies. In this way, the paper offers a solution at a high level to the issues of normative evaluation that are sometimes found problematic, particularly in economics.

A review of the four background theories was published in 2006 (Olsen, 2006), and the possibility of a moral economy rapprochement has been suggested in a number of works on which we touch in this paper (Ellis, 2000; De Haan, 2002; Folbre, 1996). However the rapprochement reached here is moral in a number of senses which are left out in both neoclassical and new institutionalist economic theory. 1) we are committed to progressive action in the way that Anderson argues is rational and Sayer argues is inevitable for public actors (Anderson, 2003; Sayer, 2001, 2000b); 2) the role of values and valuation is made very explicit so that commonsense norms are taken seriously and are neither rejected nor ignored by the theorist; and finally 3) the need for human flourishing is thought to be urgent and pressing (Lawson, 1997) so that there is little time for idealised equilibrium-based mathematizations of bondage (Basu, 2005; Basu and Van, 1998).

Thus, we offer a critical theory based upon our practical engagement with village life in southern India. We will present the theory in two stages here: first a list of some important underpinning innovations about the 'agent' who makes labouring decisions; and second a series of assertions that comprise a theory of strategic decision-making in the labour 'field'. Crucially, decisions in the labour field are linked up with decisions in other fields through second-order and third-order strategic thinking. (See Olsen, 2015: Strategic Structuralism, chapter in a book, *Philosophy of Social Justice,* forthcoming, Green Economics Institute.) In section 3 we present our data sources and methods of analysis. Fourthly we do a theme-wise analysis of the habitus, household deliberation, and status issues as they relate to labouring strategies. Fifthly a hypothesis is tested using the 39 case-study households to show that strategies cannot simply be read off from structural underpinnings. We describe two particular cases to illustrate the variety of strategies that people in these villages are using. And finally our conclusion comments on the more general benefits of using this particular social theory framework - linkages with policy intervention; transdisciplinarity; and transposable middle-range theoretical concepts.

1a) Underpinnings in How Agents are Conceptualised: Partially Independent Yet Also Interpermeating

The underpinning notions are also covered in earlier papers (Olsen, 2008; and Olsen and Neff, 2007) but are reviewed here in order to remind us that a 'decision maker' is a complex thing and that decision-making patterns should not be expected to be homogeneous over space or time. The new theory offered in this paper, however, shows that structural underpinnings create the basis for typologies (or configurations) which indicate patterns in the flexibility or inflexibility of social relations. This is important in informal rural labour markets (which is the topic of this paper's empirical work) but also much more widely in labour theory, too. A quick analogy might illustrate our idea of the structural underpinning of a typology of social relations.

If you put two strong magnets together, they may match up and stay connected. The structure of the magnetic metal causes this. On the other hand, if one magnet is then reversed in its position, the magnets will push each other away; again this is structurally determined.

If you take non-deterministic social systems, you have a kind of plastic egg - plasticene egg situation. One egg is plastic and does not bend, so the plasticene egg meets a hard wall when they are put together. But the plasticene can bend, melt, reshape, and get around (or under or over) the plastic egg. The plastic egg is a bit like a large organisation in a formal labour market. The plasticene is like a rural worker family of whom one migrates, one rents land, two go off to school, and one negotiates a daily wage for 'kuulie' (daily-paid casual) work.

If both eggs are made of plasticene, however, as when employee meets employer in informal rural labour markets, then it depends on the inner detailed structure of each egg how they act when they meet. We can now consider boiled eggs, mud eggs, goose eggs and easter eggs and how things 'are' when two types of eggs meet. A complex range of interactions are possible but these are structured in a non-deterministic (yet trans-factually effective) way by the inner structure of each egg. Of course context also matters to the resulting 'omelette'.

This metaphor may have resonance for those who work on formal (highly structured) and informal (less clearly structured) parts of labour markets.

1b) Explicit Treatment Of The Agents Who Do Labouring And Make Decisions

In our theory, persons are not the only type of agent but they are an important building block of agency (Table 1: Characteristics of Agents). We will use the word 'agent' to refer to individuals as well as to larger corporate entities such as couples, households, families, and non-governmental organisations. In order for the larger corporate agents to act, there has to be human involvement and deliberation among the involved individuals. A good example in the rural South Indian context is 'self-help groups' (Edward and Olsen, 2005), which in Andhra Pradesh are usually all-female, arise either indigenously or in the context of urban bank promptings, hold monthly local meetings and keep a membership list, arrange weekly or monthly savings from members, and distribute money in the form of loans to individual members conditional upon their good repayment and savings behaviour. The self-help groups act as peer guarantors for loans and have thrived in the context of Indian regulatory policy that mimics – but also adapts – the Grameen Bank model of Bangladesh. A self-help group is an agent but the women within it are also agents.

We want to stress three aspects of agency that were missed out in neoclassical and new institutionalist universalistic modelling. Firstly, we would argue that agents use their imaginations to act as creative producers of innovation and dreams. When people act, their vision of future achievement motivates them to do things (or, as Anderson has put it, rational attitudes cause us to express ourselves actively in ways that demonstrate our positive evaluation of specific chosen future states of affairs, Anderson, 1993). We found through field work that shared dreams of future states of affairs act as important motivating and guiding factors for sustained periods of time for entire households as well as for individual agents and groups. Exploring the imagination and vision of an agent requires a qualitative method since empathy and openness need to be shown in order for a narrative describing the vision to emerge.

By contrast, the 'individual' in neoclassical theory and the 'principal' and other 'agents' in new institutionalist theory are barely human, have a limited range of objectives – mainly acquisition of money or property or profit - , and are not seen as diverse in the ways that real human agents with visions are diverse. One can criticise these theories for economism – an excessive focus on the commercial world.

Our second innovation is to recognise and welcome emotion in agents' decision-making about the economy. Nussbaum has directed our attention to emotions such as shame, guilt, pride and joy in her work on development capabilities (Nussbaum and Glover, 1993; Nussbaum, 1999). The role of emotion, we have found, is both disciplining and enabling. Some negative emotions support the self-disciplining and social disciplining of people toward conformity with social norms. However it is also possible for emotions like confusion and anger to lead people to break old norms and to begin to create new norms (Anderson, 1993). We found, too, that love and caring as positive affect sometimes caused people to conform to patriarchal or obedient norms, but at other times caused them to take risks and to dare to migrate to cities or otherwise take on new roles (e.g. Panchayat President, self-help group leader, or employee) in order to try to gain the best life for their loved ones. We wanted to *notice emotions* through qualitative research methods in order to enrich the capacity for social economics to make linkages between the commercial sphere of paid work and the non-commercial sphere of caring and loving activities. This tactic has paid off although more work remains to be done.

Thirdly, in the spirit of the feminist work of the Gender and Development (GAD) school, we wanted our own attitude about the divisions of labour in the villages to be one of neutrality and non-judgemental interest in what village people felt were appropriate behaviours in their work and non-work roles. To put this differently, we want to challenge the gender division of labour in society, but not to challenge individual agents' decisions about the best way to perceive and act out caring roles at a particular time. One way of phrasing this delicate balancing act is this: The gendered *patterns* that we observe can be the basis of generalisations but are not normatively preferred by us. The gender *roles* that people choose to identify with, engage in or act out are often damaging to both men and women because of the restrictions on women's range of roles and because of the limited amount of active caring within the family that Indian rural men are usually expected to do. The gender *norms* are an object of study suited to both qualitative and quantitative social research methods about which we want to form normative evaluations. We wanted respondents to present some of their roles and norms to us, which they did, and we can explore how these are relevant to labour market outcomes in both the micro and macro dimensions.

This particular type of feminist orientation aims to avoid essentialising men and women into either their current (patriarchy based) social roles or into some model of equality that is implicit in our minds as authors. Instead we try to enable an ongoing recognition that social class and caste both interact with the norms for gender and how agents interpret their appropriate actions given the existing set of norms. The gendered division of public labour, especially paid labour but also unpaid productive work and political activities, is changing rapidly in India. Village women, for instance, are joining in new forms of work all the time (notably in Panchayat politics, in construction work as migrants, in cow management work, and in employment as local white-collar service providers both paid and unpaid – village-level examples include childcare manager and Self-Help Group leader). In this context, just as in urban India and in other countries, the private division of domestic labour comes under intense pressure. To give some idea of the pressure that exists, note that among the 5000+ suicides of desperately frustrated farmers in Andhra Pradesh between 1997 and 2007 a good proportion have been women. Most of those people who killed themselves had high household debts and had utilised the woman's jewels as collateral with private or bank moneylenders, and in most cases marital discord was a contributing factor to the suicide (Chindarkar, 2007). One study that used a method of interviewing the women from matched post-suicide families and same-class neighbouring families found that household disputes were a major differentiating factor (Venkateswarlu, personal communication, 2004). Thus our orientation toward gender issues is one of high sensitivity and we hope this to be clear not only in our empirical field work and analysis but also in the resulting grounded theory.

Figure 1: Aspects of the Agents in the Rural Informal Labour Markets

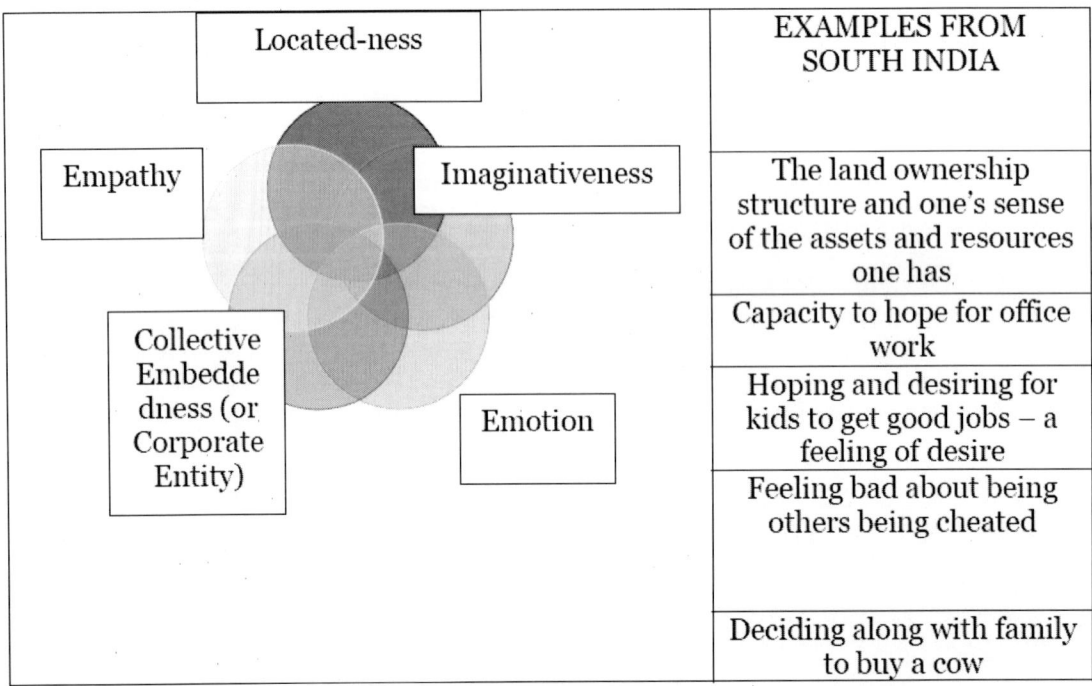

	EXAMPLES FROM SOUTH INDIA
	The land ownership structure and one's sense of the assets and resources one has
	Capacity to hope for office work
	Hoping and desiring for kids to get good jobs – a feeling of desire
	Feeling bad about being others being cheated
	Deciding along with family to buy a cow

Figure contents: Located-ness, Empathy, Imaginativeness, Collective Embeddedness (or Corporate Entity), Emotion

With these provisos in mind, we want to approach the labouring agent as summarised in Figure 1 and Table 1. These indicate the kinds of things agents do (Table 1) by virtue of their nature (Figure 1). However in Table 1 the variation among agents from rather habit-oriented to quite reflexive (discussed by Archer, 2000, 2003, 2007) is reflected in notes on the kind of agency usually associated with complex second- and third-order strategies.

In the next section we show the frequency of different *types of* resistance, exit, innovation, and conformity among the 39 couples who were interviewed in 2006/7 as part of this study/by the research team. The frequencies will demonstrate *qualitatively* the absence, presence and preponderance of different types of act in the couple's strategies vis-à-vis the rural informal labour market. They are not intended as counts or cardinal measures but as indicators of the nature of the differentiated configurations. We found that the behaviour and strategies within one social class were far more diverse than either the Bourdieuvian or the Marxian structuralist theories might initially suggest. The theoretical framework set out here is thus very original and may offer a suitable framework for further empirical research about transformative strategies both within and beyond the rural scene.

2 *Explicit Treatment of the Agents Who Make Decisions About Labouring*

The rest of this section explains important contributions from Anderson, Nelson and Habermas that support the approach to strategies offered here. The theory of strategies is offered in Section 2 (summarized in Table 2) involving a recognition that complex agents make decisions in an ongoing loop of reflection, feedback and consideration as well as habitual behaviour. Section 3 explains the retroductive methodology that was used to pluck out evidence from two village scenes over a period of years, leading to the grounded theory of strategies. In sections 4-5 a small sample of cases is summarized whose strategies at the most basic level as well as the 'second-order' and 'third-order' levels are described in detail. Finally Section 6 takes a theme-wise approach to the data we have in this study, offering a discussion of class, wealth and selected upward mobility strategies. We conclude by returning to the issue of 'schools of thought' and argue that our theory offers *bridges to other schools of thought* but also goes beyond them to a higher plateau of critical reflection on our data. This is an economics aimed at social justice.

2a) *Good Social Theory Avoids Methodological Individualism*

The work of three theorists has helped us to avoid using a model that reduces the world of labouring to individuals. Firstly, Nelson's warnings about dualisms in economic thinking are helpful in reminding us that caring is not necessarily *separate* from the world of paid work (Nelson, 2003). Nelson has repeatedly argued that an androcentric view of the world places commerce at the centre and domestic work in a periphery, but that this false ideology ignores the real centrality of trust, care, concern, mutuality and shared values within the very workplaces – and even banks - that are highly commercialized. Nelson's argument can be read to suggest that individualistic economics both encourages (while describing) and promotes selfish behaviour. By contrast, our approach will tend to suggest that larger corporate units are potentially good *in themselves* because they involve deliberative decision-making and public airing of concerns, whereas the worker who is lonely and isolated may suffer from anomie and will be less able to respond flexibly to problematic changes in the world of agriculture, to ill health, or to climate change. A series of feminist studies of solidarity in larger class- and occupational-group contexts (Jackson and Pearson, 1998) and our village experiences support Nelson's argument that androcentrism is consistent with individualism whereas caring is consistent with a world of relationality and mutuality as well as connectedness (Nelson, 2003). We as researchers should avoid an androcentric viewpoint and should have a balanced awareness of the value of the corporate life in the village community.

2b) Value is Contested

A second argument that underpins our attention to educational strategies as well as to labour-market and tenancy strategies is Anderson's concept of separate spheres of valuation. Anderson argues that the use of a single measure of value, such as money value or profitability, to compare incommensurable spheres of life is very dangerous to human well-being (Anderson, 1993). Her work is very different from the liberal author Walzer who argued that a free market in the market sphere ensures the possibility for further freedoms in other spheres (Walzer, 1983). Anderson argues that practices within different spheres and are not comparable, have their own inherent system of values, and use practice-specific expertise (similar to Schatzki (2002), Schatzki, Knorr-Cetina, *et al*.., eds (2001), Reckwitz, 2002)). The problem of who should do paid work, how to allocate a family's time, and where to work cannot simply be boiled down to an optimal decision-making problem using a monistic scale of utility, she argues. The New Home Economics (Becker, 1981; Ellis, 2000a) uses the kind of utilitarian monistic valuation that Anderson warns us against. In this paper, instead, we allow the respondents to speak for themselves in their delicate ethical balancing acts. We propose that second-order moral thinking (having strategies about strategies) and third-order thinking (described later) are normal human ways to achieve a sufficient sense of clarity about today's action whilst reserving the capacity to change the strategy or admit an error later on. The kind of ethical thinking we assume takes place is much more like that described by Wolfe who, in a USA context, showed that people do not adhere to their own stated moral principles but instead take into account the interpersonal peculiarities and situational specifics in making each intricate judgement during a caring and concerned ethical life (Wolfe, 1989 and 2001). Wolfe showed that ethical thinking is not the preserve of philosophers of ethics, but rather is the bread and butter of daily life for ordinary Americans. Lamont, too, conducted empirical work showing extensive moral reasoning among French and US male workers (Lamont, 2000). These are our exemplars. We avoid using as a reference point the mathematizable time-choice models of New Home Economics or the algebraic formulations found in Basu's formal political economy (Basu, 2005).

2c) Agents are Deeply Co-Mutual (ie. Coexisting and Overlapping)

A third area of social theory helps in exploring the relationship between the person and larger agents. This interface requires deliberation (i.e. talk and communication among people). In the villages studied, some couples had reached an ongoing unity of purpose and a strongly united voice but they did engage in deliberations – usually in the evening – to maintain this equilibrium. Some considered this equilibrium valuable and worth achieving. Other couples were clearly at odds with each other. In a few cases the husband and the wife were making separate and autonomous decisions. Habermas explores the concept of the good in situations like these where there are underlying potential conflicts of interest. His work offers two lessons and is a rich area to explore further. The first lesson is that the agents who act are not simply individuals because knowledge is socially constructed at the level of larger agents – such as NGOs – whose solidarity and indeed very existence is centred around a common core of ongoing discourse (Habermas, 1981: 100). Pusey, 1993, pages 75-83, shows that Habermas's analysis of ongoing knowledge construction leads explicitly to a theory of strategic action. Within a grouping, such as a couple, that attempts to achieve full equality and autonomy, open and public deliberation is important, says Habermas. It may be hard to achieve. Applying his logic to the farmer or worker couple, of course we have to doubt the underlying equality of the partners within the couple. Most village couples don't even pretend to have democracy in the home, as an NGO might. Persistent patriarchy and male domination surround and partially pervade most couples. 'Knowing' what is good, in such a context, may be difficult. It is a struggle. We thus find in Habermas the notion of the suppressed general interest, referring to the oppressed or marginalized persons' voices being collectively (systematically) not just personally silenced. A woman may know what she has to do, but not know what would be good for her. Thus in the context of inequality she may do what is not good for her. Extensive self-involvement in the internalisation of norms, e.g. patriarchal norms, is not the only source or cause of this collective silencing. There are also social causes (Habermas, 1986: 175). In summary from Habermas we learn of difficulties with overcoming our social enculturation, even within 'couples' or groups that claim to be achieving unity or equality.

2d) A Critical Realist Approach to Dialogue

This lesson was rather pessimistic but there is a hopeful side of Habermas, too. A second lesson from Habermas's work is that our own discourse about these groupings can try to move forward in rational ways toward dialogues-as-equals even if we cannot achieve our aim in full (Habermas, 1998). Habermas provides a benchmark, not a goal or teleology, for development researchers.[i] A pessimistic reading of Habermas would have us give up, but a critical realist reading would explore the nature of actual dialogues and try to create public scenes which encourage moves out of oppression and toward human self-actualisation (Giri, 2005, 2008). In this endeavour methodological individualism has no role to play.

Habermas also points out that dealing strategically with the 'community' or larger agent still leaves the outside world, or 'strangers', as a problematic area for moral strategic thinking (Habermas, 1998:14-15). Here Habermas explains at length that methodological individualism as a foundation for neoliberal thinking cannot deal with the real diversity of concrete moral systems that exists in a society where we have we/us/them. (*Ibid.*, pp. 10-16). "With the transition to a pluralism of worldviews in modern society, religion and the ethos rooted in it disintegrate as a *public* basis of morality shared by all.' (*Ibid.*, p. 10). By citing Habermas' argument we are disagreeing with Bourdieu, Archer, and Nussbaum who all have claimed at some point in writing that the third-world societies (Kabylia; pre-industrialised countries; and India, respectively) are not modern and that they do have a more coherent social foundation for morality than do "western" societies.[ii] In our view, India's rural areas have a confused, mixed, and diverse moral stage on which different forces and interests use ideology to play out their strategies. India, as described in our rural village study, has a place in late modern society (Chouliarakis and Fairclough, 1999) and is neither pre-modern nor simply modern.

3 Strategies of Agents as a Middle Range Theory

A number of writers have commented on labouring strategies in both 'development' and 'western' contexts. For example, the idea that farmers have strategies was set out by Ellis (2000b) who portrayed the household as if it were a rational actor or a unified decision-making body. Ellis aimed to explore how diverse livelihoods worked better for poverty reduction and the avoidance of vulnerability to shocks. His work led to the policy advice that intervention should facilitate diversity of livelihoods rather than encouraging monocropping or mono-product farmers. De Haan also used the concept of strategies when he described the decision to migrate in the context of repeat, circular migration in Bihar, north India (De Haan, 2002). Like Ellis, De Haan uses a mixture of qualitative and quantative data to describe the types of migrants and other workers and their strategies. De Haan advocates the use of mixed methods because of the additional insights that qualitative research gives about the meaning of strategies for the actors who hold them (De Haan, 2007). Bourdieu (1998) also mentions strategies explicitly in his work on practical reason. Interesting comments on strategies are found in the cross-disciplinary work of Anderson (1993), too. She shows that having a strategy for achieving good outcomes in one field is not sufficient − nor independent of − strategies in other fields. Anderson cites neither Bourdieu nor any Marxist authors, but her work makes an interesting and plausible contribution. She says that the values intrinsic to each sphere of daily life are not commensurate with the values of other spheres (this claim is also found in the work of the realists Nussbaum, 1999 ; Sayer, 2000b, and MacIntyre, 1985). For some readers Anderson will therefore be taken as a moral relativist, but she intends to be taken as a moral realist. For moral realists, like MacIntyre, values arise in the context of given human situations. The good is really 'good' in a given situation because of the nature of that situation. For these realists, a situation can be quite closely defined, so we do not arrive at universal notions of the good, but having set up a particular empirical context our knowledge of the good is constructed mainly through exploring what is (really, already, *a priori*) good there and then.[iii] The 1993 Anderson work is thus not moral relativist, but rather ontologically complex. Anderson takes the argument further − she says that people have second-order strategies which reconcile the necessary interventions of each field upon other fields. Thus she says, although the values are not commensurate, people engage in deliberations and comparisons of states of affairs, and they then proceed to make second-order judgements about what to do. In seeing these second-order decisions as processual, reactive, judgementally rational, and carefully gauged, Anderson prizes the qualities of the wise human who is communicative and can discuss the pros and cons of particular actions while taking into account their effects on multiple fields. For her, this framework leads toward a critique of neoclassical theory's utilitarian calculus. For us, the framework leads further – toward a theory of strategies and some further implications for structuralism.

3a) Reconceptualising Agents and Strategies

Consider Table 1 which describes different types of agents – the ones at left having rather simple, narrow strategies for particular fields, and the ones at the right having complex, ethical, interwoven strategies. Moving from left to right we move toward political, public engagement and caring about a wide range of effects of one's actions.

Table 1: Characteristics of Socio-Economic Agents

All have		Some Have		A few have	E.g.
E.g.			E.g.		
Locatedness	Know our assets	**Reflection**	Plan cleverly	**Image management**	Do some hiding of motives
Vision	Imagine job goals	**Wide Scope**	Consider three 'fields'	**Wide Range**	Deliberately encompass inter-temporal planning
Feelings	Become angry if cheated	**Consideration for Others**	Vicariously care about/with others	**Public Sensibility**	Make public statements, advertise
Co-Mutuality	Being both wife and tenant	**Empathy**	Recognise others' and own interests	**Conflict Resolution**	Plan how to deal with disputes

Both Table 1 and Figure 1 express some ontological assumptions that are being made here about agents. We place this conception within the widely accepted sociology of structure-agency dynamics, preferring the version represented by Elder-Vass (2007). For Elder-Vass and Archer, structures and agency do not simply exist in a mutually constituting duality. Instead they affect each other through time, and the emergence of change occurs although there are also enduring outcomes that repeatedly arise from durable underlying structures (Elder-Vass, 2007). In this context "structures" – such as class and caste - are seen as consisting not only of their component parts, but also as having some characteristics that cannot be reduced to the properties of the agents themselves. Structures, such as the land-holding structure, the relationships among court/law/owner/tenant (Sayer, 1992), and the norms about share-cropping, also exist independently of the individual agents which populate the categories that comprise the structure. Thus when one landlord loses their land the inequality of a landlord / peasant rural landholding structure may remain in place. The impact of a small change on a 'structure' depends on whether the change is simply an exit of an agent from that structure or instead whether it causes a profound alteration in that structure.

Further details of the strategies of agents within this theoretical framework are contained in Table 2. Here you see simple strategies, more complex strategies, and finally a third type which are ethically thoughtful ("third-order") strategies described in sentences.

Table 2: Characteristics of Strategies

2(a) first-order strategies

An agent develops	An orientation	To a goal	And plans the steps to get there	And plans responses to feedback

... → and acts.

2(b) second-order strategies

An agent develops	An orientation	To a goal	And plans the steps to get there	And plans responses to feedback

... → and acts.

2(c) third-order strategies

An agent develops	An ethical evaluative standpoint	About a set of goals in a set of 'fields'	Of a set of agents and the underlying structures,	Taking into account impact on self	And plans the steps to take, sooner or later	And plans or deliberates on responses to feedback
				And effects on more than one agent(s)		

...→ and acts.

This theorization of strategies was only implicit in the works by Ellis and De Haan cited above. We can find related theories of human action among psychologists such as Csikszentmihalyi (2002 and 2003); Rogers (1980); and Heron (2000). The aim of the approach is always to create a theory that helps people to move forward, as for example Csikszentmihalyi has advised readers on how to conduct 'good business' based on his concept of happiness as a flow of action toward chosen goals (2003). Thus there are reverberations from this theory of strategies that go beyond development studies.

This framework is a transdisciplinary approach to socially grounded agents and their decision-making. One begins to see numerous dynamic processes at work here; the agent who is conscious of structure may work to challenge some existing structures, but their strategies for change must work from an initial basis consisting of socially structured (or at least normed) starting-points (Elder-Vass, 2007). Behaviour cannot just be deviant or unique but must grow into innovation from a basis that combines old habits with creativity. Our insertion of 'strategies' into the structure-agent relationship is an explicit way to insert one mode of creativity into the dynamics of morphogenesis. The potential for creativity is derived in part from the complexity of the agent itself, who is not just an individual.

Examples of strategies are provided in Table 3 below to illustrate the diversity and complexity of household strategies for labouring. They have strategies for paid as well as unpaid labour, and these are then woven into second-order strategies for education and other spheres of life.

Table 3: Household Agents' Strategies – Examples

Case	Strategies	Second-Order Strategies
Bangarappa (Workers)	Managing a milch cow, renting in land, getting assigned land, planting rainfed crops, living alone, not having electricity, wanting to grow more crops	Single-man household, combining livestock work with arable land
Rajitha (Small farmers, 2.5 acres wet and 0.5 acres rainfed land)	Managing rented land, holding onto tenancy relationship 20 years, managing livestock, wanting to own land, saving up money, getting government subsidy for house building	Joint household, very focused on agriculture
Yasmeen and Jayanth (Workers)	Marrying outside muslims, working hard, children aiming for high education, hoping for jobs, wanting move to town, admiring those with service sector jobs, disliking farming, worrying about water shortage	Elder generation sacrificing for grandchildren's future success, hoping for an urban / service-sector future
Sita and Chandran (Workers)	Arguing about wages and discrimination, wanting decency in labouring, praying regularly, keeping pets, educating both children well, sending boy child away to technical college	Nuclear family with girl living at home, girl studies 5 miles away, boy 20 miles away, hoping for an urban / service-sector future

Source: Field study, 2006, Peddapalli and Chinnapalli villages. The case-wise data are selectively shown on www.ruralvisits.org in more detail.

3b) The complex agent embedded in the structure-agency dynamic

The structure-agency model has been subjected to numerous debates about its underlying causality (notably Stones, 2005) and we take the position that causal mechanisms are many within the open system that we describe as the social structures of the economy.

(1998). For example he studied the purchase of new homes by groups of French residents and was able to demonstrate the continuing relevance of his concept of habitus (Bourdieu, 2005). The habitus or concretely experienced social subjectivity is a entity which precedes individual action but helps to condition all human action. One's habitus is a set of dispositions that arise in a given social context They are not one's property nor are they completely malleable, but the set of dispositions can be changed, ignored, resisted, or obeyed and is in any case very complex. In Bourdieu's relatively recent study of home buyers, the petit bourgeois among them had aspirations for large impressive self-owned houses which went beyond what their economic means could easily afford (Bourdieu, 2005). This was a social observation that Bourdieu was making, not just a record of a series of incidentally similar individual decisions. In this sense Bourdieu's regional ontology for France is highly social and abstract, and goes beyond what any methodological individualist could conceive of. However within his social ontology there is scope for studying individual difference, as seen in various empirical works by him and his teams (Bourdieu, 1986; Bourdieu, et al., 1999).

While accepting the important role that is played by habitus in formation of agents' strategies, we also stress that the agency aspect of the structure-agency dynamic allows for action to change social reality and not merely to respond to it. Technical terms from critical realism help to distinguish 'morphogenetic' from morphostatic actions. The former cause change in the system of values, while the latter reinforce existing social values. In this paper we are going to use the term 'resistant' to refer to morphogenetic actions, 'conforming' to refer to morphostatic actions, and other terms such as 'avoiding', 'innovating', and 'exiting' for actions whose impact on the local labour market is unclear. Realists have noted that norms vary so much from place to place and from time to time that one has trouble, empirically, in knowing whether a given action is intentionally morphogenetic (change-causing) or simply reflects a different background. The present study began with the explicit intention of working out what aspects of people's labouring decisions were *constrained* to follow existing social norms (e.g. accepting a very low wage, or doing daily agricultural labour known as kuulie work) or were *freely chosen* as desired actions (a status usually thought of as mutually exclusive with *acting under constraint*). Ultimately we found a wide scope for freedom to engage in strategies of either resistance or conformity or something rather different such as avoiding a scene by leaving it. Action within this scene is still, however, constrained by an agent's resources and hence by their intersecting structural location.

These sorts of considerations arose previously in three important debates that we mention briefly here: (a) the debate about whether women are constrained to give primacy to their caring roles, and as a result perform poorly in labour markets (Folbre, 1997, Kabeer, 1994); (b) the debate about livelihoods strategies in which Ellis (2000a, 2000b) claimed that diversified livelihoods were better than monolithic single-source rural strategies – but this left him seeming to claim that some farmers weren't doing what was best for themselves -; and (c) an interesting series of papers about labouring migrants in India, of which those by de Haan explained the rationales behind the cyclical migration strategies very clearly in terms similar that the ones we are using here (De Haan, 1999, 2002), while Breman sees the migrant more as a pawn in an exploitation game whose main resources are their assets and their 'primordial loyalties' arising in their home village and their caste group or family (Breman, 2003). The migration literature has excellent insights into why individuals choose particular types of contracts (Rogaly, 1997, 2003), and it offers possibilities and exemplars for studying the allocation of time by households from a non-Beckerian (hence non-universalistic), somewhat ideographic, locally-based and hence strongly grounded viewpoint. All three of these literatures have shown a tension between choice and constraint, and often the authors come across as arguing that the labouring family is *both constrained and also at the same time free* to choose the strategy which they, *ex post*, have been observed to have taken. We find this to be less of a contradiction if we do not presuppose *choice* and *constraint* to be mutually exclusive conditions for a given decision. For instance if you want to do more irrigated production, you can *choose* to dig a well and you are simultaneously *constrained* to place the well either on your own land or on land of a nearby, cooperative farmer or your own brother. Resolving the paradox between choice and constraint is not difficult at the micro level, but what is needed is a stronger statement of why neoclassical theories of optimal choice are not adequate as social theories. By offering an alternative we help to build that case.

Table 4: Examples of Agents Who Developed Third-Order Strategies

Agent	Goal	Orientation	Feedback	Deliberation	Acts
Kistappa	Karma	Likes Voluntary Social Work	Likes encouragement, hopes god will respond	Does not consult wife	Helps in temple and school
Sai (also called *Anna*, brother)	Good human relations	Values high land productivity	Discusses cultivation, responds well to events	Calmly and kindly discusses with male tenant	Still just supervising agriculture (not 'doing'), talks in public with others
Govt of AP	Land productivity	Wants to increase water retention	Like to encourage silt removal, likes bund strengthening, prefers more responsive places	Created tank user groups, invoked consultants, hired World Bank and took its advice	Pays for works, sub-contracts works, funds user groups
Govt of India	Increase rural child education	Have banned a wide range of child labouring	Probably MNC-prompted, decided to bank child maids on govt property, did not attack private sector maids	Party-political, undertook internal consultations	Made child labour illegal, sent police to enforce, fined the employers, put up small stickers
Shantamma	Help self and others	Likes self-help groups, teaches literacy, does tailoring, invokes husband's help	Accepts training, enforces rules on default, keeps records, meets outsiders, satisfies Int'l Donor NGO	Long discussions within self-help groups, visits training centre at NGO site	Runs for president of a group of self-help groups
Other social activists	Help self and others to get higher wages	Similar to Shantamma above	Similar to Shantamma above	Similar to Shantamma above	Runs for political office OR manages Ambedkar local society

The insight offered when we look at strategies involves seeing agents as co-mutual and complex in themselves.

4 Data Set and Methods

We approach the villages as scientific realists, recognizing that structures and institutions arise as emergent properties of all the detailed properties of a village at a point in time. Our knowledge about the structures, norms, institutions and labour relations is a fallible reflection of the real characteristics of the objects which are being studied. To some extent, however, those things are also being socially constructed, and the researcher engages in a reconstructive activity of interpretation which will, inevitably, become somewhat transitive with the objects of study to the extent that those objects, such as social class, have an enduring existence over time (see Gidwani, 2001). Thus by concentrating on workers and farmers we help to construe *'kuuliemanishyulu'* and *'ryotulu'* (workers and farmers, respectively, implying low and high status, respectively, at the same time) in particular and sometimes novel ways. Notably we do not believe that workers without land should have lower social status than farmers. That does not change the social fact that in these villages they currently do. Thus within a realist framework we are agents of change or of conservatism, but the objects of study cannot freely be reconstrued in false ways. We try to offer true accounts worthy of the readers' attention.

The methodology used was data triangulation within the context of realist assumptions (Danermark, *et al.,* 2001). We also did a detailed review of literature about five economic schools of thought prior to setting up the interviews. We created both survey data and interview data. The first survey had been conducted in 1994 using a sample of 115 households drawn randomly from full village lists of two villages. From this sample, 26 households have been located in 2006 and for these, plus 13 more, a new questionnaire was completed in 2006 using face-to-face structured interviewing. Both the questionnaires covered land and other assets, land tenancy, the household members' education, usual work, and secondary work if any. The first set of questionnaires also covered labour, land tenancy, and credit extensively. From these the household social class in 1994 was worked out using the social classes of worker, worker with land, small farmer, landlord, salaried household, and self-employed trader. When selecting 39 households in 2006, no salaried or merchant households were deliberately chosen. However 2 households later were found to have salaries coming in. For the 26 households that can be traced from 1994 to 2006, mobility by social class is very low (Kendall's Tau-a 0.27, significance 1.9%, showing an ordinal association). All 3 farmer households have had to become workers because of drought and groundwater shortage leading to lower arable land production in the years 2003-2006/7. Two landlord households have dropped down to worker-farmer households, i.e. they began doing kuulie labour and they stopped hiring as supervisors. These are signs of increasing poverty due to the bad conditions for agriculture in the 1996-2006.

The distribution of the five main social classes among the quota sample interviewed 2006 appears in Figure 2 and Table 5.

Table 5: Class Mobility of the Households in the Case-Study Research

	Social Class Mobility Matrix for 26 Panel Data Cases	Worker 1	Worker-Farmer 2	Farmer 3	Supervisor, i.e. Landlord 4	Total
Class of Household in 1994	Worker	100% (3)	-	-	-	100%
	Worker-Farmer	27% (4)	60% (9)	13% (2)	-	100%
	Farmer	-	100% (3)	-	-	100%
	Supervisor, i.e. Landlord	-	40% (2)		60% (3)	100%
Total Number of Households	Total in 1994	(6)	(14)	(3)	(2)	(26)

Source: 2006 non-random sample contrasting various workers with tenants and landlord households, derived from a 1994 random sample a
cross all social classes in two villages.

Further evidence showing the distribution of the five main social classes among the quota sample selected for interviewing appears in Figure 2.

Figure 2: Social Class, Education, and Assets of 39 Households Including 2 Case Studies

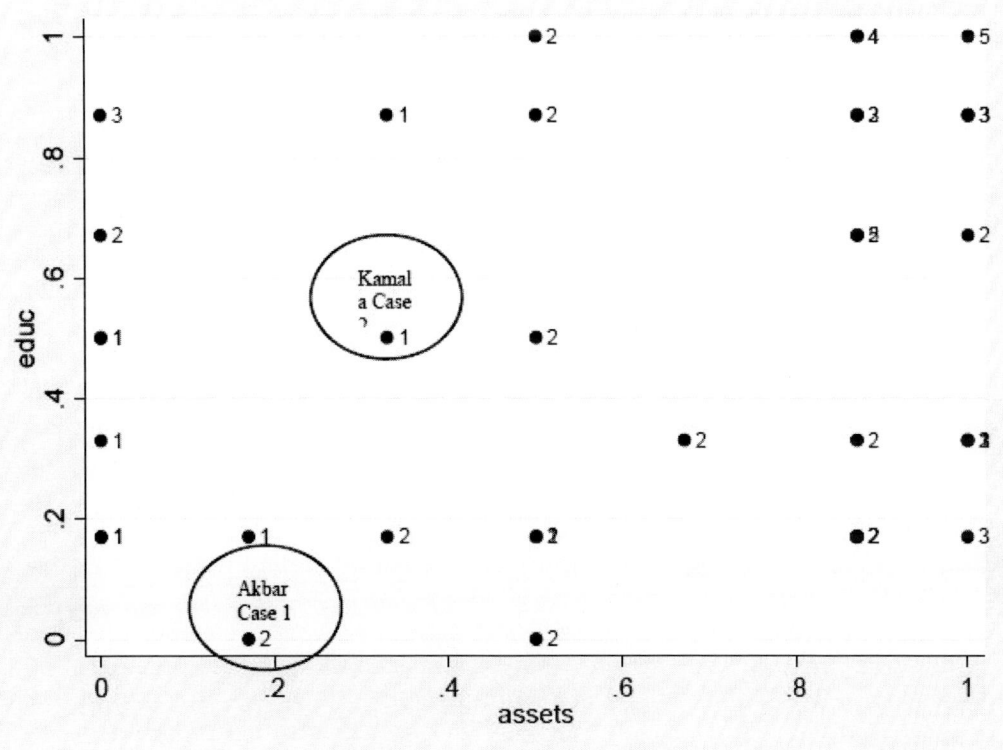

In Figure 2, the social classes are spread upon two axes. Vertically we have a fuzzy set ranking of household education (see Ragin, 2000)). If all adults of a household had high school education or higher, and the children were in school, the fuzzy set was 1.0, and if all were illiterate and not in school the fuzzy set was 0.0. In between we set the ordinal markers to 0.17 or 0.33 to indicate that some adults were illiterate but that either the kids were in school or at least one adult had primary school education (more for 0.33 level). We set the markers at .67 and .87 if all kids of school age were in school but not all the adults had any education (this fuzzy set method is described in Ragin, 2008a and 2008b; education sharing by proximity is described by Basu and Narayan (2001). This vertical axis represents the household's overall access to human capital (formal education).

The horizontal axis represents the assets of the household. Again an ordinal fuzzy set was arranged: 0 for no assets, 1 for having land and 3 of the following: bulls/cows, a well, a tractor, buffaloes. In between 0.17 reflected having sheep or goats only; 0.33 for a radio, T.V., or bicycle as well as a small animal; 0.5 for any cow, bullock, or buffalo; 0.67 for any land possessed (besides the house plot); and 0.87 for land plus at least two of the other possible assets. The horizontal and vertical rankings are strongly associated with social class itself (Kendall's tau-a 0.41 for class by assets, p=.0001; and Kendall's tau-a 0.29 for class by education at household level, p=.0044). In each case n=39 and we have 99% confidence in a pattern of association.

However, note that education is only weakly associated with class itself. Future social mobility may be higher than past mobility, because within households there are mixed education levels. Note that the non-randomly selected sample of 39 households is biased toward class 2, the workers with a little land. The 2006 questionnaire survey also included ten Likert scale attitude questions about their views on different forms of agricultural labouring such as exchange labour, casual labour, child labour. Data about the previous year's crops were also recorded in the questionnaire.

The interview data arose from one semi-structured interview with each of the 39 people selected. Initially a quota sample of men and women from worker, farmer, and tenant households was planned. Most couples insisted on being interviewed together. The women did not want to be left out, and the men were insistent on being interviewed, too. So the voices of both the man and the woman of each main couple in the household are on our tapes, and were transcribed in Telugu then in English.

These interviews were coded in NVIVO software and a 'casebook' of household attributes was created. During our analysis we studied whether strategies could be read off from – and were caused by – the structural location of a household in the caste-class system. This proved impossible because strategies themselves are so complex. The actions embedded in a strategy mean different things depending on whether the household wanted to leave agriculture, or expand their farming. Some families tried to diversify within agriculture, too. Thus even the renting of land proved to have several meanings ranging from a desperately poorly-paid form of agricultural work to a source of self-confidence and autonomy and finally to exciting investment plans for a few (e.g. silk, tamarind). Therefore no statistical analysis of the qualitative strategies data is conducted.

However, we are able to code within each interview a series of types of acts which are typically either 'conformist' or 'resistant' within the local social milieu, with respect to casual daily-paid 'kuulie' work. The conformist acts include doing unpaid labour for the employer at their house, acting respectful toward them, and accepting work from several different employers. The resistant acts reported included renting land in order to avoid kuulie work, picking a preferred employer over one whose behaviour is considered bad, and refusing to do the unpaid work when asked. A variety of other conformist and resistant acts were found, too. We also noted that 'exit' was a strategy used by many labourers who had (or had a wife or son) migrated to a nearby town or city for work. These are still workers, but they exit the kuulie labour market. Notable also were innovative acts like growing silk or renting land with tamarind trees, precisely to get revenue without doing kuulie. All these were coded with the number of different *types* of act, within a category, counted up for each household case. The act types are summarized in Table 6.

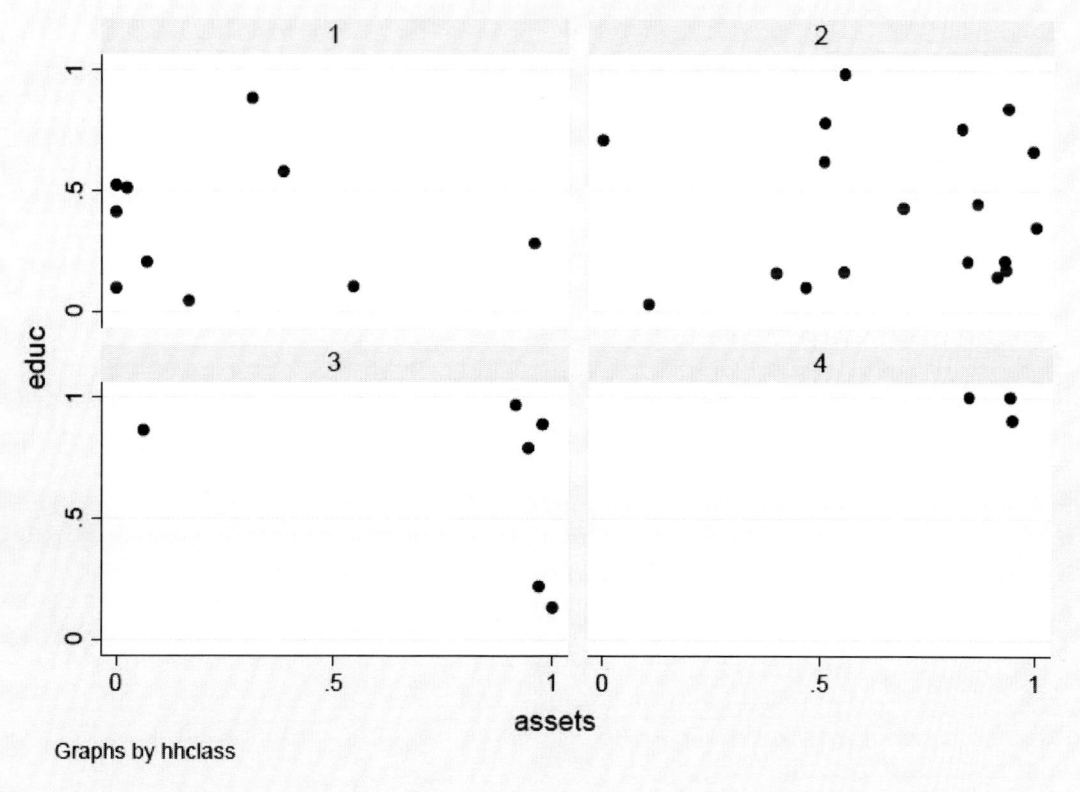

Figure 3: Household Class and Education Poorly Associated Using Household Level Fuzzy Sets

Note: Household class 1=worker, 2=worker with land, 3=farmer, 4=landlord.

The survey also included ten Likert scale attitude questions about their views on different forms of agricultural labouring (exchange labour, kuulie labour (casual), tenant work, and peasant farming work) as well as which they would like their girl and boy children to do as an occupation. Finally details of the previous year's crops were obtained.

The overall methodology is thus data triangulation within the context of a detailed pluralistic review of literature from five economic schools including one feminist school ('Gender and Development').

During our analysis we studied whether strategies could be read off from – and were caused by – the structural location of a household in the caste-class system. This hypothesis was falsified because strategies in themselves are so complex. The actions embedded in carrying out a strategy, or those actions visualized by an agent when planninga strategy mean different things depending on whether the household wants to leave agriculture, or expand their farming. Some families tried to diversify within agriculture, too. Thus even the renting of land proved to have several meanings ranging from a desperately poorly-paid form of agricultural work to a source of self-confidence and autonomy and finally to exciting investment plans for a few (e.g. silk, tamarind). Therefore no statistical analysis of the qualitative strategies data is conducted.

However, we are able to code within each interview a series of types of acts which are typically either 'conformist' or 'resistant' within the local social milieu, with respect to casual daily-paid 'kuulie' work. The conformist acts include doing unpaid labour for the employer at their house, acting respectful toward them, and accepting work from several different employers. The resistant acts reported included renting land in in order to avoid kuulie work, picking a preferred employer over one whose behaviour is considered bad, and refusing to do the unpaid work when asked. A variety of other conformist and resistant acts were found, too. We also noted that 'exit' was a strategy used by many labourers who had (or had a wife or son) migrated to a nearby town or city for work. These are still workers, but they exit the kuulie labou market. Notable also were innovative acts like growing silk or renting land with tamarind trees, precisely to get revenue without doing kuulie. All these were coded with the number of different *types* of act, within a category, counted up for each household case. The act types are summarized in Table 6.

Table 6: Actions Vis a Vis the Local Informal Labour Market, Classified From Resistant to Conformist[1] - Count of Number of Types Per Household

Social Class	Type of Act ⇒ Number of House-holds ⇓	Conform	Avoid exploita-tion, staying within locality, e.g. renting land	Exit from the locality's labour market	Resist	Inno-vate	Join in collective action
1	10	1.2	1.2	.6	.4	.8	.6
2	18	0.9	0.7	.3	.9	.8	.5
3	6	1	0.5	.5	.7	.5	0
4	3	3	0.3	.3	.3	0	0
5	2	0	1	1	1	1	1
All	39	1.1	0.8	.5	.7	.7	.4

Note: The mean number of reported actions of each type is given. Many households reported no actions of some types and these zeroes are included. The sample is 39 selected households in two Indian villages 2006/7. The unit of analysis is the couple who gave each interview (usually together).

5 Themes in the Qualitative Data: Habitus, Silencing, and Status

Four kinds of habitus were relevant to the study of labouring decisions in the villages. We will describe each one and then comment briefly on problems relating to gender silencing and to status, because these were important themes that arose from the qualitative data.

5a) Multilithic Habitus

The habitus, according to Bourdieu, is the socialized subjectivity that exists above and beyond what individuals think are their own personal norms. The habitus is related to the '*Doxa*'. *Doxa* is Bourdieu's word for the social rules that play an almost lawlike role because of their deep embeddedness. An example of a *doxum* (rule) in modern society is the law of private property and the knowledge one has of trespassing, even while one is doing it. An example of doxa given by Bourdieu is the nature of an appropriate response to receiving a gift. We know the appropriate response, and even if we don't give that response we feel a lot (guilt, shame, embarrassment) if we don't give that response (Olsen and Morgan, 2010). Several laws apply, and there are even laws about how we resist or refuse gifts. Altogether, with so many 'laws', society actually doesn't follow laws, nor are human agents restricted in their behavior to the acts specified in the tacit 'laws'. So few scholars apply Bourdieu's theory of the doxa.

The habitus, by contrast, is the whole set of possible behaviours upon which we draw, and it is not lawlike, in Bourdieu's approach. This is a useful theoretical concept (Olsen and Morgan, 2010). We argued (2010) that rules in society are often more like mezzorules, half applicable, and half unused, leaving agents more or less free, depending on the situation. Our creativity is also relevant to our actions.

Our research on labour strategies showed that there are numerous doxa upon which people draw and that sometimes they conflict with each other (Olsen and Neff, 2007). Two examples can illustrate.

First there is a Hindu tradition of festivals and worship in which colourful displays play an important role. Women participate in preparing for these festivals, and when workers are asked to do 'unpaid work' for landlords sometimes this involves women gathering and preparing the items such as flowers, leaves, or coconuts for the festival. For Muslims, however, worshipping icons is anathema and the *things* for the festival have no meaning. Meanwhile inside Muslim homes the Koran is treated in certain respectful ways, women act in certain ways, and these acts are seen as important reflections of inner worshipfulness. Thus two sets of ritual doxa co-exist. People in these villages often participate in the festivals of each others' religion, and people are careful to avoid causing offense by breaking the doxa of the other group. (Muslims are about 9% of Andhra Pradesh's population, and 9% in Chittoor District, Statistical Abstract of Andhra Pradesh, 2006. Directorate of Economics and Statistics, Govt of Andhra Pradesh, Hyderabad. Pg. 53.)

Secondly for workers, there are doxa about how to act in front of a landlord: one should be quiet and respectful and not swear or spit. These doxa extend to include the worker feeling alienated when working as a *kuulie* on an employer's land. This alienation has been expressed often to me as not caring to work fast on that land.

However for the peasants, who own their land or work rented land, the feeling toward the land is very different. Positive status derives from the (same) work activities; pride is felt about being a ryot; and a sense of belongingness can pervade the work – even if one is just a tenant – because of seeing the arable land enriched from year to year. Putting manure on the land is a prized activity (if the land is owned or rented) because of its enriching effect. The ryot of 'farmer' class can hardly imagine the feeling of alienation that workers talk about when they discuss kuulie work and kuulie wages. For field work, two sets of 'doxa' co-exist in the same society.

Because of these background norms, it is not always clear what constitutes good behaviour of a worker. Most workers try to construe themselves as good, saying for example that if necessary they will stay at night to watch the irrigation water flow in the channels, but there is also a limit to their patience and willingness to work without pay. At breaking point they draw upon some other habitus – some habit of resistance and independence – to refuse the demands of an unfair or uncaring landlord.

The point that the habitus – or social norming resources upon which they draw – is multilithic is enhanced when we consider the gender division of labour. On the one hand in Andhra Pradesh rural women are singled out publicly as forthcoming, autonomous, capable farmers and workers. Their labour force participation rate is the highest in the whole of India except for in the far Northeast (Olsen and Mehta, 2006). The government and local officials laud their involvement in women's groups, childcare facilities and micro-credit self-help groups. On the other hand they are also expected to be docile, submissive, and, in the rural areas at least, to accept beatings if the husband doles them out. A woman worker can draw upon either of these traditions – the women's empowerment tradition or the patriarchal submissiveness tradition – in responding to an employer's offer of work. The habitus of women workers seems especially split when we consider that role of housewife is highly respected and adored, yet neither Farmer class women nor Worker class women can conform to the urban image of a leisured home-maker that is put forward in the cinema and TV in the region. Many women identified themselves as *housewife* first, and *farmer* as secondary work – but only among the better-off families where household activities such as *puja* (hindu worship), elaborate cooking or handcrafts took place. The worker women just called themselves *kuulies*.

So far this section has suggested that the habitus is multilithic rather than monolithic, and that the traditions upon which people draw for 'normal' behaviour are sometimes contradictory. We will turn now to gender and status as illustrations.

5b) Silencing of Women

It proved easy to interview women, but difficult to get them to be interviewed alone. The woman's 'voice' is therefore adjusted to allow for her husband's presence. Young wives, in particular, acted very quiet and docile, and would defer to the husband's better knowledge in many areas. Older women were much more dominant in their families and would be out-spoken but still avoided refuting anything their husbands said. The study had aimed to separate the experience and voices of women from those of men but it proved impossible. We noticed that in any case the women are very differentiated among themselves by class, caste and education. So generalisations about 'the women' would not have held much content anyway. Lots of evidence about the gender division of labour emerged in this study, but the data given in this paper is nearly all at the household unit of analysis for the basic reason that in the interviewing staff could not easily separate the two sexes for one-to-one sessions. Tejokiran and Aktawallah in particular did not think it especially a priority to have one-to-one sessions interviewing women, and they felt that this was impractical and unreasonable since they are unmarried young men. In practice a study of separate women's voices needs a strong focus on that as well as careful planning.

The silencing of women is a strong feature of Indian politics, too, although there are numerous exceptions. One local Sarpanch (local government president) was female and she came from the dalit community, for example. Women are also active in the self-help group leaderships. Thus while we assert that women are agents in their own right, we are sad that we cannot give much evidence about women themselves here.

5c) Status

The emphasis that Bourdieu placed on habitus arose because he found that low status people emulate their 'betters' whilst trying to resist their power. If you emulate your opponent then you are not transforming the system but rather joining it, he argues. This emulation took the form of language (avoiding slang; Bourdieu, 1991), gift-giving (1977), and consumer culture (high culture preferences in food, housing and banking (2005). He suggested that one draws upon a tacit knowledge of social norms when deciding how to strategically oppose any opponent. Whilst we agree with this claim, we would stress that social norms are differentiated by religion, by locality, by class, and by gender. Therefore we have a multiverse of habiti not a single habitus.

When we look at the data with respect to social status, we find there is not a single ladder of status after all. Instead there are proud *kuulie* women of great strength; there are strong Muslim women who stay inside their homes and observe Purdah; there are respected farmers who take pride in their land but then decide to sell it and shift to an urban job situation (thus dumping the village status ladder for a jump to a new urban status ladder). Absentee landlords are notoriously unpredictable when they visit their villages precisely because they no longer fit into, or accept, the old norms of the locality. They may be generous, or abusive to locals and to workers; they may gamble, or they may come to do useful bargains. No one knows what to expect. Indian rural life is getting more like this because so many workers of all classes have relations living in various cities now. The habitus of rural villages is becoming diverse.

In this context agency is rather unpredictable. We have shown so far that class, education, assets and social mobility show strong structured patterns, excepting children's education which is mixed both within and between classes. Resistance is found even in the 'farmer' class. At present, due to drought and poverty, even farmers are being forced toward doing kuulie work. In that context they often do complain about the low wages and long hours. These complaints translate into refusing some employers' requests, refusing to do unpaid labour, and so on. It is harder, and more meaningful in social change terms, for a dalit worker to make these refusals in the landlord's face. One reason why tenancy is so popular is that a tenant does not supply kuulie labour to the market at the peak demand times of year. Cow-raising and exiting the village as a seasonal migrant are other common ways to avoid kuulie work.

6 Could Structures Predict These Strategies and Actions? No

Table 6 lists the kinds of resistant and conformist behaviour that may be observed among workers, employers, couples and NGOs in this area. Table 6 showed that the prevalence of these is spread widely across the classes in the villages. Table 7 gives examples.

Table 7: Examples of Different Acts in Informal Rural Labour Market (All Examples Are Relative to Kuulie Work)

AGENT	RESISTANCE (R)	EXIT BY DEPARTURE FROM SCENE (E)	CONFORMITY (C)	INNOVATION BY TRYING ANOTHER INSTITUTION WITHIN SCENE (I)	COLLECTIVE ACTION (CA)
MAN or WOMAN	Negotiate, shame, criticize, bargain Get bullock or cow pair to do well-paid kuulie work	Try for a job, get urban education, avoid doing unpaid labour, get a cow to avoid doing kuulie labour	Accept given constraints, ask landlord for help, accept given terms & conditions, negotiate within given parameters	Try for cow owning, try to get land on rental	Join SHG, run for office, create Rural Education Society, collectively negotiate EGS
Person of EMPLOYER household	Shame, criticize, shun, or hit worker(s) Threaten them with withdrawal of offers of work/land-rental	Absentee landlordism	Keep on employing workers at lowest possible wages	Buy tractor and have a driver as employee; use permanent labour; tie permanent labour by lending to them;	Run the tank users' association and run the Panchayat in order todominante government funded investment activities
COUPLE	Same as above	Same as above	Same as above	Try a new occupation such as flower selling, silk, beedi	Same as above
NGO	Collectively represent interests in milk, cow, vet, fodder markets, or in EGS, tank silt removal, and tank users' group	Attract people into doing new jobs such as doll-making, transport, small hotel or other	Encourage women to accept given division of labour but advise them on non-labour areas such as reproductive health	Teach women and men to do tailoring, to collectively rent land or do trading/storage/milling	All the strategies shown at left count as collective NGO action – but who 'does' things? (really) – leaders, all members, or "the NGO" as an actor?

The categories of action were operationalised to indicate the number of different *types of acts of* resistance, conformity, innovation etc. that were mentioned during the interviews. Our operationalisation then allows a test of whether resistance (to employer's demands) could have been predicted by a household's social class location. This test fails, and Kendall's tau also shows no significance for any combination of any of the categories (see Table 6) against household social class, against education at household level, or against assets. These tests seek ordinal-by-ordinal association, so the metric that appears for education and assets is irrelevant. Furthermore a measure of the frequency of acts of resistance has not been attempted here. Instead only mentions of resistance are counted, ignoring repeats, because the categories in Tables 5 and 6 arose as part of the grounded learning that occurred *after* the survey and interviews had been conducted. With what we now know, we can conduct further research on the frequency of conformity and resistance, etc. We advise that a wide range of classes (not just workers) be involved in such research because there are signs of all six types of act among all the rural social classes.

Figure 4 illustrates resistance as it is spread by class, education and assets per se.

Figure 4: Resistance (Types of Acts) by Class, Education and Assets of Households

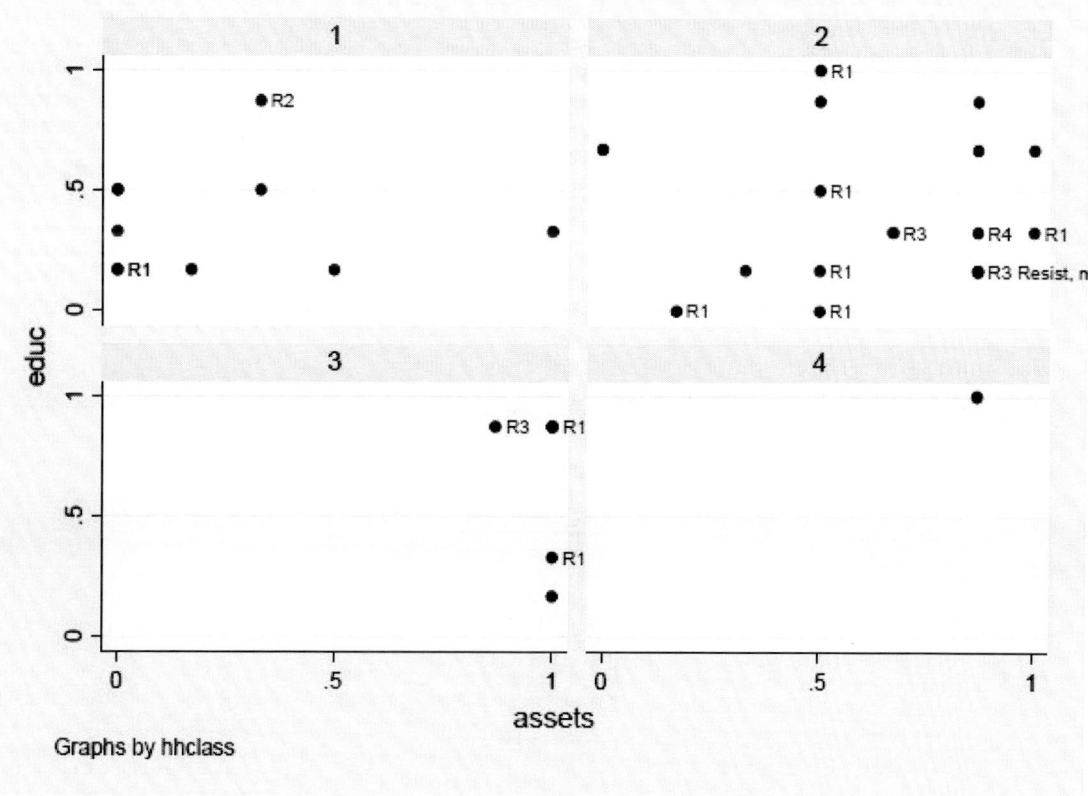

Graphs by hhclass

Note: Household class 1=worker, 2=worker with land, 3=farmer, 4=landlord. "Education" is a fuzzy set at household level, and "assets" is a fuzzy set indicating rising economic resources at household level.

The dots without any R in Figure 4 are those couples who did not mention resisting employers' demands. In particular it is notable that resistance is found even in the 'farmer' class. At present, due to drought and poverty, even farmers are being forced toward doing kuulie work. In that context some do complain about the low wages and long hours. These complaints translate into refusing some employers' requests, refusing to do unpaid labour, and so on. It is harder, and more meaningful in social change terms, for a dalit worker to make these refusals in the landlord's face. As described in a separate paper (Olsen and Neff, 2007), avoiding the landlord altogether is much more popular. This is one reason why tenancy is so popular; it keeps people out of the kuulie labour market at crucial times of year. Cow-raising and exiting the village are other ways to avoid kuulie work. Exit and avoidance with the village- by adopting other activities – are also evenly spread across the classes (see Table 6). Innovation and joining collective action groups are less common and their spread is shown in Figures 5 and 6:

Figure 5: Economic Innovation by Class, Education and Assets

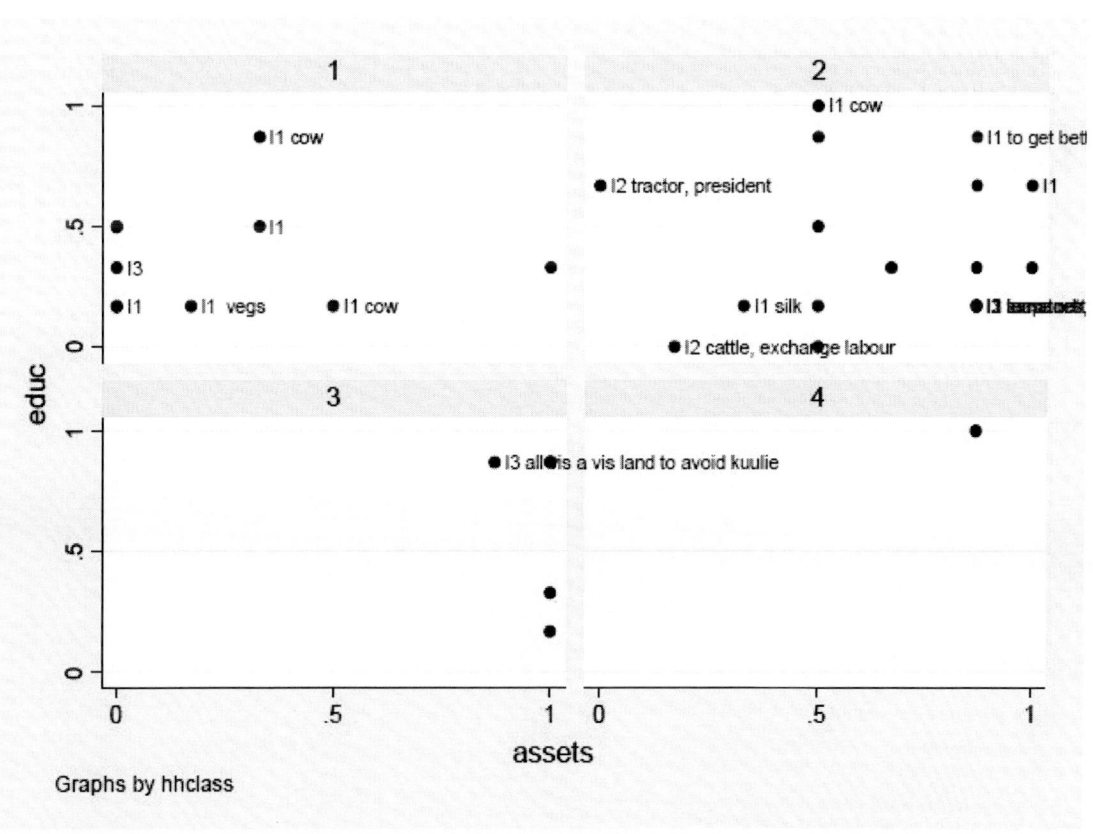

Graphs by hhclass

Note: Household class 1=worker, 2=worker with land, 3=farmer, 4=landlord.

Figure 6: Joining Collective Action Groups (e.g. Micro-Credit, Chit Funds[iv])
by Class, Education, and Assets

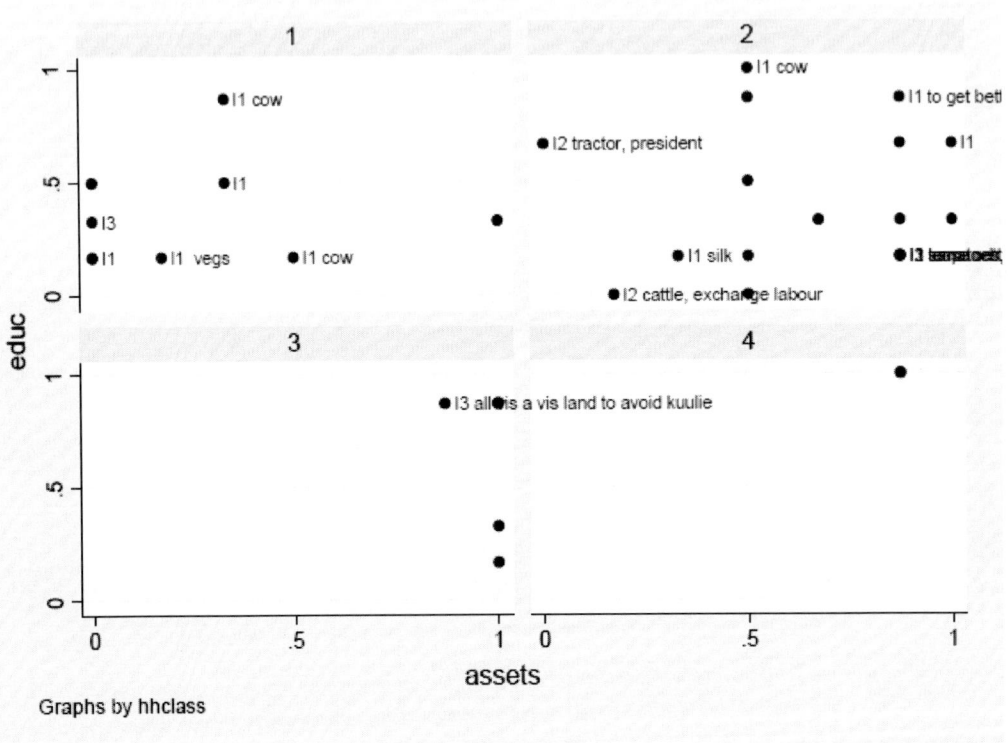

Graphs by hhclass

Note: Household class 1=worker, 2=worker with land, 3=farmer, 4=landlord.

Joining a collective action group was not limited to women but was strongly gender-divided. Women joined official self-help groups – and have done for over 15 years – but men join in chit funds. There is occasional cross-over among migrants to cities. We coded the collective action regardless of the context in which they reported it. Clearly, as seen above and in Table 5, it is not concentrated in any particular social class. It affects all the other strategies for that couple because it creates the hope or reality of a new line of credit.

In this section we tested the claim that a structuralist might make, that the strategies of agents can be read off their class location. There was no evidence of this except with respect to high-end asset investment schemes, e.g. the tractors of the village are all owned by Farmer or Landlord class households. In the village labour market huge differentiation exists. At the same time, agency at the couple level is just one way of broaching structuralist questions about causality. Further research would look at gender, caste and religions as structuring factors, too. Our results support the paper's strong emphasis on recognizing agency as a qualitative factor shaping people's futures.

7 Two Cases to Illustrate Workers' Strategies

The two case studies below illustrate how strategies are set out by worker families. Neither has any land, but each has two cows, and both couples are able to work in farming as tenants from time to time. The first case household is less poor, was classified as Class 2 Kuulie With Land, has a diversified livelihood, and is entirely able to avoid doing *kuulie* work. But the people in the second household have to do *kuulie* work and feel they cannot avoid it.

Case 1: Sonu and Akbar, a Muslim couple who do farming. Their poverty is great; their home is a single room and they have no bike, radio, nor of course t.v. Like most Muslims in the rural areas of Andhra Pradesh they have been poor through several generations. But by innovating and having a diversified livelihoods strategy they have achieved a capacity to avoid *kuulie* work. They perceive themselves as *ryots* (peasants), not kuulies. They strongly prefer renting land in to doing casual paid work. They have *beedi* (cigarette rolling) work to do as well. This is a cottage industry performed as piecework in the home. Their main land rental ended due to the drought and groundwater shortage, but this year they are trying again to rent some land to try to earn cash for other investments. The adults of the household are illiterate. Their two daughters aged 12 and 7 are still in school. They and the wife regularly roll *beedies* whenever they can to earn some money. Although he dislikes it, the husband, Akbar (age 37) does admit to doing agricultural labour (*kuulie*) sometimes.

Case 2: Kamala and Ramayya, a dalit couple. These two workers are illiterate and have tried to increase their earnings by sending the husband to work in service in the nearby town. They own a bicycle. Kamala, the wife, takes up the 'drought works' (in other words Employment Guarantee Scheme) in the village whenever she can. She thus uses the EGS innovation offered to poor workers to get some experience outside the usual *kuulie* situation. On the whole Kamala and Ramayya otherwise conform in many ways to the usual behaviour of kuulies: they do unpaid labour for the landlord and they work for him when called for. Kamala spoke during the interview.

Kamala: We do small works for them. If it is a heavy work they will

pay us. If they ask us to arrange water for their fields, we will certainly oblige and do the work. We do not do the work out of fear.

J. Rangaswamy: Do they give money for the small works?

R: No, they do not. Out of affection we do the work. [. . .] we do unpaid work on the festival days. Like arranging *thoranalu* [*festoons made from mango leaves*], arranging water for the cattle -- for this work we do not expect any payment.

They also report doing these sorts of unpaid work for other employer landlords. However they perceive that they are forced to do this:

Kamala: We will 'adjust' [*i.e. accept what they are told, and not argue with the landlord*] because we are poor you know. We are not rich so we cannot argue with the rich. Regarding *koru* [*sharecropping*] share. We shall give according to the terms and conditions as fixed at the time of giving the land for *koru*. We do not like to give even a single grain to the landlord.

The implication is clear – they do what they have to do, and don't like it. They rent land whenever they can. Their son, now 17, has education at the high school level.

Two important points stand out in these two vignettes. Firstly, although both are poor working class families with low assets and adult illiteracy, they respond in different ways and have different strategies. One avoids *kuulie* while the other engages in it. Both attempt to do tenancy, but one couple perceives themselves as peasants while the other acts respectful toward the landlord and does services for them. The fact that the more resistant couple is Muslim is highly relevant, yet many Muslims in this area simply work as *kuulies* and they are all very poor. The selected household with *beedi* making activity is among the less poor of the village. The more conformist couple, Kamala and Ramayya, are 'harijan' i.e. dalit people. As a result can we expect to be able to predict their strategy and their behaviour toward the landlords? No; only by asking them do we find out that they *act* respectful and helpful but they *feel* coerced and poor. Their strategy to escape the situation is not to negotiate better wages but rather for the man to work in the town for higher wages.

Thus the strategies could not be 'read off' the structural location at the lower part of the social class spectrum.

8 Conclusion

We have developed this mixed-methods paper to try to persuade readers to take up a strategies-oriented approach to labour relations. We have shown that the theory fits the rural Indian labourers' decisions about casual work and tenancy very well. By examining a series of cases in depth, we gained a good understanding of labouring strategies which adds to our existing knowledge.

The overall approach to rural labourers' strategies put forward here (and also in Olsen, 2008) has two concrete advantages. First, it is relevant to policy interventions because a knowledgeable policy maker or grass-roots activist can aim to facilitate people's existing strategies or can try to remove obstacles to achieving people's visions. We have found close links between our understanding of strategies and our grasp of how people decide where/when/who to send out to do Employment Guarantee Scheme works. We feel we could now advise government on these works although more research in diverse districts is also required. We also urge government and NGO staff to take up the strategies approach themselves for further (local) study. They might use the methodology advised by Lemon (et al., 1999) to study sustainable agriculture with an insider's view yet with an interdisciplinary team of experts facilitating the research. A clear advantage of the strategies approach is that the theory is pluralistic by having links with institutional economics (Olsen and Morgan, 2010), with political theory (especially on the local specificity of 'the good'; and on how to deliberate about moving forward from now to next (Habermas, 1986, 1998), with feminist theories (Kabeer, 1999), and with sociology and the livelihoods debate in development studies (Ellis, 2000b).

Secondly, with this kind of transdisciplinary social science we increase our capacity to talk across / over / through the walls that currently separate some academic disciplines. We are not like sheep and cows in different fields: we are human. Let us talk about power and strategies; emotion and strategic action; religion and gender; patriarchy and strategies to change it; and so on. In this sense the strategies approach to agency has much in common with the livelihoods approach to peasantries (Ellis, 2000b). A theory of strategies enables to continue the conversation about livelihoods while recognizing the cultural, religious, emotive and normative aspects of people's lives.

Obviously we have used a realist approach (cf Peyton Young, 2001). A structuralism that is realist is not determinist. Instead it is usually critical realist. The advantages of a strategic structuralism satisfy three criteria for 'persuasiveness' as put forward by Morgan. He says there are "three ways that a proposition, concept or theory might be persuasive":

> - It is dialogically immersed in a commonly acknowledged
> problematic, including disputed areas of argument situated to
> alternative theoretical formulations of some proposed

ontological entity.
- Its extension from the initial philosophical sources from which it derives its plausibility is unambiguously elaborated in a way that is appropriate to the object that is considered.
- It is enhanced through the presentation of applied research that accords with its principles.

J. Morgan, 2001 (Vol 5 No. 1 *JCR*)[2]

Strategic thinking about strategies is a welcome, plausible, and empirically grounded contribution just as Morgan urges.

References

Anderson, E. (1993). <u>Value in ethics and economics</u>. Cambridge, Mass. ; London, Harvard University Press.

Anderson, E. (2003). Sen, Ethics and Democracy. *Feminist Economics* **9**(2): 239-262.

Archer, M. (). <u>Structure, agency and the internal conversation</u>. Cambridge, Cambridge University Press.

Archer, M. (2007). <u>Making Our Way Through the World: Human Reflexivity and Social Mobility</u>. Cambridge, Cambridge University Press.

Archer, M. S. (2000). <u>Being Human: The problem of agency</u>. Cambridge, U.K. ; New York, Cambridge University Press.

Basu, K. (1999). "Child labor: Cause, consequence, and cure, with remarks on international labor standards." <u>Journal of Economic Literature</u> **37**(3): pp. 1083-1119.

Basu, K. (2005). "New Empirical Development Economics: Remarks on Its Philosophical Foundations." <u>Economic and Political Weekly</u> **XL**(40): 4336-4339.

Basu, K. and P. H. Van (1998). "The economics of child labor." <u>The American Economic Review</u> **88**(3): 412.

Basu, K., A. Narayan, et al. (2001). "Is literacy shared within households? Theory and evidence for Bangladesh." <u>Labour Economics</u> **8**(6): pp. 649-665.

Becker, G. (1981). <u>A Treatise on the Family</u>, Boston: Harvard University Press.

Bourdieu, P. and R. Nice (1977). <u>Outline Of A Theory Of Practice,</u> Cambridge and New York: Cambridge University Press.

Bourdieu, P. (1986). <u>Distinction: A social critique of the judgement of taste</u>. London, Routledge & Kegan Paul.

Bourdieu, P. (1991). <u>Language and Symbolic Power</u>. Cambridge UK: Polity Press.

Bourdieu, P. (1998). <u>Practical Reason: On the Theory of Action</u>. Stanford, Calif., Stanford University Press.

Bourdieu, P. (2005). <u>The Social Structures of the Economy</u>. Cambridge UK, Polity

Press.

Bourdieu, P., et al. (1999). <u>The Weight Of The World: Social suffering in contemporary society</u>. Stanford, Calif., Stanford University Press.

Breman, J. (2003). <u>The Labouring Poor In India: Patterns Of Exploitation, Subordination, And Exclusion</u>. Delhi, Oxford: Oxford University Press.

Chindarkar, N. (2007). "A Comparative Analysis of Farmers' Suicides in Andhra Pradesh, India", *Methodological Innovations Online*, 2:2, online journal.

Chouliaraki, L. and N. Fairclough (1999). <u>Discourse in Late Modernity: Rethinking critical discourse analysis</u>. Edinburgh, Edinburgh University Press.

Csikszentmihalyi, Mihaly (2002, 2nd ed.). <u>Flow: The Classic Work on How to Achieve Happiness</u>, London: Rider & Co.

Csikszentmihalyi, Mihaly (2003). <u>Good Business: Leadership, Flow and the Making of Meaning,</u> London: Hodder and Stoughton.

Danermark, B., *et al.* (2001). <u>Explaining Society: An introduction to critical realism in the social sciences.</u> London, New York, Routledge.

De Haan, A. (1999). "Livelihoods and poverty: The role of migration--a critical review of the migration literature." <u>The Journal of Development Studies</u> **36**(2): 1.

De Haan, A. (2002). "Migration and livelihoods in historical perspective: A case study of Bihar, India." <u>Journal of Development Studies</u> **38**(5): 115-+.

De Haan, A. (2007). "Conceptualizing social exclusion in the context of India's poorest regions: a contribution to the Qual-Quant debate", Q-Squared Working Paper No. 39, URL http://www.q-squared.ca/papers39.html, accessed Aug. 2007.

Edward, P. and W. Olsen (2006). "Paradigms and Reality in Micro-Finance: The Indian Case." <u>Perspectives on Global Development and Technology</u> **5**(1-2): 31-54.

Elder-Vass, D. (2007). "For Emergence: Refining Archer's Account of Social Structure." <u>Journal for the Theory of Social Behaviour</u> **37**(1): 25-44.

Ellis, F. (2000a). "The determinants of rural livelihood diversification in developing countries." <u>Journal of Agricultural Economics</u> **51**(2): 289-302.

Ellis, F. (2000b). <u>Rural Livelihoods and Diversity in Developing Countries</u>. Oxford, Oxford University Press.

Folbre, N. (1997). Gender Coalitions: Extrafamily Influences on Intrafamily Inequality. <u>Intrahousehold Resource Allocation in Developing Countries</u>. L. Haddad, John Hoddinott, and Harold Alderman. Baltimore and London, Johns Hopkins University Press.

Frankel, F.R., and M.S.A. Rao, eds. (1989). <u>Dominance and State Power in Modern India: Decline of a Social Order</u>, Delhi, Bombay: Oxford University Press.

Gidwani, V. (2001). "The Cultural Logic of Work: Explaining Labour Deployment and Piece-Rate Contracts in Matar Taluka, Gujarat." <u>Journal of Development Studies</u> 38(2): 57-74 and 75-108.

Habermas, J. (1981), <u>Reason and the Rationalisation of Society, Vol. 1,</u> Translated from German by Tom McCarthey. London: Heinemann.

Habermas, J. (1986) <u>Autonomy and Solidarity: Interviews,</u> Ed. P. Dews, London: Verso.

Habermas, J. (1998, original 1996). The Inclusion of the Other. Studies in Political Theory. Cambridge: CUP.

Heron, J. (2000). Co-Operative Inquiry: Research into the Human Condition. London, Sage.

Jackson, C. and R. Pearson (1998). Feminist visions of development : gender, analysis and policy. London, Routledge.

Jary, D. and J. Jary, eds. (1991) "Social Structure", in The Harper Collins Dictionary of Sociology, NY: Harper Collins.

Kabeer, N. (1994). Reversed Realities: Gender hierarchies in development thought. London ; New York, Verso.

Kent, R. (2008). Using fsQCA: A Brief Guide and Workshop for Fuzzy-Set Qualitative Comparative Analysis, Working Paper, Cathie Marsh Centre for Census & Survey Research. Mimeo, forthcoming on www.ccsr.ac.uk.

Lamont, M. (2000). The dignity of working men : morality and the boundaries of race, class, and immigration. Harvard, Harvard University Press.

Lawson, T. (1997). Economics and reality. London ; New York, Routledge.

Lemon, M., ed. (1999).Exploring Environmental Change Using An Integrated Method, in the Environmental Problems and Social Dynamics series, London: Gordon & Breach Scientific Publishers.

MacIntyre, A. (1985 (orig. 1981)). After Virtue: A Study in Moral Theory. London, Duckworth Publishers.

Morgan, Jamie (2001) The Soul: Plausibility and Persuasiveness in Realism, Journal of Critical Realism, 5:1.

Nelson, J. A. (2003). "Once More, With Feeling: Feminist Economics and the Ontological Question." Feminist Economics 9(1): 109-118.

Nussbaum, M. (1999). "Women and equality: the capabilities approach." International Labour Review 138(3): 227-245.

Nussbaum, M. and J. Glover, Eds. (1995). Women, culture and development : a study of human capabilities WIDER studies in development economics. Oxford, Oxford University Press.

Olsen, W. K. (2006). "Pluralism, Poverty, and Sharecropping: Cultivating Open-Mindedness in Poverty Studies." Journal Of Development Studies 42(7): 1130-1157.

Olsen, W.K. (2008) Beyond Sociology: Structure, Agency, and Strategy Among Tenants in India, Journal of Asian Social Science, forthcoming 2008.

Olsen, W.K., and D. Neff (2007) Informal Agricultural Work, Habitus and Practices in an Indian Context, Working Paper NO. 79, Global Poverty Research Group, www.gprg.org, accessed Sept. 2007.

Olsen, Wendy, and S. Mehta (2006) "The Right to Work and Differentiation in Indian Employment", Indian Journal of Labour Economics, 49:3, July-Sept., 2006, pages 389-406.

Olsen, W. (2009) "Exploring Practical Horizons of Beyond Sociology: Structure, Agency, and Strategy among Tenants in India", Asian Journal of Social Science 37, 366-390, DOI 10.1163/156853109X436775.

Olsen, W., and J. Morgan (2010) "Institutional change from within the informal sector in Indian rural labour relations", International Review of Sociology – Revue Internationale de Sociologie Vol. 20, No.3, 535-555, DOI 10.1080/03906701.2010.511919

Peyton Young, H. (2001) Individual Strategy and Social Structure: An Evolutionary Theory of Institutions, Princeton, Princeton University Press.

Pusey, M. (1993). Jürgen Habermas London, Routledge.

Ragin, C (2008b, forthcoming), Redesigning Social Inquiry: Fuzzy Sets and Beyond, University of Chicago Press.

Ragin, C. (2008a, forthcoming), 'Qualitative Comparative Analysis Using Fuzzy Sets', in Rihoux, B. and Ragin, C. (eds), Configurational Comparative Analysis, Sage Publications.

Ragin, C. C. (2000). Fuzzy-set social science. Chicago ; London, University of Chicago Press.

Reckwitz A (2002) "Toward A Theory Of Social Practices: A development in culturalist theorizing", European Journal of Social Theory, 5(2), 243-63.

Rogaly, B. (1997). "Embedded Markets: Hired Labour Arrangements in West Bengal Agriculture." Oxford Development Studies 25(1): 209-223.

Rogaly, B., D. Coppard, et al. (2003). "Seasonal migration, employer-worker interactions, and shifting ethnic identities in contemporary West Bengal." Contributions to Indian Sociology 37(1-2): 281-310.

Rogers, C. (1980). A Way of Being. Boston, Houghton Mifflin.

Sayer, A. (2000a) Realist Social Science. London: Sage.

Sayer, A. (2000b) "Moral Economy and Political Economy", Studies in Political Economy, 61: 79-103.

Sayer, A. (2001). "For a Critical Cultural Political Economy." Antipode 33(4): 687-708.

Sayer, A. and R. Walker (1992). The New Social Economy: Reworking the division of labor. Cambridge, Mass, Blackwell Publishing.

Schatzki, T. R. (1996). Social Practices: A Wittgensteinian approach to human activity and the social, Cambridge: Cambridge University Press.

Schatzki, T. R., K. D. Knorr-Cetina, et al. (2001). The Practice Turn in Contemporary Theory. London: Routledge.

Stones, R. (2005) Structuration Theory, Traditions in Social Theory series, Basingstoke, Palgrave Macmillan.

Walzer, M. (1983). Spheres of Justice: A defence of pluralism and equality, Oxford, Robertson.

Wolfe, A. (1989). Whose Keeper? Social Science and Moral Obligation. Berkeley, University of California.

Wolfe, A. (2001) Moral Freedom: The impossible idea that defines the way we live now, NY, London: Norton Press.

[1] Please note that the **actions** are classified here, but that the evidence we have are their **descriptions** in semi-structured interviews which are not simply being taken as factual accounts. Instead, the appearance of an incident or action in an interview account reflects the speaker's decision that the action was strategically meaningful for them and that it was important to include that action in their account of their labouring practices and decision-making. There were numerous ways that an interview could lead into descriptions of resistance, conformity, exit etc. We did not count reports of third-party resistance in annotating the accounts.

[2] Ironically Morgan (2001) was arguing that the case for transubstantiation is plausible but not persuasive. The importance of persuasiveness is that many arguments – such as some arguments for God - are plausible yet they are not all important enough or well-argued enough to deserve any attention.

---

[i] We are grateful to Prof. Reinhart Koβler of the Albert Ludwig University of Freiburg for the insight that Habermas does not have to be taken to mean that democracy can only be achieved in perfect speech situations.

[ii] If necessary we can provide the references.

[iii] A caveat: the epistemology of knowing about the good is not being neglected, but the ontological argument is being put forward very clearly and deliberately. Knowing is part of the cycle of knowing-about-something, but the characterization of that 'something' is the ontological step which realists take an interest in.

[iv] A chit fund is a revolving savings association. People meet in a fixed group informally either weekly or monthly. They share their fixed savings input. Each week one person takes the whole pot. Without loans, this chit fund acts effectively as a source of a lump sum from time to time.

Photo by Miriam Kennet. Decent Public Transport. Here a tram in Kassel Germany helps greately towards social justice for everyone.

Photo by Miriam Kennet. Objections to flights in Berlin.

Photo by Miriam Kennet. Tree at the boat show in Pangbourne

Photo by Miriam Kennet.Traffic lights for cyclists in Berlin